T0413178

Knowledge Mobilization in TESOL

Knowledge Mobilization in TESOL

Connecting Research and Practice

Edited by

Sardar Anwaruddin

BRILL

SENSE

LEIDEN | BOSTON

All chapters in this book have undergone peer review.

The Library of Congress Cataloging-in-Publication Data is available online at http://catalog.loc.gov

Typeface for the Latin, Greek, and Cyrillic scripts: "Brill". See and download: brill.com/brill-typeface.

ISBN 978-90-04-38876-5 (paperback)
ISBN 978-90-04-39246-5 (hardback)
ISBN 978-90-04-39247-2 (e-book)

This book is printed on acid-free paper and produced in a sustainable manner.

Printed by Printforce, the Netherlands

Contents

Foreword: Teachers' Engagement with Research

This volume draws upon pedagogical issues identified by a diverse group of English language teachers from around the world. Within this volume, we meet teachers who present a panoply of unique and interesting perspectives on the teaching of English. These teachers endeavor to connect academic research with classroom practice, with the professional goal of supporting their students in the learning of the English language. What is unique about this book is its focus on teachers' firsthand accounts of how they endeavored to utilize academic research for their classroom practice. From these contributors, we hear interesting stories and gain valuable knowledge and insights into their professional development, as they strive to support their students. Through the stories of this diverse group of teachers, we come to recognize that many common themes are revealed when teachers use academic research for practical classroom purposes.

This volume is a must-read for any and all academics, as well as the general reading public, who wish to obtain a superior understanding of how teachers struggle and succeed in the difficult work of translating theory into practice for the benefit of students. The book has taken on a huge challenge: that of reconciling elements of the Great Theory-Practice Divide. This volume is not only timely, it is a great boon in that it dares to identify issues related to language teaching and learning. It also allows us to recognize the advantages of research utilization when teachers communicate across vast distances to promote their own and others' professional development. The book offers the opportunity to re-conceptualize professional learning for teachers. The English language teachers who have contributed to this book have identified, spoken to, and acted upon the challenges and opportunities of professional development. The accounts of research-informed pedagogical practice that we see within the covers of this volume have much to offer the fields of TESOL and Applied Linguistics.

Karyn Cooper
Ontario Institute for Studies in Education
University of Toronto, Canada

Foreword: What is the World Coming to?

What is the world coming to? I have heard this expression more times than enough, particularly in the context of yet another harried teacher of English trying to make sense of just one more essay filled with approximate English. While some of these teachers may be English as a second or additional language teachers, some of them are also regular English language teachers bemoaning the fact that their students spend more time on video games than on discovering the beauties of the English language.

What is the world coming to? After some years of pondering this question, as if it were a question rather than an observation, I arrived at an answer. The world is coming to English. This has been a long time coming, however. It did not happen and will not happen overnight. How the world is coming to English has been a story more than a thousand years long. From the colder northern slopes of Scandinavia and Denmark, the Angles, Jutes and Saxons descended upon the "Emerald Isle," ultimately displacing, at least temporarily, the Celts, Picts and Britons who called this place home.

As time passed and the Angles, Jutes and Saxons settled in for the long haul, significant adjustments occurred in terms of intermarriage, culture and trade. The Jutes, hemmed in between the Angles and the Saxons and, according to varying accounts of their origins, were among the first to become absorbed into what later became known as the Anglo-Saxon community. This was the end of the beginning, as various groups wrestled with one another for supremacy amid the cultural mélange that was simultaneously developing.

While the Celtish groups remained indomitable, and the Jutes began to disappear into the newly Anglo-Saxon culture, the Angles gradually gained the upper hand. The prefix, "Anglo-," is believed to have come from Anglia, a peninsula located on the Baltic Sea, along the shore of what is now known as Schleswig-Holstein in Northern Denmark. The Anglo-Saxon culture lent its name to the general surroundings. The people became known as Anglo-Saxons. They spoke "Angle-ish" and named their home "Angle-land." No need to translate this term.

Now, all of this history transpired in the days of the post-Roman conquest of Britain. This is significant because history tends to repeat itself. Relinquishing our hold on the history and culture of the United Kingdom for a moment, let us concentrate on language. English is a rich and beautiful language. It has the largest word pool of any language and is considered by many non-native speakers to be one of the hardest languages to learn. Personally, I reject this last point, because all languages contain elements of idiomatic speech, and it is this part that tends to amaze and confound newcomers to the language—any language.

It has been said that there is really no such thing as a true synonym in English. I can agree with this observation because each word that we claim as an English word has origins and contexts that separate it, even slightly, from its meme.

The widespread use of Latin as a *lingua franca* contracted and failed just as the Roman Empire itself contracted and failed. "Anglish" and, eventually, English replaced Latin as the language of the court and the commons. This continues today. In centuries past, Latin was the common language of science. Latin, because it was considered to be a "dead" language, allowed scholars around the globe from various cultures, traditions and languages to converse, to collaborate and to create together even though, given their language of origin, they would otherwise not be able to understand one another without the abilities of a skilled translator.

Times and tides have changed. As Latin fell from favor, English began its ascendancy as the language of a new world order. Not only did English become the new *lingua franca* of science, it also became the language of computers and information technology. As more innovation followed, English became the standard for medicine, as well as for international commerce and trade. This occurred not so much as a result of pride but more as a result of necessity. English was already a dominant language, due, in part to British colonialism and American "manifest destiny," and was spoken, to some degree, in various corners around the world.

I am always amazed, as I travel the world and walk up and down in it, how easy it is to find someone who speaks English, and how readily, willing and able they are to converse with you, to practice their English proudly and to become friends. For many, choosing to learn English has become fashionable, if not necessary. This takes me to a remembrance of my numerous sojourns in China, where I was editor of a textbook series that helped untold numbers of Chinese students learn English. I raise this as an object lesson; so, please remember that this is an observation and has little enough empirical basis. Thus, what follows is an assumption that may prove false. However, hopefully, it stands as a case in point.

While spoken Chinese may vary from region to region, the language is united by the written "word" in the form of pictographs. Virtually unfathomable to foreigners, Chinese pictographs number in the thousands. Imagine, if you will, a small child, struggling to learn to read and write in the traditional way. Now, numerous scholars of the English language, such as Jim Cummins and Colleen Capper, suggest that it may take anywhere from three to ten years for a student, for whom English is not the language of origin, to gain mastery of the English language. I suspect it may take as long for students for whom English *is* the language of origin, perhaps longer. After all, what is mastery, anyway? Does one ever truly *master* a language?

Let us return to that student somewhere in China striving to master thousands of pictographs. Given the enormity of the task, I ask the same question. Does anyone really master Chinese, as it is written? I imagine that it would take a tremendous amount of time and energy to gain an intimate knowledge of the written pictograph. I also suspect that true mastery of the Chinese written language would be relatively rare, possibly similar to true mastery of the English language. However, the issue of the pictograph remains. English has a very economical symbol base. With twenty-six letters, one can produce any word or sound in English that one can imagine. However, the Chinese written language remains less flexible than this, bogged down in a plethora of pictographs.

Thus, it is my opinion that becoming literate, let alone gaining mastery of the Chinese written language, would be difficult, with true mastery residing in the halls of the wealthy and privileged, those who have the time, resources and energy to invest in developing a deep understanding of the intricacies of the written word. In Japan, a similar situation has arisen, and the crafty Japanese have developed a simplified language, an inter-language called Hiragana, that allows for ease and speed of communication. I wonder that the Chinese may benefit from something like this. And I wonder if that inter-language might not be English. Of course, this sounds like an arrogance. It is not meant as such, but simply to say that English has become the "go-to" language of so many systems such as science, medicine, technology and commerce that, by default, perhaps it could serve to further develop Chinese national and international systems.

Needless to say, this is not unbroken terrain. While it may seem on the surface that learning English in China may make some small sense, not everyone is on board. There are always contextual differences. This is an example of "big picture/little picture" thinking. While it may make sense for students to learn English, many of their parents are struggling to learn Cambodian or Vietnamese because these are the trading partners of right now, not tomorrow. Among these co-existing stresses are additional tensions relating to culture, heritage, beliefs and values associated with the learning of new languages.

Tensions relating to culture, heritage, beliefs and values are not only the province of language learning. These are also some of the issues related to globalization. Our world will never become *less* globalized than it is at the moment. As the neo-liberal juggernaut gains strength, allegiances and alliances around the globe, languages fall in favor of English. As the language of dominance, English is not only the language of colonialism, it is also the language of neo-colonialism. Empire building continues apace, the only difference between now and past empires is the alarming fact that new colonizers do not have allegiance to any particular country. They are truly global in perspective. And the weapons of destruction and dominance are financial and economic in nature. To learn a language is to learn a culture. Clearly, the learning of English as a second, third or even fourth language may represent an excursion into either the comforting world of inclusive language or the otherwise terrifying world of the hostile takeover, resulting in economic domination.

In some cases, there is no chance to win. Several years ago, I was in the rain forest of Belize, in a tiny village that time appeared to have forgotten. However, not all is what it seems. Many years earlier, the entire area was given over to rain forest. Then, the wheels of "justice" declared the rain forest as a reserved area and this small town was created just outside of the perimeters of the rain forest. Many people who were born and raised in the rain forest were displaced. Many had to learn to function anew in the relatively modern society of the small tribal village. However, the issues did not stop here.

Children went to a small public school named, ironically enough, after Saint Jude, the patron saint of lost causes. Attendance was relatively relaxed, even for the teachers. This was a half-hearted attempt at formal education and I was interested to discover the reasoning behind such a lackadaisical attitude. What I discovered was that this was a no-win situation in the making. Not only had the townspeople been displaced from the way of life they had been born into, they were also impaled upon the horns of a dilemma. Out of approximately 150 elementary school-aged children, there were two scholarships available to allow promising academically minded children to pursue a secondary school education in the not-so-nearby large town. Slightly more than one percent of the children in the community would have an opportunity to proceed to high school.

The statistics are depressing. However, not all children were determined to get an "advanced" education. Their choices, however, were grim. They could vie for the scholarships and, if successful, live in a larger town and, hopefully, gain employment to further their aspirations. Conversely, they could stay in their small community and, given the education they would receive at the public school, eventually take up the family business. Family businesses here are pretty marginal, to say the least; however, the choices were to stay home and engage in subsistence farming or go to the large town, bereft of friends and family, and perhaps become "successful," however success may be measured.

In a place like this small town, the dilemma appears stark and hard-edged. However, it has played out like this, to some extent or other, in a variety of venues, ever since the Industrial Revolution. Since its inception, circa 1760, from the beginnings of the Industrial Revolution, machinery was developed that made life much easier, if redundant. Machines replaced human labor and left many people without gainful employment. Youngsters were unemployed, often for the first time in their short lives. It was at this point that childhood was invented. The invention of schools followed not far behind in an attempt to keep these young people away from public mischief and to instill in them a modicum of language, learning and culture.

It has been said by some that our current technological revolution is nothing more than a continuation of the Industrial Revolution. Thanks to the development of the microchip, huge sums of money can be moved effortlessly around the globe. Terrorists no longer need to leave the comforts of their home in order to wreak havoc on the rest of the world. Corporations, national, transnational and supranational have become border lords, almost in a parody of the city-states of yore. As the world grows smaller, it also grows more diverse in some ways, and more confusing in others. Perhaps the learning of a language such as English can serve as somewhat of a unifying force in the face of so much fracturing of countries, cultures and ways of being.

I am not arguing for assimilation but for preservation. Just as in Canada, we have had issues around the separation of our French-speaking contingent to potentially form its own country. These issues, in some incarnation or other, tend to hover about many cultures and peoples. As Michael Ignatieff noted in his book, *Blood and Belonging,* the surest way to lose the French culture in Canada is to separate. It comes down to trading partners and, he believes, the US would be the major trading partner of the newly minted French-speaking country, not France, and the Americans would not tolerate French in their trade negotiations. To remain under the umbrella of Canada, with all its flaws, serves to protect the Francophone culture.

Similarly, the spread of English as a second or additional language may adopt the same stance. It may be better to learn a language that one may utilize for one's own posterity in order to ensure one's eventual survival, than to merely accept the eventual conversion of all languages, remote as that may seem, to the English language. I have heard this cast in terms of eggs and bacon—the chicken is involved but the pig is committed. One side of the coin, the chicken, represents acquiescence. The obverse of that same coin shows the pig has, passively or not, accepted its fate. Is this a dilemma? Is a world order where English represents the voice of major industry and institutions a taken-for-granted assumption?

This volume represents a firewall, of sorts. It draws from around the world. Between the covers of this book, we meet all sorts of people from all around the world. We hear about their stories, their trials and tribulations and, yes, their successes. We see how a diverse group of teachers endeavored to connect academic research and classroom practice with the same professional goal: to support their students' learning of the English language. Through these renditions, we come to view the world differently, not as separate cultures that have nothing in common, but as pieces of patchwork made into one whole.

This wholeness, however, is not sameness. That which gives us life and strength, the cultures within which we thrive and succeed, are as real and distinctive as they ever were. What has changed is the unity with which we arrive at the goal of learning English. Rather than merely tolerating the study of English as an evil necessity, perhaps it is time to embrace it as a unifying force, a force that can allow us to communicate across vast distances in ways that are easily understood. Perhaps it is time to re-conceptualize the study of English as a measure of unity that has the potential to bring different and dissident sides together at the same table. This is my hope for this book and for other books in the same vein to follow.

Reference

Ignatieff, M. (1993). *Blood and belonging: Journeys into the new nationalism*. Toronto: Penguin.

Robert E. White
St. Francis Xavier University, Canada

Figures and Tables

Figures

Tables

Acknowledgements

I am grateful to the many people who have supported my research and the completion of this volume. First of all, I would like to thank the language teacher-researchers who contributed chapters to this book. Their enthusiasm and courage to share authentic experiences of connecting research and practice made this volume possible. Further, their willingness to review each other's chapters and provide constructive feedback is greatly appreciated.

The roots of this book lie in my doctoral study at the Ontario Institute for Studies in Education (OISE). I am thankful to OISE for encouraging me to be curious in my work. I owe much to Dennis Thiessen, Karyn Cooper, and Rubén Gaztambide-Fernández.

I am eternally grateful to the Social Sciences and Humanities Research Council of Canada (SSHRC) for funding my two-year postdoctoral study. I am fortunate to have had the institutional base provided by the Faculty of Education at St. Francis Xavier University. Dr. Robert White's support has been tremendous.

Many colleagues at the York University English Language Institute offered encouragement and thoughtful reviews. I thank all of them, especially Michael Koslowski and Kris Johnston. Additionally, the support of colleagues who anonymously reviewed some of the chapters in this volume may go unspoken, but not forgotten.

Importantly, I owe special thanks to my wife Shirina Aktar for her encouragement throughout this book project.

Last but not least, I am grateful to the staff at Brill Sense for their professionalism, care, and support.

Notes on Contributors

Chris Banister

(MA TESOL, BA Hons., PGCHE) teaches academic and business English at Regent's University London. Chris has previously worked in wide ranging ELT settings in London and Istanbul. He holds an MA in TESOL from the University College London Institute of Education and his dissertation research focused on vocabulary lists for academic English. His teaching and research articles have appeared in edited books and refereed journals.

Leigh Bennett

is a lecturer in the English for Academic Purposes department at Akita International University, Japan. He has previously taught English in South Korea, Japan and the U.K. His research interests include the academic writing struggles of students during their tertiary studies and corpus linguistics in language education.

Xin Chen

(PhD Candidate in Literacy, Culture and Language Education) teaches academic writing at Indiana University in Bloomington, USA. Previously, she worked as a program administrator of Business English training in China. Her research interests include multilingual students' development of English academic literacy, translingual literacy and international education. She has published articles in *INTESOL Journal* and *TESOL Newsletter*. She also co-authored a book entitled *Teacher Training and Professional Development of Chinese English Language Teachers* (Routledge, 2017).

Tiffany Johnson

(MA, TESOL) is currently studying Arabic full-time in the Middle East and plans to teach in a Foundations English Program when she completes her studies. Previously, she worked as an ESL specialist at a K-12 private international school in the United Arab Emirates before earning her Master's degree at Eastern Michigan University. Tiffany's research interests include learner autonomy, adult education, and materials development.

Kendon Kurzer

(PhD, Education; MA, TESOL) is currently a lecturer in the University Writing Program at the University of California, Davis. His primary research interests include the intersection of writing across the curriculum, L2 writing, and written corrective feedback. He has published in the *TESOL Quarterly, Assessing*

Writing, and *Foreign Language Annals*. He also serves on the editorial board of the *Journal of Response to Writing*.

Nguyen Thi Thuy Loan

(MA, TESOL; PhD, English Language Studies) teaches English for Academic Purposes and English Language Teaching Methodologies at Kalasin University, Thailand. Her research interests include genre analysis, English written discourse, and L2 writing instruction. She has published in journals including *ESP Today, The Asian ESP Journal, The Asian EFL Journal, The Indonesian Journal of Applied Linguistics, The Iranian Journal of Language Teaching Research,* and *3L Journal.*

Cynthia J. Macknish

(EdD, TESOL & Applied Linguistics) has taught various levels from elementary and secondary to undergraduate and graduate levels in Canada, the Bahamas, China, and Singapore. Currently, she enjoys teaching ESL and TESOL as associate professor at Eastern Michigan University. Prior to this, she developed and taught post-secondary ESL, EAP, and teacher education courses in Singapore. Her research interests include service learning, language pedagogy, assessment, and critical literacy.

Michael McLelland

(MA, TESOL) currently teaches ESL students in metro Detroit, Michigan. He has accepted a position and plans to teach at a university in Danang, Vietnam beginning in 2019.

Brian Morgan

(PhD) is an associate professor in the English Department of Glendon College, York University, in Toronto, where he teaches courses in content-based EAP, language teacher education, and graduate courses in applied linguistics. His primary research area is in critical theories and their potential implementation across English language teaching contexts.

Donna M. Neary

(MA) teaches high school Social Studies to English language learners in Louisville, Kentucky. Previously, Donna worked for museums including the Kentucky Historical Society and the Kentucky Derby Museum curating exhibitions and planning programming for visitors. Her articles have appeared in *The Public Historian, Louisville Encyclopedia, Encyclopedia of Kentucky, Ohio Valley History, Pioneers of American Landscape Design II,* EdSurge.org, and JCPSforward.org. She has written several community histories.

Gina Paschalidou

holds BA in English Language and Literature from the Aristotle University of Thessaloniki, and MEd in TESOL from the Hellenic Open University, Greece. She is a teacher of English in Greek State Secondary Education. Gina's research interests include student motivation, content and language integrated learning, material design, and cross-language mediation.

Ayşenur Sağdıç

(MA, TESL) is a PhD student in Applied Linguistics at Georgetown University and an EAP instructor. Ayşenur has several years of experience in teaching adult EFL and ESL learners in Turkey and in the USA as well as in teaching English composition and research skills to undergraduates. Her research area includes classroom-based adult second language acquisition with an emphasis on second language pragmatic development, instruction, and assessment.

Nashwa Nashaat Sobhy

(PhD, Applied Linguistics) currently teaches language and education subjects at San Jorge University in Spain, and is a member of the UAM-CLIL research group at the Autonomous University of Madrid. Her research has centered on teaching and learning through English as an additional language, with specific focus on language pragmatics and academic discourse functions. She has written chapters in edited books published by John Benjamins, Brill, and Peter Lang. Nashwa has also published articles in *Intercultural Pragmatics* and *RESLA*.

Lorena Valmori

(PhD, Second Language Studies) teaches English to high school students in Modena, Italy. Previously she taught Italian as a second language in the UK and the USA. She also taught English and teaching methods in the Department of Education and Humanities at Università of Modena and Reggio Emilia, Italy. Her teaching experience has informed her research interests in motivational dynamics, identity, and emotions in second language learning. Her articles have appeared in *Language Teaching* and *System*.

Robert E. White

(PhD) is Associate Professor in the Faculty of Education at St. Francis Xavier University in Nova Scotia, Canada. Robert's research interests lie in social justice and equity education, globalization, critical pedagogy, leadership and qualitative research. Robert has had a lengthy career in the public school system where he taught English as a Second Language.

Mobilizing Research Knowledge: Insights from the Classroom

Sardar Anwaruddin
St. Francis Xavier University, Canada

The term *research* has always occupied a privileged position in academic discourses. Historically, it has been linked to the scientific authority to produce legitimate knowledge. In recent decades, the idea of research has escaped the academic discourses of the ivory towers of universities and has mingled with public discourses. Nowadays we often hear people talk about research-based practice. The utterance of the word research by a greater number of people does not make research any less legitimate or powerful. Instead, it suggests that people are now more capable of accessing research evidence than they were in the past. They are also more aware of the potential benefits of using research-based knowledge in their personal, social, and professional lives. While it sounds promising that an increasing number of people are familiar with the idea of research, their understanding of research and its usefulness may vary significantly. Furthermore, what qualifies as research and the extent to which research can improve practice remains highly contested.

In this book, research is conceptualized as a planned activity which follows recognized method(s) to find answers to a worthy question. As Arjun Appadurai (2006) wrote, to conduct research means "to make disciplined inquires into those things we need to know, but do not know yet" (p. 167). Thus, the most important aspect of research is to ask the right question that should be answered from an inquiry. Another important characteristic of research is that its findings need to be made public. They must remain subject to public criticism and further empirical tests (Stenhouse, 1981). In this sense, the concept of research is inherently dialogical and self-critical.

As for contributions that research makes to the knowledge base in the field of education, two broad categories of research may be identified: education and education*al*. When the aim of research is to produce knowledge for its own sake, it is generally referred to as education research. Here knowledge creation is an intellectually stimulating activity, and the researcher is not overly concerned with improving the practice. On the other hand, when the primary aim of research is to improve practice, the preferred term is education*al* research. In this context, knowledge generation is viewed as a practical activity (see Whitty, 2006 for further discussion on this topic). In this book, I follow this distinction between education and educational research, albeit with a cautionary note that at times the lines between them may become blurred. I am concerned primarily with research that aims to generate knowledge that may be helpful for practitioners in diverse social and cultural contexts. As Lawrence Stenhouse (1981) wrote, "research is educational to the extent that it can be related to the practice of education" (p. 113).

The "Awful" Reputation of Educational Research

Historically, educational research has attracted criticism from stakeholders such as teachers, parents, administrators, and members of the public concerned about educational improvements. Carl Kaestle's (1993) article "The Awful Reputation of Educational Research" highlighted key criticisms levelled against educational research in the 1970s and 1980s. One of the main criticisms was that research had little to no influence on teachers' classroom practice. Mary Kennedy (1997) put forward four hypotheses to explain this apparent lack of influence of research on practice:

> (a) The research itself is not sufficiently persuasive or authoritative; the quality of educational studies has not been high enough to provide compelling, unambiguous, or authoritative results to practitioners. (b) The research has not been relevant to practice. It has not been sufficiently practical, it has not addressed teachers' questions, nor has it adequately acknowledged their constraints. (c) Ideas from research have not been accessible to teachers. Findings have not been expressed in ways that are comprehensible to teachers. (d) The education system itself is intractable and unable to change, or it is conversely inherently unstable, overly susceptible to fads, and consequently unable to engage in systematic change. (p. 4)

While some of the problems that Kennedy (1997) identified still exist, considerable advancements have been made to make research more meaningful and usable for practitioners.

For example, we now have sophisticated channels of communication between researchers and practitioners. There are many researchers who design and conduct studies in collaboration with practicing teachers. Increasing numbers of teachers are members of professional organizations such as

TESOL and IATEFL and attending academic conferences to learn about the latest research in their area of work. Many teachers are also joining interest-driven online communities where they exchange research-based knowledge. Researchers are now publishing papers in open-access journals as a way of reaching greater readership in diverse contexts around the world. Government and non-government funding agencies now require researchers to explain how they will disseminate their findings beyond the academic circle. While these developments do not necessarily eradicate all material and cultural barriers that prevent teachers from utilizing research-based knowledge, they certainly make research more accessible and potentially relevant to the practice of teaching.

There is a growing body of work that focuses on the dissemination and utilization of academic research. A few different terms are being used to describe this body of work, including research dissemination, research exchange, and knowledge mobilization. I prefer the term knowledge mobilization (KMb), which is concerned primarily with the question: "How can research-produced knowledge be better 'mobilised' among users such as practising educators, policy-makers and the public communities" (Fenwick & Farrell, 2012, p. 1)? My work is inspired by the Canadian model of knowledge mobilization, which is gaining considerable popularity both within and outside Canada. The government of Canada is committed to increasing the impact of research so that it may bring about positive social change and improve the quality of life. In this light, knowledge mobilization has been defined as:

> the reciprocal and complementary flow and uptake of research knowl-edge between researchers, knowledge brokers and knowledge users—both within and beyond academia—in such a way that may benefit users and create positive impacts within Canada and/or internationally, and, ultimately, has the potential to enhance the profile, reach and impact of social sciences and humanities research. (SSHRC, 2018, p. 30)

As this definition suggests, knowledge mobilization provides an alternative view of the traditional, one-way process of research conducted by university-based researchers, where findings are simplified and integrated into curricu-lum materials by mediators/brokers, and then teachers adopt the materials to improve their practice. This one-way view of research dissemination has dominated the field for a long time and has failed largely due to its inability to address the sociocultural and material contexts of the schools in which research-based knowledge is supposed to be applied. Contrary to this trans-fer model of research use, KMb encourages reciprocity between researchers and practitioners where both parties complement and learn from each other's expertise and experience.

Although the concept of knowledge mobilization is promising, much of what is being done under the banner of KMb still suffers from the earlier transfer model of research utilization. There is no doubt that contemporary initiatives of KMb include more effective communication links, thanks to the advancement in information and communication technologies. For example, one KMb initiative[1] locates published research papers that have practical implications for classroom teachers. The papers are then summarized in "plain" English. These summaries are published on the Internet and are freely accessible to all. A similar initiative has been implemented by the Centre for the Use of Research and Evidence in Education (CUREE) in the United Kingdom. This project locates and disseminates "the most useful research" to support teachers' professional development. It endeavours "to help teachers make informed decisions about the most effective and efficient approaches to use in their own context[s]" (CUREE, 2018, p. 1). While these initiatives are worthy of praise for their efforts to reach out to teachers in diverse contexts, their selection processes for research studies remain unclear and questionable. CUREE does not provide information on which research is summarized and published, and why. Moreover, we do not know how the summarized research may be meaningful in individual teachers' unique contexts. Ultimately, the dialogical character of knowledge mobilization is absent in this one-way transfer model of research dissemination.

Research and Classroom Practice in Applied Linguistics and TESOL

The concept of knowledge mobilization is particularly relevant to the field of applied linguistics because the field itself was built on the premise of *application*. The foundational goal of applied linguistics was to apply linguistic knowledge to real-world language-related problems. As Kaplan and Widdowson (1992) wrote, "Applied is a technology which makes abstract ideas and research findings accessible and relevant to the real world; it mediates between theory and practice" (p. 76). Over the years, applied linguistics has evolved to become a diverse field of study, which draws not only from linguistics (i.e., the scientific study of languages), but also from other fields such as education, psychology, anthropology, sociology, media and communications studies, and cultural studies. Today, applied linguistics is broadly understood as "an international, multilingual field concerned with issues pertaining to languages and literacies in the real world and with the people who learn, speak, write, process, translate, test, teach, use, and lose languages in myriad ways" (Duff, 2015, p. 57). Although the field is now understood in such broad terms, it has not lost its foundational spirit of application. As James Simpson (2013) wrote in his introduction to *The Routledge Handbook of Applied Linguistics*, "Applied linguistics is the academic field which connects knowledge about language to decision-making in the real world" (p. 1). In light of these definitions, it is essential to understand how research-based knowledge is being mobilized in this practice-oriented field.

Many researchers, practitioners, and policy-makers have lamented the so-called research-practice "gap" in applied linguistics. An oft-cited criticism is that research has failed to sufficiently improve classroom practice. From Duff's (2015) broad definition of applied linguistics, I now focus on a specific area of study, namely, Teaching English to Speakers of Other Languages (TESOL), which is also widely known as English Language Teaching (ELT). Like other sub-fields of education, TESOL has been subject to the criticism of the so-called research-practice gap. David Block (2000) wrote that this gap was due to three main reasons: differences in the status of researchers and teachers, their different stances towards knowledge, and membership in different discourse communities. Similarly, Simon Borg's (2009) study with 505 teachers of English from 13 countries identified teachers' low level of research engagement. Many teachers participating in Borg's study reported that a lack of time, inaccessibility of published research, and a lack of practical relevance were among the key barriers to their engagement with research. Furthermore, teachers who participated in Nassaji's (2012) study believed that "the knowledge they gain from teaching experience is more relevant to their teaching practices than the knowledge they gain from ... research" (p. 350). This line of criticism challenges the relevance of academic research to teachers' classroom practice. Commentators such as Medgyes (2017) go as far as to portray researchers as "mere extras in the language-teaching operation" and claim that the blame should be put on "researchers, who are reluctant to admit that their work may not be so relevant as they would have us believe" (p. 494).

Recognizing this negative attitude towards research and a perceived lack of practical relevance to classroom practice, the TESOL International Association Research Agenda (2014) "calls for more attention to how practitioners can use research" (p. 2). This current edited volume responds directly to this call by showcasing how in-service teachers apply research-based knowledge to their pedagogical practice. It also sheds light on personal, social, and institutional factors that help or hinder teachers' research utilization. While the transfer of research evidence, for example, from university to school, is a fairly straightforward activity, the uptake and use of research evidence by practitioners is very complex. This complexity is due to the fact that "at the level of practice, research-generated knowledge must compete for the attention of practitioners with other forms of knowledge, including tradition, professional expertise, and various forms of data, including students' test data" (Cain, Wieser, & Livingston, 2016, p. 531). Therefore, knowledge mobilization requires careful attention to the complexities, potentials, and challenges of utilizing research-evidence to improve pedagogical practice.

What This Book Aims to Do

One of the dimensions of knowledge mobilization addressed in this volume is co-production of knowledge by academic researchers and classroom teachers. Because KMb is understood as a reciprocal process of knowledge construction and utilization, teachers are not merely implementers of research. Instead, they are treated as active constructors of knowledge. Teachers make practical teaching decisions based on their understanding and contextually-responsive modifications of research evidence. Thus, the principal aim of this book is to feature in-service teachers' first-hand accounts of research-informed practice. This is important because teachers who engage with research should be able to demonstrate why and how their pedagogical decisions are effective. Their accounts should also "be made public, open to scrutiny and available for future reference" (Burns, 2014, p. 4). The contributing teachers' experiences and insights, as presented through the chapters of this volume, will provide practical implications for individuals and organizations interested in making research more impactful in the field of TESOL.

It should be noted that there is a group of commentators who doubt the usefulness of research for second/foreign language teaching. They contend that teaching is too complex an activity to be informed by the findings of systematically conducted research studies. They suggest that teachers learn from their own experience and intuition and share such learning with peers (e.g., Medgyes, 2017). Others challenge this suggestion on the ground that there is no way of distinguishing good experiences from bad ones. Therefore, experience cannot be a reliable source of professional knowledge. Many teachers teach the way they were taught. More than four decades ago, Dan Lortie (1975) documented this kind of teacher learning, which he explained through the notion of the *apprenticeship of observation*. However, critics of this model of professional learning argue that it "can lead to the danger of entering a vicious circle of received wisdom which is never questioned, and which blocks change. The simple recycling of experience from one professional to another cannot be the way the profession progresses" (Paran, 2017, p. 500). My opinion is that learning from experiences and stories is an important component of teachers' professional development. However, this does not cancel out the possibility of learning from systematically conducted academic research. Instead of embracing an *either-or* approach, this book aims to explore whether or not, and under what circumstances, research can make contributions to language-teachers' professional learning and development.

The Story behind This Book

All chapters of this volume are written by practicing teachers of English as a second/additional language. These teachers were requested to follow a three-step writing process:

Step 1: Each author chose a research article from a peer-reviewed journal within the field of TESOL/ELT.[2] They were encouraged to find an article that had practical implications for pedagogical practice.

Step 2: After reading the article, the teachers thought about how the article might inform their teaching. They revised or updated their curriculum by incorporating the article's findings and recommendations. Then, they implemented the new curriculum.

Step 3: After teaching the research-informed curriculum, the teachers wrote a paper reflecting on their experiences. Some guiding questions for them included, but were not limited to: What worked and what did not? How did the article inform their practice? How did their students respond to the research-informed curriculum? What were the challenges to implementing the article's recommendations? What would they like to tell colleagues interested in research utilization?

An Overview of the Chapters

In Chapter 1, "Improving the Effectiveness of International Students' Peer Review in an English Academic Writing Course," Xin Chen describes her utilization of a peer review model. She integrated this model—published in *TESL Canada Journal*—into her curriculum of a composition course designed for first-year international students at a university in the United States.

In Chapter 2, "Implementing Peer-Feedback in Paragraph-Writing Classes at a Thai University," Nguyen Thi Thuy Loan reports on her experience of facilitating editing and revising activities with third-year English majors at a Thai university. She drew research-based insights from an article on using peer-feedback in ESL writing classes, which was published in *ELT Journal*.

In Chapter 3, "Revising Essays Collaboratively," Gina Paschalidou discusses her experiences of applying collaborative revision to her teaching at a lower secondary school in Greece. She utilized research on collaborative writing in second language writing published in *ELT Journal*.

In Chapter 4, "Dynamic Written Corrective Feedback in a Community College ESL Writing Class Setting," Kendon Kurzer reports on his utilization of a method of providing grammar feedback known as dynamic written corrective feedback. He utilized research on this topic, published in *Language Teaching Research*, while teaching lower intermediate ESL students at a suburban community college in the United States.

In Chapter 5, "Bringing the Academic Vocabulary List into the Classroom: Student Lexical Investigations," Chris Banister discusses how he applied research on academic vocabulary to his curriculum of business English for a group of exchange students at a UK university. He turned to research on frequency-based vocabulary teaching published in *Applied Linguistics*.

In Chapter 6, "Operationalizing 'Defining' from a Cognitive Discourse Perspective for Learners' Use," Nashwa Nashaat Sobhy describes how she adopted "defining" as a cognitive discourse function (CDF) to teach a content and language integrated course entitled Theory and History of Education at a Spanish university. She drew on CDF research published in a book entitled *Conceptualising Integration in CLIL and Multilingual Education*.

In Chapter 7, "From Researchers to L2 Classrooms: Teaching Pragmatics through Collaborative Tasks," Ayşenur Sağdıç focuses on her research-informed teaching in an intermediate level English for Academic Purposes (EAP) course at the Intensive English Program of a public university in the United States. She utilized research on collaborative pragmatic tasks published in *Foreign Language Annals*.

In Chapter 8, "From False Myths to Achievable Goals: Developing Language Learning Awareness in the L2 Classroom," Lorena Valmori shares her experiences of research-informed teaching at a technical high school in Italy. Drawing upon research on language learners' beliefs published in *The Modern Language Journal*, she endeavoured to re-design her EFL curriculum to increase students' awareness of their learning processes.

In Chapter 9, "Reflecting on Academic Service-Learning Research in a University Intensive English Program," Cynthia Macknish, Tiffany Johnson, and Michael McLelland discuss their curriculum revision to enhance students' language learning and to help them make contributions to the local community.

In this endeavour, the authors turned to research on academic service learning published in *TESOL Journal*.

In Chapter 10, "'I Saw Wonderfull Things in There': Reflection on an Art Museum Field Trip for High School English Language Learners," Donna M. Neary describes her curriculum intervention involving a field trip to an art museum. Her starting point was research on the educational value of field trips published in *Education Next*. Neary discusses how the field trip provided opportunities for recently migrated ESL students to connect their home cultures with life and education in the United States.

In Chapter 11, "Blending the Styles: Exploring Students' Views on the Merging of the Creative with the Academic," Leigh Yohei Bennett ponders his attempt to integrate creativity in the design and teaching of an EAP writing curriculum at a liberal arts university in Japan. He drew inspiration from research on creativity and academic writing published in the *Journal of English for Academic Purposes*.

Four Insights Gleaned from the Chapters

There is no shortage of research-based recommendations in the TESOL/ELT literature. Perhaps, this is one of the reasons why many teachers are unwilling to turn to research for professional development. For them, research evidence is strangely inconclusive. And teachers have very little time and patience to try to make sense of seemingly contradictory research findings. As Claire Kramsch (2015) wrote, research-based proposals are often "bewildering for the practitioner who is at the same time under increased pressure to measure and evaluate success through multiple choice tests so as to justify his/her own existence" (p. 458). Against this challenge, the teachers who contribute to this book engaged in a practical experiment with research-based recommendations. Their reflections on research utilization have yielded important insights which I describe in four broad terms: context-responsive praxis, personal theories of research-based knowledge, epistemological pluralism, and reciprocal dependence. This categorization is done at the risk of simplification; however, my intention is to present my understanding of the contributing authors' research utilization in a manageable way and, at the same time, to initiate further discussions on teachers' engagement with academic research.

Context-Responsive Praxis: Teachers' application of research-based knowledge to classroom teaching reflects their context-responsive praxis. By the term *praxis*, I refer to a notion different from the meaning of *practice*. While practice denotes any activity in general, praxis refers to particular ways of doing something, which involve an ethical consideration. In this Aristotelian view of praxis, knowledge is inseparable from practical wisdom. An actor performs a task in ways that are morally right and informed by prudent choices. In this light, teaching is not a purely technical activity where the end goal is pre-determined and achieved by applying precise methods. When the teachers featured in this book engaged with research, they took professional context in their ethical consideration, and adapted research evidence in order to meet their contextual needs. This is aligned with my earlier study where teachers' reading and understanding of research became synonymous with attending to contextual circumstances (Anwaruddin, 2016, 2017). To varying degrees, all eleven chapters show that teachers adapted research-based proposals to suit the needs of their students. In general, the participating teachers' attentiveness to context supports Judy Sharkey's (2004) finding that teachers' awareness of context is a critical factor in curriculum development and implementation. Hence, contextualization is a necessary strategy to make research meaningful for practice.

Personal Theories of Research-Based Knowledge: Good teaching requires instant decision making. For example, when two students raise hands at the same time, who speaks first? Due to the complexity and unpredictability involved in teaching, it requires teachers to develop ethical values over time. Teachers' practical experience and wisdom play an important role in the development of such values that guide instant decision making in the classroom. Research-based recommendations may become helpful when teachers have read, interpreted, and personalized the recommendations for their own contexts and students. However, such personalized views of research are not static; they change depending on cultural, material, and human circumstances. Therefore, it is safe to say that teachers develop their own personal theory of research-based knowledge, which may lack the methodological coherence of scientific inquiry, but which is "sufficiently flexible to guide action in varied and constantly changing contexts" (Cain & Allan, 2017, p. 721). The teachers featured in this book demonstrate such a personal theory of research-based knowledge developed through attentiveness to both macro and micro contexts of teaching and learning in order to make changes in curriculum and instruction. For example, in Chapter 7, Ayşenur Sağdıç shows how she took ownership of research by critically evaluating its findings in light of the unique demands of her teaching context.

Epistemological Pluralism: We have different ways of knowing. Our natural inclination, cultural background, academic training, and professional socialization determine the method(s) of knowing we prefer. Today, most disciplines in the humanities and social sciences are faced with an epistemological complexity. After the "post" turn (e.g., postmodernism, poststructuralism, and postcolonialism), disciplines of academic inquiry no longer subscribe to a single meta-narrative of how we come to know something and how we validate the method of our knowing. The epistemological landscape is now marked with diversity of methods, and most scholars would agree that such diversity is a good thing. It enriches our experience of being in the world and trying to make sense of it. Commenting on the field of instructed second language acquisition and the educational and societal complexities involved in it, Lourdes Ortega (2005) argued that "it behooves us all not only to respect but also to engage intellectually with work resulting from epistemologies different from our own" (p. 436). Such epistemological openness is crucial for the practice of teaching, which requires practical wisdom and ethical judgment based on different kinds of knowledge. The teachers featured in this book show epistemological openness in their engagement with research. They respect the researchers' knowledge, but critically assess its contextual validity and usefulness, while remaining committed to the development of their personal theory.

Reciprocal Dependence: For a long time, research and practice have been understood as dichotomous. A common-sense belief was that research—as a systematic and rigorous activity—produces valuable knowledge that should be used to improve practice. Therefore, research findings have been translated into "usable knowledge" for contexts such as schools, hospitals, and stock markets. In this view, researchers' propositional knowledge has always enjoyed more prestige and power when compared to practitioners' practical knowledge. However, one recent line of thinking in educational studies maintains that we should move beyond the dichotomy of research *versus* practice, and that we should embrace research *and* practice as two equally valuable sources of knowledge. For example, Catherine Snow (2015) argued that it is erroneous to view researchers as the producers of knowledge and practitioners as the users of knowledge. Educational improvement is dependent on a reciprocal model in which "researchers need to acknowledge the realities of practice and practitioners need to acknowledge the commitment to rigor in research" (Snow, 2015, p. 461). This kind of reciprocity is productive because both researchers and teachers benefit from each other. The chapters in the current volume attest to this reciprocal dependence. The authors not only document what worked and what did not in their classroom context, but they also initiate a dialogue in which researchers can re-evaluate the knowledge that they have generated.

Looking Ahead

Working with the group of teachers for this book project has led me to believe that we need to stop thinking about research-based evidence as the panacea for all educational ills. We also need to stop believing that research-based evidence is more valid and useful than teachers' practical knowledge and wisdom. In one context, research evidence may be very helpful, while in another context, a teacher's life-experience can be the most important factor in making pedagogically effective decisions. Furthermore, we need to keep in mind that research sometimes yields conflicting results. Inconclusive and/or contradictory findings are major areas of criticism for which educational research has attracted what Kaestle (1993) called an "awful reputation." However, I would like to underscore that inconclusiveness and contradictions do not make research worthless; rather, they "help us construct complex answers to complex phenomena, though of course they may sometimes lead us to re-examine evidence and possibly reject it" (Paran, 2017, p. 502). Therefore, an important conclusion from the knowledge mobilization project presented in this book is that research-based evidence, while not the only source of knowledge, can certainly enrich teachers' pedagogical knowledge and practice.

The chapters in this book suggest that effective utilization of research in the classroom is achievable and that the future holds exciting possibilities. The challenge for the TESOL field is how to locate, read, interpret, adapt, and utilize research-based evidence in manners that will be transformative for teachers and students, as well as the researchers who generated the evidence in the first place. One promising area of work is knowledge mobilization, which opposes earlier efforts to transfer research evidence from universities to schools, from laboratories to classrooms. The linear models of one-way transfer of research knowledge have already proven to be counterproductive. The contemporary wave of knowledge mobilization aims at focusing on the complex processes of generating and utilizing research evidence. In my view, knowledge mobilization involves four broad steps: generation, transfer, interpretation, and utilization. In the field of TESOL, we have recently seen some initiatives to bring research-evidence to a broader audience through various media such as user-contributed blogs. ELT Research Bites (2018) is an example of how research studies are summarized in simplified language so that busy teachers may keep abreast of recent developments in the field and potentially reflect on the impacts of these developments on their teaching practice.

While initiatives such as the ELT Research Bites are an important step, dissemination of evidence is not enough. We need to know how practitioners read, understand, and apply evidence to their classroom practice. Such knowledge is important not only for other teachers who may be interested in turning to research-evidence for professional learning, but also for researchers who generated the evidence. This speaks to the self-correcting nature of research as an intellectual activity. After learning about the uptake of research evidence, researchers may re-examine the method, validity, and social implications of their findings. In this way, successful knowledge mobilization holds the potential to blur the traditional boundary between researchers and practitioners. Due to its emphasis on reciprocity (SSHRC, 2018), knowledge mobilization provides opportunities to go beyond dissemination of research and encourage re-examination of research. The four insights discussed in this introductory chapter and demonstrated throughout the book can be helpful to address the complexities and challenges in designing future knowledge mobilization projects in TESOL. To reiterate, the insights are (1) paying attention to contextual realities, (2) developing personal theories of research-based knowledge, (3) embracing epistemological pluralism, and (4) nurturing reciprocal dependence between researchers and teachers. By considering these insights for knowledge mobilization in TESOL, researchers and teachers could respond to Graham Hall's (2018) call for connecting research and practice "in ways which are supportive, motivating and sustainable in [teachers'] daily working lives" (p. 40).

As the chapters of this volume will demonstrate, one beneficial and sustainable way of teachers' engagement with academic research is to take an interpretive approach to assessing the validity and applicability of research-based recommendations in local contexts of practice. Because each context is unique, such interpretive reading of research requires that the teacher take stock of a variety of pedagogical, political, and cultural factors that constitute the distinctive character of the context. As Brian Morgan (2016) writes, effective teachers are aware of the sociopolitical context within which they teach. It is their professional responsibility to identify issues that negatively impact their pedagogical practice. Morgan (2016) suggests that teachers create a blueprint for action that will respond to their identified issues, which impede pedagogical innovation. Turning to academic research and taking an interpretive approach to understanding its implications can be helpful to implement such blueprints for action. Thus, critical examinations of the nexus between research and its practical use in the classroom may be a vehicle for teachers' professional learning and development.

Notes

1 https://oere.oise.utoronto.ca/
2 One author chose a book chapter.

References

Anwaruddin, S. M. (2016). Language teachers' responses to educational research: Addressing the "crisis" of representation. *International Journal of Research and Method in Education, 39*(3), 314–328. doi:10.1080/1743727X.2016.1166485

Anwaruddin, S. M. (2017). Engagement with research, teacher learning and educational leadership: Towards an interpretive-ecological approach. *International Journal of Leadership in Education,* 1–14. doi:10.1080/13603124.2017.1394495

Appadurai, A. (2006). The right to research. *Globalisation, Societies and Education, 4*(2), 167–177. doi:10.1080/14767720600750696

Block, D. (2000). Revisiting the gap between SLA researchers and language teachers. *Links & Letters, 7,* 129–143.

Borg, S. (2009). English language teachers' conceptions of research. *Applied Linguistics, 30*(3), 358–388. doi:10.1093/applin/amp007

Burns, A. (2014). 'Systematic inquiry made public': Teacher reports from a national action research program. *Research Notes, 56,* 4–6. Retrieved from http://www.cambridgeenglish.org/images/170903-research-notes-56-document.pdf

Cain, T., & Allan, D. (2017). The invisible impact of educational research. *Oxford Review of Education, 43*(6), 718–732. doi:10.1080/03054985.2017.1316252

Cain, T., Wieser, C., & Livingston, K. (2016). Mobilising research knowledge for teaching and teacher education. *European Journal of Teacher Education, 39*(5), 529–533. doi:10.1080/02619768.2016.1256086

CUREE. (2018). *About us.* Retrieved from http://www.curee.co.uk/about-us

Duff, P. A. (2015). Transnationalism, multilingualism, and identity. *Annual Review of Applied Linguistics, 35,* 57–80. doi:10.1017/S026719051400018X

ELT Research Bites. (2018). Retrieved from http://www.eltresearchbites.com/about/

Fenwick, T., & Farrell, L. (2012). Introduction: Knowledge mobilization. In T. Fenwick & L. Farrell (Eds.), *Knowledge mobilization and educational research: Politics, languages and responsibilities* (pp. 1–13). London: Routledge.

Hall, G. (2018). Theory, theories and practice in ELT: 'Believing and doubting.' In J. Mackay, M. Birello, & D. Xerri (Eds.), *ELT research in action: Bridging the gap between research and classroom practice* (pp. 37–40). Faversham: IATEFL.

Kaestle, C. F. (1993). The awful reputation of educational research. *Educational Researcher, 22*(1), 23–31.

Kaplan, R. B., & Widdowson, H. G. (1992). Applied linguistics. In W. Bright (Ed.), *International encyclopedia of linguistics* (Vol. 1, pp. 76–80). New York, NY: Oxford University Press.

Kennedy, M. M. (1997). The connection between research and practice. *Educational Researcher, 26*(7), 4–12. doi:10.3102/0013189X026007004

Kramsch, C. (2015). Applied linguistics: A theory of the practice. *Applied Linguistics, 36*(4), 454–465. doi:10.1093/applin/amv039

Lortie, D. (1975). *School teacher: A sociological study.* Chicago, IL: University of Chicago Press.

Medgyes, P. (2017). The (ir)relevance of academic research for the language teacher. *ELT Journal, 71*(4), 491–498. doi:10.1093/elt/ccx034

Morgan, B. (2016). Language teacher identity and the domestication of dissent: An exploratory account. *TESOL Quarterly, 50*(3), 708–734. doi:10.1002/tesq.316

Nassaji, H. (2012). The relationship between SLA research and language pedagogy: Teachers' perspectives. *Language Teaching Research, 16*(3), 337–365. doi: 10.1177/1362168812436903

Ortega, L. (2005). For what and for whom is our research? The ethical as transformative lens in instructed SLA. *The Modern Language Journal, 89*(3), 427–443. doi: 10.1111/j.1540-4781.2005.00315.x

Paran, A. (2017). 'Only connect': Researchers and teachers in dialogue. *ELT Journal, 71*(4), 499–508. doi:10.1093/elt/ccx033

Sharkey, J. (2004). ESOL teachers' knowledge of context as critical mediator in curriculum development. *TESOL Quarterly, 38*(2), 279–299. doi:10.2307/3588381

Simpson, J. (2013). Introduction: Applied linguistics in the contemporary world. In J. Simpson (Ed.), *The Routledge handbook of applied linguistics* (pp. 1–7). New York, NY: Routledge.

Snow, C. E. (2015). Rigor and realism: Doing educational science in the real world. *Educational Researcher, 44*(9), 460–466. doi:10.3102/0013189X15619166

Social Sciences and Humanities Research Council (SSHRC). (2018). *Knowledge mobilization.* Retrieved from http://www.sshrc-crsh.gc.ca/funding-financement/programs-programmes/definitions-eng.aspx#km-mc

Stenhouse, L. (1981). What counts as research? *British Journal of Educational Studies, 29*(2), 103–114. Retrieved from http://www.jstor.org/stable/3120018

TESOL International Association Research Agenda. (2014). Retrieved from https://www.tesol.org/docs/default-source/pdf/2014_tesol-research-agenda.pdf?sfvrsn=2

Whitty, G. (2006). Education(al) research and education policy making: Is conflict inevitable? *British Educational Research Journal, 32*(2), 159–176. doi:10.1080/01411920600568919

CHAPTER 1

Improving the Effectiveness of International Students' Peer Review in an English Academic Writing Course

Xin Chen
Indiana University Bloomington, USA

Introduction

Peer review helps students benefit from feedback through comparatively plain peer language (Gielen, Tops, Dochy, Onghena, & Smeets, 2010) and better understand the writing as well as revision process (Mendonca & Johnson, 1994; Villamil & de Guerrero, 2006). Many English as a Second Language (ESL) writing teachers have realized the importance of prior training and scaffolding for students to reap the benefit of peer review (e.g., Hu, 2005; Liou & Peng, 2009). However, there is scant research done on the motivation for students' implementation of the peer-review skills taught by their instructors. For example, international students from East Asian countries tend to rely more on the authority (such as teachers) for knowledge and trust than their peers' comments on their work. Furthermore, their culture of courtesy and being afraid of "losing face" in front of others may prevent them from candidly critiquing others' work face-to-face. On top of that, how effectively students can incorporate peer comments in revision still remains under-researched.

I teach first-year composition to international students at a research university in the United States. Most of my students are from Asian countries and had little experience of English academic writing or peer review prior to coming to the U.S. One of the learning outcomes of the course I am teaching is to make the students understand that writing is a process and they will learn how to employ strategies of pre-writing, drafting, and revising in the process. By taking this course, they are also expected to have the ability to produce substantial revisions of drafts, as distinguished from editing and proofreading. According to the curriculum, all the students will do peer review for their drafts of major writing assignments throughout the semester. However, when I observed my students' interaction in class during the first month, I found that most of them were quite passive in peer review and few of them took peers' comments into serious consideration when revising their work. How to motivate those students to improve their peer-review skills and help them benefit more from peer review in the writing process has become one of the biggest challenges I face when teaching this course. Therefore, I planned to do an action research study to improve my feedback pedagogy, especially the instructions on peer review. The questions guiding my research are: (1) What are the factors in peer-review activities that impact first-year international students' implementation of peer review skills? (2) How can writing teachers help those students make good use of peer feedback on their drafts for effective revision? The study is primarily based on the research findings from Lam's (2010) article, which proposed a peer review training workshop to coach EFL students in effectively giving and responding to peer feedback. His training approach aimed to raise students' consciousness through analyzing the effectiveness of their peer feedback and evaluating the extent to which peers' comments were incorporated into their subsequent revisions. Considering it well suited to my research goal, I integrated Lam's (2010) recommended training approach into my curriculum and pedagogy with some adjustments for the ESL context. I also assessed the learning outcome of my students and reflected on my own teaching practices.

Review of Literature

In order to take informed action, I drew upon relevant literatures to make my research plan. First of all, prior training and appropriate scaffolding is essential in preparing students to give critical comments as well as workable suggestions on their peer's writing and helping them to realize the value of peer review. Min's (2005) study proposed four characteristics of comments that facilitate students' revision and used them as guidelines for training: clarifying writers' intentions, identifying problems, explaining the nature of problems, and making specific suggestions. According to Min (2006), it is crucial to explain the nature of problems and provide constructive suggestions in the review to make the peer comments reliable because writers may not be convinced to adopt peer comments in their revision if there is no justification. Built on that, Lam's (2010) article demonstrated how to conduct a peer review training workshop to coach students in giving and responding more effectively to peer feedback. His training approach aimed to raise students' consciousness through analyzing the effectiveness of their peer feedback and evaluating the extent to which peers' comments were incorporated into their subsequent revisions (see Table 1.1).

TABLE 1.1   Lam's (2010) four-step procedure of peer review

Procedure	Purpose	Examples
1. Clarifying	To elucidate writer's intentions	"Do you want to say…" "Could you explain why you think…" "Do you mean that…" "What is the purpose of this paragraph…" "Why did you put…in this paragraph?"
2. Identifying	To search for problematic areas	"Do you realize that…and…are incompatible?" "It sounds to me that this issue you presented is too subjective." "It seems to me that… and…should not be compared in this dimension."
3. Explaining	To describe the nature of problems	"You may be wrong here because…" "This example may not be suitable to illustrate the idea of the topic sentence." "This quote may not be relevant to what you are discussing. You should say…instead."
4. Giving suggestions	To provide workable suggestions for modifications	"Why don't you change the idea from…to …?" "I think you should give more information about…in the second-last paragraph?" "You might use the word…rather than…" "You need to add a phrase concerning the disadvantage of…here."

Lam's study was conducted at a Hong Kong university with 30 non-English majors attending the training workshop. The participants were all Cantonese-speakers and enrolled in a writing course designed for all first-year students. Given that Lam's (2010) research context is similar to mine, and the workshop had generated positive results for students, I adopted his training approach in my pedagogy while also making some adjustment to ensure that the approach fits my own instructional goals. Then I held teacher-student conferences on revision to follow up the training. I structured the conferences based on Anderson's (2000) suggestion on the role of the teacher and the student in a writing conference and employed the specific research questions in teacher-student conferences on revision to assess the learning outcomes. Since the writing conferences are designed as a supplement to the training sessions, Anderson's (2000, 2005) books have provided me with practical guidelines to assess and help student writers individually. After that, I also reflected on my own teaching practices for improvement.

Methodology

Context and Participants

The writing course I teach is a one-semester compulsory for-credit course which every first-year international student whose first language is not English has to take. The course aims to develop students' writing abilities in various genres and prepare them for writing academic essays. This class meets three times a week, with 50 minutes of duration for each class. There are 15 international students enrolled in the class. The module of this course includes four units. For each unit, the students are assigned one short paper (500–600 words) and one major essay (1000–1500 words). These writing assignments are used to assess their writing ability in different genres. Students review their peers' first draft of the major essay in every unit, so peer review is a significant part of the curriculum of this course.

Nevertheless, I realized that the learning outcomes regarding peer review were not as satisfactory as expected. The quality of students' comments on their peer's writing was not good enough. Many of the students tended to focus on the sentence-level issues (e.g. grammar and mechanics) rather than the "larger picture" of the paper, i.e. the thesis, organization, and logic flow. Moreover, when I compared students' multiple drafts, few of their peer's comments were adopted in the revision. Thus, in the Spring semester 2017, I wanted to improve my feedback pedagogy with an emphasis on scaffolding peer review to make it more beneficial for international students. I first conducted a focus group interview with three of my former students. I emailed all the students enrolled in the same writing course in the Fall semester and invited them to a discussion on peer review activities. Three of them were willing to participate in the focus group. From their interviews, I found that even if prior training had been provided, giving specific and constructive feedback to their peers remained a challenge for those international students. In addition, they were not motivated to implement the peer review skills because they perceived peer comments less valuable and felt reluctant to critique each other fact-to-face. Furthermore, the students did not appreciate the usefulness of peer feedback due to their failure in interpreting their peers' comments for revision. Similarly, when I checked my students' work in Unit 1 in the Spring semester (after they did peer review for the major essay), I observed that fewer than half the peer comments were actually adopted in revision. Concerned about students' inability to give effective peer feedback, and their seeming resistance to incorporating peer comments into revision, I intended to design a series of peer review training that would be more systematic than the existing one so as to better facilitate students in giving and evaluating peer comments. More importantly, I wanted to provide more instructions on how to analyze peer feedback for effective revision.

My peer review training process consisted of three classes including modeling, practicing, and analyzing, which allowed me to provide the 15 students with sufficient training and scaffolding for peer review. After that, I assigned the peer review as homework and asked the students to reflect on their learning by posting in an online discussion forum created for this course. My purpose was to compare the results of different forms of peer review so as to identify some factors that impact students' learning outcomes. For this project, I had four focal students Annie, Ben, Christy and David (pseudonyms are used for their privacy), who were willing to participate in my research and improve their revision strategies. I interviewed them about their experiences of peer review activities, thoughts on the peer review training, and co-analyzed with them their revision process based on peer comments. Data collection included audio recording of the interviews as well as the individual writing conferences with the four students, their multiple drafts of writing, and their entries in online discussion forum.

Lesson Plans

I planned three sessions to conduct the systematic training of peer review and then asked the students to do peer review for their draft of the major essay in Unit 2. The training was done in three classes successively within a week, each lasting 50 minutes. The first session was an in-class demonstration and modeling. During the training, I took an essay composed by my former student (with his permission) as a writing sample and demonstrated to the students how to make comments on it using Lam's (2010) four-step procedure. Techniques for implementing each step were also modeled to them in class. I emphasized that contents of a piece of writing was as important as its form and I instructed the students to start examining the argument, structure and organization in the writing sample rather than editing the grammatical issues.

In the second session, I invited the students to practice the four-step procedure with another authentic writing sample from my former student (with her permission) and provided them with procedural guidelines for the peer review activity (see Appendix A), which was adapted from Lam's (2010) Procedures Concerning the Operation of Peer Review Sessions. The objective of this session was to assess whether the students were able to identify both the rhetorical-level and sentence-level problems in writing and explain them accordingly. They were also expected to provide constructive suggestions for revising the sample essay. After that, students were asked to form pairs, exchange the writing sample they reviewed with their partner, discuss the quality of the peer marking, and check if they had missed any substantial problems. Then I invited each pair to talk about their peer review to the whole class and commented on their sharing so as to reinforce the students' understanding of the four-step procedure.

In the third session, I asked the students to bring their first draft of the major essay in Unit 2 along with the procedural guidelines (see Appendix A) and do peer review in class. I also gave the students a sheet of Peer Review Guidelines (see Appendix B) adapted from Lam's (2010) Guidance Sheet for Peer Reviewers. It was a hands-on practice for students to implement the skills they learnt from the previous training sessions. After class, students were assigned to revise their first draft based on their peer's comments. Then I provided my comments on their second draft and invited all the students to visit me during office hours to discuss how to use feedback from both their peer and the instructor to improve writing.

Post-Training

Writing Conferences
After the three training sessions in Unit 2, all students were asked to revise their first draft based on the comments they received from peers. Then they submitted the second draft for teacher feedback. In order to get a better sense of how students perceived the training and responded to the peers' comments, I conducted a 30-minute semi-structured interview with the four focal students (see Appendix C for the interview protocol). Then I held individual writing conferences with each of them to further assist them in analyzing the peer comments and incorporating them into their own subsequent revisions. I referred to Anderson's (2000) prediction on the role of the teacher and the student in a writing conference to structure the individual writing conferences with my students (see Table 1.2), and employed the specific research questions in teacher-student conferences on revision suggested by Anderson (2005, p. 181) to guide my feedback pedagogy.

Online Discussion Forum
After the students became familiar with the procedures and guidelines of peer review in Unit 2, I assigned the peer review for their major essay in Unit 3 as homework. The purpose of this assignment was to see whether the students can finish the task independently at home and whether giving more time will make a difference in their implementation of peer review skills. Each student was assigned one peer's draft after they submitted their own drafts

TABLE 1.2   Structure of a writing conference (adapted from Anderson, 2000)

The teacher's role	The student's role
In the first part of the conversation	
– Invite the student to set an agenda for the conference	– Set the agenda for the conference by describing his/her writing work
– Ask assessment questions	– Respond to the teacher's research questions by describing his/her writing work more deeply
– Read the student's writing	
– Make a teaching decision	
In the second part of the conversation	
– Give the student critical feedback	– Listen carefully to the teacher's feedback and teaching
– Teach the student	
– Nudge the students to say how he/she can use what has been taught	– Ask questions to clarify and deepen his/her understanding of the teacher's feedback and teaching
– Link the conference to the student's independent work	– Attempt to apply what the teacher has taught
	– Commit to trying what the teacher has taught after the conference.

in class. I asked them to do peer review according to the same guidelines in Unit 2 (see Appendix B) at home and then bring the paper they reviewed with their comments to the next class. Then they had face-to-face conversations with the peer whose paper they reviewed and discussed plans for revision in class. The students were also invited to post their thoughts on the process of doing this assignment in the online discussion forum created for this course. I participated in the online discussion and compared the results of peer review in Unit 2 and Unit 3.

Findings and New Understandings

According to the students' reflections posted in the online discussion forum and the interviews with the four focal students, all of them were positive about the peer review activities as well as the training they had received. Most of the participants realized the value of peer review and appreciated "another pair of eyes" to look at their writing. Annie said in the interview: "In the peer review we are able to both learn from others and correct our own mistakes. It is a good way for us to improve our skills based on others' opinions" (Annie, personal communication, 2017). Christy also remarked: "The most I like about the peer review is that people can learn something from others during the process. I can also know how others think about my essay and immediately change the problems" (Christy, personal communication, 2017). In his reflection, Ben wrote: "In the peer review, students can exchange their thoughts for academic writing. Peers can also point out my error which I may not know." David suggested that peer review even helped to create his audience awareness: "I thought it was helpful for us to read others' thoughts and give them feedback because we were able to know the reader's point of view" (David, personal communication, 2017).

The data also indicated that the training made a difference in students' perception of peer review and enabled them to become independent writers. Christy admitted that before the training, she thought peer review was just to tell the writer whether she liked or disliked about his/her work, which was often judgmental rather than critical. However, the training provided very specific guidelines for her to look at peers' work. It also enabled her to be more evaluative about her own work so that she can revise the drafts more critically. David reported that the training sessions gave him more confidence in reviewing others' writing and it also made him trust peers' comments more. Ben used to have negative experiences in peer review because he thought his peers tended to give "superficial" comments, which was not helpful in his writing. But after the training, he felt the peers had become more reliable and he had received more "good-quality" comments. Furthermore, he had learnt how to analyze the comments and incorporate them into revision from the individual writing conference.

Another finding is that teachers' participation in the peer review would make students more accountable for such activities and help them respond to peers' comments more critically. As Rollinson (2005) proposed, teacher intervention is a crucial factor to ensure students' effective implementation of the peer review skills they learn in class. Annie wrote in the reflection: "I prefer to have peer review in the online discussion forum with the teacher together. Because in the group I am able to get advice from different aspects and I can receive more valuable information." Ben's words in the interview also revealed the significance of teacher participation in the peer review activities: "Sometimes, I cannot get some professional suggestion from the peers, and different person has different ideas, so they are not consistent. If the teacher is also participating in the discussion, we will be more serious about the activity and the teacher can help if I do not agree with my peers' comments" (Ben, personal communication, 2017). Additionally, the individual writing conferences I held after the peer review activities turned out to be beneficial to all the focal students. The follow-up instruction on analyzing and incorporating peer feedback in revision can also be regarded as teacher support, which proved to be necessary to ensure the effectiveness of peer review.

The last point of note is that international students usually need more time to read and write in English. Assigning peer review as homework enabled them to think more carefully about giving feedback. They can also revise their comments if they were not confident enough or not satisfied with their first attempt. Students were found to have given more critical comments and constructive suggestions in Unit 3, when they did the peer review at home.

Pedagogical Implications

Conducting action research and utilizing research-based knowledge in pedagogical activities was a precious learning process for me as a writing instructor. It helped me know more about my students as writers. Overall, the prior training and follow-up instructions were successful in facilitating students' effective peer review as well as their revision based on peer feedback. Accordingly, recommendations could be made to foster better implementation of peer review activities in the ESL writing class. Nevertheless, new issues in feedback pedagogy also emerged from the research and provoked me to think more for future studies. For example, from my observation, if a strong student was paired with a weak student, usually the weak student would receive more constructive suggestions from the strong student. Therefore, how to strategically pair the students for peer review to ensure the maximum benefits for students with varying proficiency levels is a problem that warrants further exploration.

It will be important for teachers to manage the inconsistency between peer comments and teacher feedback if there is any. I suggest that teachers review all peer comments before giving their own feedback on students' drafts and help students critically evaluate the comments they have received. In addition, two participants (Annie and David) mentioned in their reflections that they would still like to have face-to-face communications with their peers and the teacher so that they could be clearer about what the problems were and how to revise according to the feedback. Therefore, teachers should always consider including follow-up discussions in the feedback plan. Furthermore, the online discussion forum created a learning community for the students, which allowed international students to express themselves more freely. As Johnson and Brescia (2006) argue, students engaged in interactive instructional environments are supposed to "work with others to discover, construct, and participate in social collaborations that bring about meaning" (p. 57). A learning community can create that kind of environment, in which students "take control of their own learning based on their own background and previous experiences" (Brown, 2014, p. 2). Specially in an online learning community, students can take active roles to participate and express themselves while gaining a sense of value to remove the isolation that might inhibit learning (Brown, 2014). It is thus necessary for teachers to also think about how to make good use of such a community to further develop international students' academic literacy.

Reflection and Conclusion

In Lam's (2010) article, he made three recommendations for effective peer review training, which I took into consideration in my own study. The first is to use scoring guides as a starting point and help students understand the expectations in their peer review because "students usually encounter difficulties with prioritizing the marking of content or language errors, or even do not know what they should target while commenting on their peers' papers" (Lam, 2010, p. 122). Although I did not include scoring guides in my peer review guidelines, I asked the students to refer to the rubrics that I gave them for each assignment to internalize the assessment criteria. Yet I did not invite students to co-construct the scoring guides, as Lam (2010) also suggested, because I found the students were not ready to set the criteria to assess their own writing. Especially for first-year international students who might not be familiar with the Western writing conventions, helping them fully understand the criteria of their coursework and the instructor's expectations was a priority.

The second recommendation made by Lam (2010) is to promote self-editing and ask students to write a reflection about their editing process. His rationale is that if students are trained to be accountable for applying editing strategies in their own work, they can "attend specifically to any content errors in their partner's writing and may generate more constructive feedback for effective revisions" (Lam, 2010, p. 123). While I agree that teachers need to reinforce students' awareness of the importance of revision and editing in the writing process, we cannot neglect the differences between revision and editing. It is necessary for teachers to make instructional decisions about the focus of their peer review training workshop so as to avoid overwhelming the novice writers such as first-year international students. Those students might also need extra training on self-editing before they can be sensitive enough to their own errors in writing.

Lam's (2010) last recommendation about using technology to assist peer review training had the most lasting influence on me. He suggested extending peer review practice outside the classroom by guiding students to do peer review online, given that class time is limited. Besides, Web 2.0 applications (e.g. blogs and wikis) may encourage "students to give more serious and objective peer feedback because their comments are viewed by a larger audience than just their work partners" (Penrod, 2007, cited in Lam, 2010, p. 123). I made use of the online instructional tool Canvas to design peer review activities and create an online learning community, which allowed students more time for work and engaged them in thoughtful discussions. The integration of technology in peer review activities worked well in my class and it provided an alternative way for the students who were not very confident in spoken English.

In closing, it is worth mentioning that my initial plan was subject to some minor changes during the research process. Initially I intended to improve my pedagogy on peer review and teacher feedback separately. However, after consulting relevant literatures, I realized that they could be (and should be) combined. I also revised my research questions to make the investigation more focused on peer review because I found that most first-year international students did not have experiences of peer review in their previous education, let alone systematic training on peer review skills. Comparatively, students in my class had fewer difficulties in understanding and incorporating teacher feedback in revision, probably because they had had exposure to such top-down instruction from teachers as authorities. Therefore, I held individual writing conferences with the students to follow up the peer review activities and built my teacher feedback on their peers' comments so that students could learn how to integrate various points of view into their drafts to improve writing. When I assessed the students' final drafts of the major essay in both Unit 2 and Unit 3, more than half of the peer comments and almost all the teacher comments were effectively incorporated in the revision. Seeing the satisfactory results, I plan to make the peer review training part of my curriculum in future semesters and run it earlier (in Unit 1). I also hope to hold individual writing conferences with all students to follow up on the training in order to ensure their successful implementation of peer review skills as well as the revision strategies based on feedback on their drafts.

Appendix A: Procedures of Peer Review[1]

1. Read the sample essay in detail.
2. Use a pencil to annotate the essay in the areas of thesis statement, topic sentences, developing ideas and organization in various paragraphs.
3. Jot down your comments and suggestions in the order of occurrence and number the comment/suggestion one after another in the margins.
4. Then, read the sample essay again and identify some common and "treatable" grammatical errors with a pen. Do not correct the language errors. Underline or circle those errors with appropriate error codes.
5. Point out all content problems on the sample essay. If you have doubt about some problems, feel free to contact me.
6. Exchange your work with your partner. Silently read your peer's comments for about 5 to 10 minutes. Then, you need to clarify any points you are not clear about in your partner's comments and invite him/her to explain the problematic areas to you.
7. In the meantime, your partner should also explain to you why he or she thinks particular feedback points in your comments are inappropriate for the sample essay if necessary.
8. Next time, if you receive peer feedback on your own essay, you (as a writer) need to read all the comments and raise questions to your partner if you are not certain about some feedback points. Then, start revising your first draft based upon the feedback.

Appendix B: Peer Review Guidelines[2]

1. **Insert comments (*at least 5*) in the text (margins). Focus on:**
   – Introductory and concluding paragraphs
   – Thesis statement
   – Topic sentences
   – Evidence with analysis for the main claims
   – Transitions between sentences and paragraphs
   – APA citations
2. **Give overall feedback at the end of the essay (*at least 5 sentences*).**
   – Use the following guiding questions to point out specific problems and give constructive suggestions:
   a. Is the thesis statement in the introductory paragraph strong and effective?

b. Is the introductory paragraph interesting and clearly written?

Attend to the following questions (c–e) when checking the body paragraphs:

c. What are the topic sentences in each paragraph and are they supported by developing ideas?

d. What are the supporting details for the main idea in each paragraph? If you cannot identify them, please suggest one for the writer.

e. Has the paper included any real life examples or concrete illustrations to support the main idea of each paragraph? If not, please provide the writer with directions to explain the main ideas with solid examples.

f. Are the issues of the essay debatable (attracting various points of view)?

g. Is the essay coherent in terms of proper use of transitional words/ signal phrases?

h. Does the essay include the effective use of paraphrasing and sparing quotations?

i. Does the conclusion echo the thesis statement and lead the reader to a new point or realization about your argument?

j. Does the conclusion include relevant information highlighted in the previous paragraphs and moved to more general statements on the topic as a whole?

Appendix C: Student Interview Protocol

1. How did you like peer review before the training?

2. What do you think about the peer review training sessions?

3. Which aspects of the training do you think most helpful and why?

4. How much do you think the training has helped you learn how to give effective feedback?

5. What kind of peer review activities do you prefer (e.g., pair work or group discussion, in class or after class) and why?

6. Is there anything else you would like to share about your experiences of peer review and the training?

Notes

1 This sheet is adapted from Lam's (2010) Procedures Concerning the Operation of Peer Review Sessions.

2 This handout is adapted from Lam's (2010) Guidance Sheet for Peer Reviewers.

References

Anderson, C. (2000). *How's it going? A practical guide to conferring with student writers.* Portsmouth, NH: Heinemann.

Anderson, C. (2005). *Assessing writer.* Portsmouth, NH: Heinemann.

Brown, L. (2014). Constructivist learning environments and defining the online learning community. *Journal on School Educational Technology, 9*(4), 1–6.

Gielen, S., Tops, L., Dochy, F., Onghena, P., & Smeets, S. (2010). A comparative study of peer and teacher feedback and of various peer feedback forms in a secondary school writing curriculum. *British Educational Research Journal, 36,* 143–162.

Hu, G. (2005). Using peer review with Chinese ESL student writers. *Language Teaching Research, 9*(3), 321–342.

Johnson, C., & Brescia, W. R. (2006). Connecting, making meaning, and learning in the electronic classroom: Reflections on facilitating learning at a distance. *Journal of Scholarship of Teaching and Learning, 6*(1), 56–74.

Lam, R. (2010). A peer review training workshop: Coaching students to give and evaluate peer feedback. *TESL Canada Journal, 27*(2), 114–127.

Liou, H., & Peng, Z. (2009). Training effects on computer-mediated peer review. *System, 37*(3), 514–525.

Mendonca, C. O., & Johnson, K. E. (1994). Peer review negotiations: Revision activities in ESL writing instruction. *TESOL Quarterly, 28*(4), 745–769.

Min, H. T. (2005). Training students to become successful peer reviewers. *System, 33,* 293–308.

Min, H. T. (2006). The effects of trained peer review on EFL students' revision types and writing quality. *Journal of Second Language Writing, 15,* 118–141.

Penrod, D. (2007). *Using blogs to enhance literacy: The next powerful step in 21st century learning.* Lanham, MD: Rowman & Littlefield Education.

Rollinson, P. (2005). Using peer feedback in the ESL writing class. *ELT Journal, 59*(1), 23–30.

Villamil, O., & de Guerrero, M. (2006). Sociocultural theory: A framework for understanding socio-cognitive dimensions of peer feedback. In K. Hyland & F. Hyland (Eds.), *Feedback in second language writing: Contexts and issues* (pp. 23–41). New York, NY: Cambridge University Press.

CHAPTER 2

Implementing Peer-Feedback in Paragraph-Writing Classes at a Thai University

Nguyen Thi Thuy Loan
Kalasin University, Thailand

Despite its alleged disadvantages, peer-feedback has gained increased attention from practitioners in English as second or foreign language (L2/FL) writing classes. To alleviate potential problems and facilitate profitable peer-response activities, Rollinson (2005) provided practical suggestions regarding its utilization in writing classes. Following his recommendations, I organized editing-revising sessions for my two fourteen-week paragraph-writing classes with third-year English major students at a university in Thailand. At this university, English is taught as a foreign language. Here most English writing programs are still taught using the grammar-translation method, emphasizing the accuracy of grammatical structures and vocabulary. My inquiry reported in this chapter explored how students may benefit from interactive peer-feedback activities. To this goal, their peers' comments (both valid and invalid ones), and how they revised their writing based on both their peers' and teacher's feedback (correct and incorrect revisions) were recorded. Furthermore, to understand these students' thoughts and attitudes towards this learning activity, a five-point Likert scale survey and a focus group interview were conducted at the end of the course. In this chapter, I focus mainly on how Rollinson's (2005) suggestions were incorporated into the paragraph-writing curriculum, what worked and what needed to be taken into consideration in the educational settings in Thailand. This chapter is thus expected to partly reflect how in-service teachers interpret and utilize reported research knowledge in their actual teaching situations and to provide practical suggestions on how to effectively employ peer-feedback in a culturally-based context of English learning in Thailand as well as in other countries with similar cultural values.

Introduction

Due to the widespread influence of process-oriented writing instruction (Ferris & Hedgcock, 2014), which encourages the production of multiple drafts of writing with response and revision, *peer-response* (a term that is used interchangeably with *peer-review* and *peer-feedback*) has become a common practice in many L2/FL classrooms. During peer-feedback, learners work together and comment on each other's work or performance and provide feedback on strengths, weaknesses, and suggestions for improvement. Theoretically, peer-feedback can be justified and supported by various theories, including process writing theory, interactionist theory in second language acquisition, collaborative learning theory, as well as sociocultural theory (Lantolf & Thorne, 2006; Liu & Hansen, 2002; Vygotsky, 1978; Yu & Lee, 2015). The value of peer-response in the L2/FL writing classrooms at both secondary and tertiary levels has also been substantiated by various empirical studies (Min, 2006; Paulus, 1999; Tsui & Ng, 2000; Villamil & de Guerrero, 1996; Yu & Lee, 2016). It can contribute to the development of learning and increase student motivation (Hyland & Hyland, 2006). Furthermore, it may enable students to identify the weak and strong points in their writing, and hence improve their writing proficiency and help them become autonomous learners (Hansen & Liu, 2005). Moreover, through peer-review, students are assigned the role of a teacher, so they are actively engaged in their own learning and assume responsibility for their own learning progress (Liu & Hansen, 2002).

Despite the theoretical support and the empirical evidence of its facilitative role in L2/FL writing, peer-feedback has not been widely used in L2/FL writing classrooms (Yu & Lee, 2016). This could be due to various issues associated with the use of peer-review, such as time constraint, teacher roles and student characteristics (Rollinson, 2005). Furthermore, Hu (2005) wrote that students' limited knowledge of the target language and its rhetorical conventions, the "surface" nature of students' comments, and students' various inappropriate attitudes towards peer-review are likely to hinder the implementation of peer-feedback in L2/FL writing classes. Moreover, Zhang (1995) stated that cultural background is also a confounding variable of peer-feedback. Carson and Nelson (1996) reported that peer-feedback activities were ineffective for Asian students who were used to teacher-dominated pedagogies and preferred to incorporate teacher-feedback because the teacher was deemed to be the expert and the only source of authority. Similarly, Fei (2006) found that her Chinese students felt doubtful about the quality of peer suggestions, hesitated to use peer comments in revision, and had very negative perceptions of the helpfulness of peer-review. In Thailand, a couple of studies conducted on peer-feedback also indicated that Thai university students preferred teachers' feedback (Srichanyachon, 2011, 2012) and refused to give their drafts to peers for comments (Chamcharatsri, 2010).

Acknowledging these difficulties, I followed Rollinson's (2005) detailed suggestions on setting up the groups, establishing effective procedures and training for useful peer-response activities in two paragraph-writing classes at a university in Thailand. According to Rollinson, in the setting-up stage the teacher first needs to make a number of decisions regarding the group size, the number of drafts to be written, and whether or not feedback will be evaluated or graded by the teacher. For the response activity, the teacher has to choose between having students provide oral or written feedback as each alternative offers its own advantages. Decisions on whether feedback will be provided independently or in a consensus group, how much time is allowed for this activity, and to what degree the reader-writer interaction for clarification or debate will be given also need to be taken into consideration when organizing the response sessions. Furthermore, responding and self-reporting guidelines and follow-up activities (teacher-student conferences or teacher-group discussions) should also be prepared in the setting and procedures.

For the training stage, Rollinson (2005) suggests two steps: pre-training and intervention-training. The main purposes of pre-training are informing students the principles and objectives of peer-feedback, how to interact in groups and basic procedures for effective comments and revisions. These objectives can be achieved through various activities from teacher explanations, class discussions, teachers' demonstrations and non-threatening practice activities. Such organized activities aim to ensure that students will have necessary and appropriate skills to perform the acts of giving comments on their peers' writing and responding to their peers' feedback. Intervention-training is then followed to maximize the benefits of the peer-response activities for each student in the group. In this stage, the teacher needs to maintain a close contact with each group and lend help to resolve their particular problems. For example, he/she may keep notes of students' feelings and reactions to their received comments and the reasons for students' discarding of certain feedback through reading their successive drafts and the revisions, and then make suggestions for improving the readers' comments and the writers' revisions. Besides the two practical suggestions for effective peer-feedback activities, Rollinson (2005) briefly reviews what to do in "doing peer feedback" (p. 28). It includes how to locate the comments (interlineal, annotated and introductory/end) and which techniques to use (different colors for different types of comments), and these mainly stem from the pre-training activities, which will in turn reflect the teacher's priorities.

The Teaching Context

English has been taught as a foreign language and as a separate subject rather than being used as the medium of communication for decades in Thailand.

Although English is a compulsory subject for Thai students from primary to tertiary levels, it is taught more in Thai than in English (Bennui, 2008). Thai university students' English proficiency is reported to be less than satisfactory (Boonpattanaporn, 2008; Komin, 1998), and their writing is of particular concern as it is not systematically taught as a subject (Chamcharatsri, 2010; Puengpipattrakul, 2013; Srichanyachon, 2011; Wongsothorn, 1994). Furthermore, most writing programs are still taught using the traditional model emphasizing the accuracy of grammatical structures and vocabulary (Chamcharatsri, 2010; Clayton & Klainin, 1994; McDonough, 2004; Siriphan, 1988). Testing in most writing programs stresses objective-type questions, which require sentence completion, reordering sentences, reordering words and error correction (Wongsothorn, 1994; Puengpipattrakul, 2013). Students thus have very few opportunities to represent their ideas and knowledge through the written mode. Moreover, in Thai educational context, students have not been required to engage actively in class activities; therefore, cooperative work often leads to students' resistance and confusion (Kongpetch, 2006; McDonough, 2004). This could be partly due to Thai traditional belief of "silence denotes wisdom" and Thai cultural constraint about the need to avoid criticism (Puengpipattrakul, 2013; Root, 2016).

At the university where the current study was conducted, the entrance exam for candidates of the English language education program includes three sections, namely a test on their general knowledge (in Thai), an interview conducted in Thai and an English test on grammar and reading skills in a multiple-choice format. The newly admitted English major students' writing skills at this university are thus unknown. The English curriculum at the university has three obligatory writing courses: Writing 1 (paragraph writing), Writing 2 (short compositions) and Writing 3 (five-paragraph academic essays). These courses are taught in three successive terms of fourteen weeks each, starting from their third year of study. Besides two obligatory English grammar courses mainly taught in Thai by a Thai teacher of English, English major students at this university study general subjects in Thai language in their first two years. English communication courses 1 and 2 are also considered as their general subjects.

Peer-feedback was conducted in a Writing 1 course with third-year English major students who met once a week for a 14-week semester. Each class session lasted 150 minutes, using the selected course book (*Writers at Work: From Sentence to Paragraph* by Laurie Blass and Deborah Gordon). This book consists of ten chapters with ten different writing topics, and the target vocabulary and grammatical points for each topic are also presented in each chapter. Although the objective of this course is to help students develop their skills in writing an academic paragraph, very little information about paragraph writing is given in this book. That is why the chair of the English division at this university supported my curriculum innovation to improve students' writing abilities. This year, I taught this course to two classes of third-year students (32 and 28 students respectively) aged between 20 and 21 years (for the ease of reference, G1 refers to the group with 32 students while the other is G2). These students' English proficiency level is upper-elementary or pre-intermediate. The final grade for this course includes 5% for their class-attendance, 45% for their assignments allocated by the teacher, and the other 50% is for midterm and final tests (20% and 30%, respectively).

Incorporating Rollinson's Suggestions into the Curriculum

In order to both meet the course requirements and implement the peer-feedback activities in this writing course, I revised the curriculum instead of teaching the book chapter-by-chapter. In the first five weeks of the course, a genre-based approach was employed to teach students the generic structure of an academic paragraph. During this time, students were familiarized with the basic components of an academic paragraph (topic sentence, supporting sentences and concluding sentence) and how to compose each component through step-by-step instructions as well as thorough practice with the materials developed by myself. From weeks 6 to 14, the students were asked to write seven complete paragraphs of 150 words each for seven topics chosen from the course book. The topics were (1) *All about me,* (2) *Daily activities,* (3) *Your family,* (4) *Your favorite book/movie/TV show* (choose 1), (5) *Your idol,* (6) *Your future plans,* and (7) *Your memorable trip.* Students wrote the paragraph at home, and peer-feedback activities following Rollinson's (2005) suggestions were implemented in class.

In the setting-up stage, I decided to have students write three drafts), work in groups of four, selected by themselves but were encouraged to work with different peers over the course, and use indirect written feedback (using provided correction-symbols to indicate the mistakes instead of providing corrections). The first draft was checked by their peers and the writer, first independently and then in a consensus group for clarifications and suggestions on the revisions, using the responding guidelines (Appendix A). I checked their second and third drafts. Their first language was used in this interactive activity. When they submitted second and third drafts, a summary of their responses including explanations for their choice of not incorporating any suggested comments was required (Appendix B). Their comments and revisions were graded with a deduction of 1% from their obtained assignment score (45%) for irresponsible comments and ignoring the given feedback. In the three-week training period, class discussions on the benefits of peer-feedback and appropriate attitudes in peer-feedback activities and non-threatening practice activities on Topics 1 and 2 were conducted.

The training phase was conducted as follows:

1. Students write a paragraph for a given topic at home, and bring 4 copies to their next class.
2. In class, students use responding guidelines and correction-symbols, sit in groups of 4, but work independently on the first peer's writing (first individually, then in groups for clarifications) with teachers' supervision and assistance. Then they review another peer's draft (first individually, then in groups) until finishing reviewing drafts of all four members (1 hour in total).
3. Students revise their writing at home and submit the second draft with a summary of their responses in the following class (and at the same time, writing a paragraph for a new topic).
4. Teacher checks their revisions, all drafts reviewed by peers, and the revised paragraph. Teacher provides feedback on the revised paragraph (outside the class).
5. Students have 45 minutes at the beginning of the next class for follow-up activities on the second draft.
6. Students revise their second draft at home and submit the third draft with a summary of their responses in the following class (and writing for another topic).
7. Teacher checks students' summaries of revisions, the previous draft commented by the teacher and the revised paragraph, provides feedback (if any) and grades their third draft (outside the class).
8. Students spend 45 minutes for follow-up activities on the 3rd draft.

Generally, the class procedures were:

a. Follow-up activities (returning students' last assignment, asking them to read the comments, summarizing commonly-made mistakes, and explaining the comments to those who asked for help) (45 minutes),
b. Peer-feedback on the new writing (1 hour), and
c. Lessons in the book and preparation for the following writing topic (45 minutes).

Because a considerable amount of class time was dedicated to peer-feedback activities, students were asked to check new vocabulary and do grammar exercises at home. In the last 45 minutes of every class their work was corrected and ideas for their upcoming writing topic were also generated.

Findings

The revised curriculum generally worked well for this group of Thai university students despite large class size, students' low level of English proficiency, their relative lack of experience in group work, and their culturally-embedded "passive" learning styles (Kongpetch, 2006; McDonough, 2004; Puengpipat-trakul, 2013; Root, 2016). Unlike the results of previous studies (Fei, 2006; Nelson & Carson, 1998; Tsui & Ng, 2000) which showed the resistance of students with entrenched teacher-centered learning experiences to peer-feedback, all Thai students in this study showed great interest in working with peers, their positive attitude towards peers' comments, their incorporations of feedback from both peers and the teacher, and most importantly their improvements in English writing. For their 45% assignments, students had the high average scores (83% and 81.4% for G1 and G2, respectively). This success could be due partly to the well-designed and step-by-step training that made these Thai students believe that their teacher was not the only source of knowledge (Min, 2006; Rahimi, 2013; Rollinson, 2005). As revealed in the questionnaire and the interview, these students wanted to have feedback from both the teacher and peers as the former assisted them with language while the latter helped them with ideas.

Another possible explanation for the effectiveness of the peer feedback in this study is the grading of their comments and their paragraphs. As for these students who will become English teachers, gaining good scores in all subjects is what they are aiming for in order to secure a job in the future. In fact, in order to improve the country's general education, the Thai government has given teacher-students with a GPA of 3.0 or higher some favorable conditions after their graduation. Students also admitted in the interview that grading the comments made them more responsible in giving feedback and revising their writing. Additionally, some students showed their dislike for being marked five times as they believed that the more times the teacher read their writing, the higher probability that the teacher would find their weakness, which could result in lower scores. Finally, the follow-up activities and the teacher's checking their feedback and writing were reported in the interview to maintain the students' enthusiasm in this interactive activity and improve their writing as they knew they always had their teacher's continuous support and more importantly their language knowledge was consolidated and updated. As these students have hardly had opportunities to write in English, such consistent follow-up activities and feedback helped them review their written language and gradually build up their confidence in English writing. To sum up, the effectiveness of this activity and the positive attitudes of these Thai university students generally confirm Rollinson's (2005) assertion that "only if the class is adequately set up and trained can the benefits of the peer-feedback activity be fully realized" (p. 29).

Recommendations

Although Rollinson's (2005) suggestions on making peer-feedback effective in L2/EF writing classes proved to work well with these Thai university students, this inquiry has led me to make some recommendations. First, allowing your students to use their mother tongue (L1) is a must as it assists them in understanding and being understood in their peer interactions. This facilitative role of L1 in peer collaborations aligns with the socio-cultural theory that language is the most important tool to mediate language development with social interactions (Lantolf & Thorne, 2006; Vygotsky, 1978). Because the use of L1 promotes the efficiency of peer interaction, students' English proficiency levels should be taken into consideration when deciding how much L1 will be used in this activity to maximize their understanding of feedback.

Second, written feedback tends to contribute to the effectiveness of peer-feedback activities with low-level students. In addition to the benefits of written over oral feedback mentioned by Rollinson (2005), written comments reduce students' pressure in listening to peers' reading of their writing, attending to both global and local errors (e.g., structure, organization and content vs grammar, mechanics and punctuation, respectively), and at the same time providing oral comments on their peers' writing if oral feedback is conducted. Due to the absence of these Thai students' daily exposure to English communication, their deeply-rooted L1 interference (Bennui, 2008) and more improvement needed in their pronunciation and vocabulary, oral feedback would be strikingly challenging and consequently could create confusion in them.

Third, in addition to the written mode, indirect or coded feedback would be of greater benefits in facilitating these students' writing development than the direct ones. As these students are still at their developmental stage of learning the target language, providing them with corrected forms may not produce the reflection and cognitive engagement that helps them acquire linguistic structures and reduce errors over time. As Ferris and Roberts (2001) showed, consistently marking the error types, paired with mini-lessons which build students' knowledge, would yield more long-term growth in student accuracy.

Fourth, peer-feedback with L2/FL low-level students should be done inside the classroom with teachers' observation. Though carefully trained and provided with guiding questions, these students at times centered their focus on the local issues, the teacher's observing the activity and adjusting their feedback-giving behaviors is necessary. Moreover, when dealing with global errors, students often made inappropriate and confusing comments or suggestions; so, addressing such problems in time helps facilitate this peer-feedback activity.

Fifth, self-selection of peers could partly account for the success of peer-feedback activities. As stated by researchers such as Dixon and Hawe, (2017) and Nassaji (2016), the extent to which learners benefit from other learners' feedback depends on how satisfied and trusted they are with their peers.

Sixth, as students' awareness of the usefulness of peer feedback in the writing classroom is extremely important (Rollinson, 2005), and especially in Asian contexts where cultural norms "may be antithetical to the pedagogical principles" of peer-feedback (Hu, 2005, p. 332), the teacher should periodically remind students of the rationale of this practice in order to cultivate their positive attitude towards working with others as a fruitful way of acquiring the target language.

Seventh, the teacher's quick returning of student writing with feedback should engage students and increase their interest and enthusiasm in writing. In this inquiry, after receiving my feedback, students' knowledge was consolidated in an uninterrupted manner. However, with the effort and time required to check students' comments and provide further feedback, the teacher's time, strong commitment, and patience are absolutely necessary for the success of this kind of activity.

Finally, for the effectiveness of any innovative pedagogy, it is imperative to have the supportive environment from the school as well as other community members (Hyland & Wong, 2013). In fact, this study was successful because I was granted the right to revise the curriculum to enhance students' writing skills. Lee, Mak, and Burns (2016) also state that despite the teachers' relevant subject knowledge, their attempts will be impeded by the unsupportive environment of the school. School leaders therefore need to be sufficiently open-minded to allow for curriculum innovation, where appropriate and necessary, because change does not occur at the individual level only. Supportive and stimulating conditions are necessary to foster real change in practice (Fullan, 2007).

In conclusion, peer-review is a time-consuming academic process, but its benefits are undeniable. It was particularly helpful for my low-proficiency

Thai students with their reported passive learning styles. Although students' cultural backgrounds and the target language levels have been claimed to render peer-feedback ineffective or challenging, its success in this study appeared to result mainly from sufficient training with my adequate awareness of contextual differences and students' own characteristics, and then adjusting feedback strategies accordingly. As stated by Lee et al. (2016), students' reviewing of peers' writing makes them cognizant of the assessment criteria and the requirements of the writing, which enables them to progress towards the required standards. Thus, peer-feedback may help them become more self-reliant writers by developing skills to revise and edit their own and peers' writings (Rollinson, 2005).

Appendix A: Paragraph Checklist

Format

1.   Is there a title, and is it capitalized correctly?
2.   Is the first line of the paragraph indented?

Organization and content

1.   Is there a clear, focused topic sentence and controlling idea?
2.   Is there any sentence that is not related to the topic and the controlling idea?
3.   Is the paragraph organized in a logical way (for example, time order, steps in a process, reasons, effects, etc.)?
4.   Are there transitional words or phrases to help the reader know when a new support statement is going to be discussed?
5.   Is there a concluding sentence? Is there a final comment? Does it fit the paragraph?

Language and mechanics

1.   Is the paragraph free of grammar, punctuation, and spelling errors? (Refer to *"Correction Key"*)
2.   Is there a variety of sentence structures?
3.   Is there an effort to make the topic interesting and informative?

Appendix B: Response Summary

Part 1: Summary

Reported items	Format	Organization & content	Language & mechanics
Number of mistakes			
Number of mistakes corrected			
Number of mistakes left uncorrected			
Rationale for not correcting the mistakes			

Part 2: Responses

Errors	→	Corrections

Ex:

1.	(N) student	→	students
2.	(art) student	→	a student

References

Bennui, P. (2008). A study of L1 interference in the writing of Thai EFL students. *Malaysian Journal of ELT Research, 4*, 72–102.

Boonpattanaporn, P. (2008). Comparative study of English essay writing strategies and difficulties as perceived by English major students: A case study of students in the school of humanities. *The University of the Thai Chamber of Commerce Academic Journal, 28*(2), 76–90.

Carson, J., & Nelson, G. (1996). Chinese students' perceptions of ESL peer response group interaction. *Journal of Second Language Writing, 5*(1), 1–19.

Chamcharatsri, P. B. (2010). On teaching writing in Thailand. *Writing on the Edge, 21*(1), 18–26.

Clayton, T., & Klainin, S. (1994). How organization affects grammatical accuracy. In M. L. Tickoo (Ed.), *Research in reading and writing* (pp. 109–117). Singapore: SEAMEO Regional Language Center.

Dixon, H., & Hawe, E. (2017). Creating the climate and space for peer review within the writing classroom. *Journal of Response to Writing, 3*(1), 6–30.

Fei, H. (2006). Students' perceptions of peer response activity in English writing instruction. *Teaching English in China, 4*, 48–52.

Ferris, D., & Hedgcock, J. S. (2014). *Teaching L2 composition: Purpose, process, and practice* (3rd ed.). New York, NY: Routledge.

Ferris, D., & Roberts, B. (2001). Error feedback in L2 writing classes: How explicit does it need to be? *Journal of Second Language Writing, 10*(3), 161–184. doi:10.1016/s1060-3743(01)00039-x

Fullan, M. (2007). *The new meaning of educational change* (4th ed.). New York, NY: Teachers College Press.

Hansen, J., & Liu, J. (2005). Guiding principles for effective peer response. *ELT Journal, 59,* 31–38.

Hu, G. (2005). Using peer review with Chinese ESL student writers. *Language Teaching Research, 9*(3), 321–342.

Hyland, K., & Hyland, F. (2006). Contexts and issues in feedback on L2 writing: An introduction. In K. Hyland & F. Hyland (Eds.), *Feedback in second language writing: Contexts and issues* (pp. 1–19). Cambridge: Cambridge University Press.

Hyland, K., & Wong, L. L. C. (2013). *Innovation and change in English language education.* Abingdon: Routledge.

Komin, S. (1998). English language learning in the 21st Asian century. In W. A. Renandya & G. M. Jacobs (Eds.), *Learners and language learning* (pp. 263–269). Singapore: SEAMEO Regional Language Center.

Kongpetch, S. (2006). Using a genre-based approach to teach writing to Thai students: A case study. *Prospect, 21*(2), 3–33.

Lantolf, J. P., & Thorne, S. L. (2006). *Sociocultural theory and the genesis of second language development.* Oxford: Oxford University Press.

Lee, I., Mak, P., & Burns, A. (2016). EFL teachers' attempts at feedback innovation in the writing classroom. *Language Teaching Research, 20*(2), 248–269.

Liu, J., & Hansen, J. (2002). *Peer response in second language writing classrooms.* Ann Arbor, MI: The University of Michigan Press.

McDonough, K. (2004). Learner-learner interaction during pair and small group activities in a Thai EFL context. *System, 32,* 207–224.

Min, H. (2006). The effects of trained peer review on EFL students' revision types and writing quality. *Journal of Second Language Writing, 15*(2), 118–141.

Nassaji, H. (2016). Anniversary article: Interactional feedback in second language teaching and learning: A synthesis and analysis of current research. *Language Teaching Research, 20*(4), 535–562.

Nelson, G. L., & Carson, J. G. (1998). ESL students' perceptions of effectiveness in peer response groups. *Journal of Second Language Writing, 2,* 113–131.

Paulus, T. M. (1999). The effect of peer and teacher feedback on student writing. *Journal of Second Language Writing, 8*(3), 265–289. Retrieved from http://dx.doi.org/10.1016/S1060-3743(99)80117-9

Puengpipattrakul, W. (2013). Assessment of Thai EFF undergraduates' writing competence through integrated feedback. *Journal of Institutional Research in South East Asia, 11*(1), 5–27.

Rahimi, M. (2013). Is training student reviewers worth its while? A study of how training influences the quality of students' feedback and writing. *Language Teaching Research, 17*(1), 67–89.

Rollinson, P. (2005). Using peer feedback in the ESL writing class. *ELT Journal, 59*(1), 23–30. doi:10.1093/elt/cci003

Root, S. (2016). Understanding Thai culture: Exploring the effect of academic stress in students' learning orientation. *ASEAN Journal of Management & Innovation, 3*(2), 15.

Siriphan, S. (1988). *An investigation of syntax, semantics, and rhetoric in the English writing of fifteen Thai graduate students* (Unpublished PhD thesis). Texas Woman's University, Denton, TX.

Srichanyachon, N. (2011). A comparative study of three revision methods in EFL writing. *Journal of College Teaching and Learning, 8*(9), 1–8.

Srichanyachon, N. (2012). An investigation of university EFL students' attitudes toward peer and teacher feedback. *Educational Research and Reviews, 7*(26), 558–562.

Tsui, A. B. M., & Ng, M. (2000). Do secondary L2 writers benefit from peer comments? *Journal of Second Language Writing, 9*, 147–170.

Villamil, O. S., & de Guerrero, M. C. M. (1996). Peer revision in the L2 classroom: Social-cognitive activities, mediating strategies, and aspects of social behavior. *Journal of Second Language Writing, 5*, 51–75.

Vygotsky, L. S. (1978). *Mind in society: The development of higher psychological processes.* Cambridge, MA: Harvard University Press.

Wongsothorn, A. (1994). An investigation of students' writing improvement through various types of teachers' intervention. In M. L. Tickoo (Ed.), *Research in reading and writing: A Southeast Asian collection* (pp. 118–125). Singapore: RELC.

Yu, S., & Lee, I. (2015). Understanding EFL students' participation in group peer feedback of L2 writing: A case study from an activity theory perspective. *Language Teaching Research, 19*, 572–593.

Yu, S., & Lee, I. (2016). Peer feedback in second language writing (2005–2014). *Language Teaching, 49*(4), 461–493. doi:10.1017/s0261444816000161

Zhang, S. (1995). Reexamining the affective advantage of peer feedback in the ESL writing class. *Journal of Second Language Writing, 4*(3), 209–222. Retrieved from http://dx.doi.org/10.1016/1060-3743(95)90010-1

Revising Essays Collaboratively

Gina Paschalidou
State Secondary Education, Greece

Introduction

After reading the article "Collaborative revision in L2 writing: learners' reflections" by Memari Hanjani (2016), published in *ELT Journal,* I was impressed by the practicality of its methodological design and its implications for EFL essay writing. Memari Hanjani's article was almost calling for implementation in an EFL/ESL writing class, be it in a primary, secondary or tertiary education context. The article is a case study of eight Iranian tertiary students participating in an EFL writing course, who are introduced to peer-feedback as a second step to essay review after teacher-feedback is provided via a written code. The participants' perceptions on the benefits and challenges of such an approach are then gathered through semi-structured interviews which purport both positive attitudes towards collaborative revision as well as absence of the problems usually related with teacher-feedback (Ferris, 1995; McCurdy, 1992; Zhao, 2010) and peer-feedback (Lundstorm & Baker, 2009; Zhang, 1995) as two distinct approaches to revision. The article can be perceived as a hands-on step-by-step framework of pair-work revision of essay writing. Within this scope, it echoes workshops that provide practical activities to improve EFL teacher practice, enhance results, motivate students, or even make lessons interesting.

Memari Hanjani theoretically places his exploratory study within the process-oriented approach to writing and the case of multiple drafting (Bereiter & Scardamalia, 1987; Kern, 2000). Indeed, feedback, whoever the instigator is, creates the conditions for multiple reviewing, drafting and, ultimately, improving a piece of written work. Memari Hanjani also places his study within sociocultural theory since peer collaboration and revising collaboratively is a manifestation of the theory's social processes where scaffolding is used to promote learning (Lantorf, 2009). He distinguishes collaborative revision from collaborative writing,[1] teacher feedback[2] and peer feedback/review,[3] and defines it as the process whereby peers revise their drafts jointly using teacher feedback (Memari Hanjani, 2013). While we could perceive collaborative revision as an interactive process of peer revision in the sense that each peer does not only comment on the other peer's mistakes and limitations but actually engages in a joint revision of each student's written text, the author ascribes an extra element to it: a first stage of feedback provided by the teacher. The students, then, build upon this first "layer" of teacher commentary to successfully collaborate in order to improve their first drafts, and, thus, follow a process of collaborative revision.

What is sought from this approach towards essay revision is the combination of the advantages reported by research on peer feedback and teacher feedback and the minimization of the disadvantages that usually arise by the above practices. Following from the above, research questions were formed, research methodology was designed, and a real educational setting was selected by the teacher-researcher of the original article. The study's purpose was to decipher the participants' views on the benefits, difficulties and concerns of implementing collaborative revision in an EFL writing course. The subjects who volunteered to participate were eight tertiary students of intermediate level of English language competence at a private University in Iran majoring in English who formed self-selected pairs for the interactive review.

The course they attended was a writing course of fifteen 90-minute sessions focusing on core writing skills (brainstorming, organizing, developing paragraph thesis etc.—phase 1) and three genres of essays (process, compare & contrast, cause & effect—phase 2), upon which the collaborative revision activity took place. The second phase took the form of three repeated cycles of four parts: (a) in the first part (class session) a specific type of essay was discussed, (b) in the second part (homework) the first draft of the essay was written, sent to the teacher via e-mail and was commented by the teacher based on a common feedback code, (c) in the third part (class session), the essay was returned to the students in class and collaborative revision occurred in pairs, and (d) in the fourth part (homework) the final draft was written by the student and sent to the teacher who provided final comments. This cycle was repeated three times, each time with a different essay genre.

Concerning the data collection and analysis which followed, Memari Hanjani used semi-structured interviews of all the participants conducted in their native language to achieve more attention to details. The interviews were recorded, transcribed and translated into English. The data were then categorized into three types: pedagogical benefits, affective benefits, and challenges. The findings suggested pedagogical benefits deriving from the teacher guidance in the form of written feedback which was maximized by the help of the other member of the pair as shared knowledge made it easier and faster to correct their own essays. Also, spending time with the peer's essay enhanced their self-awareness and made them careful with their own mistakes. Finally, the participants found meaning in the process of helping others. Affective benefits as perceived by the students themselves were mostly associated with more self-confidence in the context of collaboration whereas individual revision was associated with more stress and less engagement with re-drafting.

Teaching EFL in Greece: My Perspective

As a teacher of English as a Foreign Language (EFL), I have always believed that avoiding spoon-feeding students makes them seek the right answers by themselves, thus enabling them to gradually become more independent. Nevertheless, this approach is not compatible with everyone and I have quite often experienced undue demands of providing my students with ready-made solutions to their language problems, such as correcting every error they made or explaining every unknown word. At the same time, it is self-evident that learners of any age, let alone adolescents, need clear guidance and step-by-step instructions to complete a task, to learn how to learn, and to learn how to revise.

Additionally, as a non-native teacher of English in Greece teaching learners of various ages from early primary students to adults for more than 15 years, I can easily identify myself with them since I have experienced and am still experiencing their difficulties and successes with English as a foreign language. For the most part of these years, I have been working with young teenagers in the context of State Secondary Education. The fact that English classes are compulsory in Greece and the common practice for the vast majority of children to learn English privately from a very young age create a challenging situation for the State EFL teachers. This situation forces them to try a variety of practices to motivate learners while at the same time expanding their EFL knowledge.

Teaching and Learning Context

The general context of my study was chosen on the grounds of "convenience sampling" (Dörnyei, 2007, p. 129), as it was the educational institution where I was teaching. The specific lower-secondary school was a recently-established specialized Music School, providing a series of music courses in addition to the regular curriculum offered by general lower-secondary schools in Greece. This meant that, typically, students spent more time on-site and were more overloaded than students of other schools. Yet, in reality, due to the distinctive nature of the school, teachers tended to set lower standards and students were assigned lighter homework. On the other hand, and probably owing to the above reasons, there was a prevailing openness in terms of pedagogical initiatives and educational innovations. So, the administration of the school approved and supported my idea, since it fulfilled not only my research interests but also practical needs of the students.

The class to which the implementation of the particular research was addressed was a class of 11 Lower Secondary School students aged 14–15. Their level of English proficiency was assessed at approximately B1-B2 (Council of Europe, 2001), based on my own judgment of their competence after five months of lessons and their attendance of 5–6 years of private EFL tuition. The English course which is officially provided by the state is a general English course below their proficiency level, thus, leaving learners unmotivated and bored. The classroom did not provide any computer equipment or other visual aids apart from the blackboard, and the students were seated in pairs. The class met twice a week for a 40-minute lesson and the experiment took place between March–April 2017, towards the end of the academic year. The reasons for the selection of this group of students were mainly the small class size and the similar level of English they shared. In addition, the particular level of B1-B2 they were at was considered a prerequisite to carry through with the writing of the essay genres which Memari Hanjani's article proposed. Finally, a relative good rapport and cooperation with each other and with me led to the selection of this particular class.

Objectives and Research Questions

The purpose of my study was to examine the perceptions and attitudes of my students towards collaborative revision in EFL essay writing. In this way, it aimed to explore if the findings of the original study could be applicable to my own students and, therefore, possibly transferrable to different age groups and learning contexts. We could consider the present study as a modified replication[4] of the original case study because the methodological design was altered to adjust to the particular context of a State Junior High School and the adolescent participants of my study, in terms which will be analyzed in the next section.

The first two research questions were similar to the question of the original study while the third was an addition. They were formulated as follows:

1.   What are the EFL students' views on the benefits of using collaborative revision to improve their essay writing?
2.   What are the EFL students' views on the difficulties of using collaborative revision to improve their essay writing?

3.   What are the EFL students' views on collaborative revision in comparison to self-correction and teacher-correction?

Methodological Design

The collaborative revision activities were incorporated in the general English course and formed a part of its writing component. Due to the limited time of the total course (approximately forty five 40-minute sessions a year), one fourth of it was dedicated to writing, that is, about twelve lessons throughout the year, which started with paragraph writing and guided composition and ended with essay writing and the collaborative revision activities.

Although there is no specific recommendation for the use of collaborative revision or multiple drafting by the official documents of the Greek foreign languages curriculum (Pedagogical Institute, 2003a, 2011) the general guidelines for all school subjects provide the theoretical framework for the implementation of such collaborative practices (Pedagogical Institute, 2003b). More specifically, the guidelines for promoting collaborative work and enhancing problem-solving skills and strategies can be said to encompass collaborative revision. This is my own interpretation of the policy documents which, as Braun et al. (2011) maintain, is inevitable within each institutional context and depends on each teacher as well.

Despite the limited in-class time, the digitally written essay as homework was rejected from the start, however convenient it could have been time-wise, because the students were not used to writing essays for the English course at home and they were definitely not accustomed to using computers for educational purposes. If such a procedure had been selected, it would have compromised the study. Consequently, the traditional pen and paper form was used to write the essays in class.

The collaborative revision activities formed cycles, as the original study, but in this study two cycles were formed, including two of the essay genres, the compare-and-contrast and the cause-and-effect types. More specifically, the whole experiment lasted for seven 40-minute sessions in the following framework:

Session 1: It included a general introduction to the study, the steps that would be followed and what the learners would have to do. It also included an explanation of the "essay feedback code" (Appendix A), slightly modified from Memari Hanjani's (2016) article. Finally, it introduced genre I and its topic, "Internet or TV? Compare and contrast the two media." A brainstorming discussion on the topic followed while the students took notes.

Session 2: It was the actual essay writing where the students individually wrote their essays using the notes they had from the previous session. They were allowed to occasionally consult their peers. Then I collected their completed essays.

Session 3: It consisted of a revision of the "essay feedback code" to cater for any inquiries and misunderstandings. The essays, after being corrected by me using the code, were handed out to the students who formed four pairs and one three-member group, all of which were teacher-selected. Then, the essays were collaboratively revised by the students and handed back to me.

Session 4: This session followed Easter holidays, so there was a gap of two weeks. I handed out the corrected second drafts of the essays to the students and then genre II was introduced with the topic "Telling lies: the causes and effects." The students brainstormed their ideas and took notes.

Session 5: The students wrote essay II individually and their manuscripts were collected.

Session 6: There was a brief revision of the "essay feedback code" due to the Easter break and the discontinuation of the experiment and the corrected first drafts of essay II were returned to the students. Then, they went on with the collaborative revision activity and at the end I was given back their second drafts.

Session 7: The final session included the distribution of the corrected second drafts of essay II to the students, a brief informal discussion and the completion of a questionnaire.

Data Collection

The semi-structured interviews of the original article were replaced by questionnaires, which were distributed and answered by all 11 participants. Questionnaires were selected for the collection of the students' views on collaborative revision on the basis of minimum time needed to be completed and the quantifiable data they could yield (Dornyei, 2003).

The questionnaire was written in Greek to ensure better understanding. It comprised of 11 questions in total (see Appendix B). Nine were closed-ended with four-point Likert-type answers (Dornyei, 2007) and two were open-ended questions. Questions 1–3 examined what part of collaborative revision the students preferred, questions 4–7 examined how the students perceived this type of revision's effectiveness, open-ended questions 8–9 prompted the participants to freely express what helped them and what hindered the process of the collaborative revision, and questions 10–11 examined their views on other types of correction (teacher- and self-correction) to cater to the third research question. Unfortunately, as was expected, the open-ended questions were not answered by the majority of the students and the decision to keep brief observation notes during the process of collaborative revision sessions was found to be essential for the triangulation of the findings from the questionnaire and helped to gain deeper insight into any discrepancies between reality and the students' comments.

Findings

Prelude: Some Preliminary Comments

The present study, partially duplicating the original one, does not explore the actual gains of the learners' writing after the collaborative revision. It rather studies the learners' perceptions and attitudes towards the process, as well as the gains and difficulties of the innovative mode of essay revision. Therefore, it does not measure improvement in written performance, e.g., which errors were located and corrected, and which were located but not corrected. This would require a very close examination of the participants' essays, which is beyond the scope of this chapter but could form a very interesting future study, as well as the examination of other parameters such as the role of the specific student-pairs and many more. What it does measure is the extent to which the technique of collaborative revision is seen as helpful, valuable, non-threatening and effective by the students themselves in terms of linguistic and pedagogical gains. The present study also briefly explores the students' perception of collaborative revision in comparison to other modes of correction, self-correction and teacher-correction (research question 3) in order to extract conclusions related to the preferable type of revision according to the students.

In general, what the students perceive as the best type of feedback and revision is not always the most effective in terms of measurable improvement. Their views may be negatively or positively influenced by various parameters, such as overall class atmosphere and rapport, the (dys)function of the particular pair, (un)familiarity with the method, attitudes towards novelties in general, time-table fit, and attitudes towards the instructor. Nevertheless, a positive view towards any specific method/approach/technique would allow for greater motivation which, in turn, would lead to deeper engagement and ultimately improvement (Dornyei & Ushioda, 2011). Thus, a positive disposition towards collaborative revision is an asset because it may facilitate the expected results.

Findings from the Questionnaire

The findings from the questionnaire showed that most students somehow liked (4 students) or clearly liked (4 students) the process of locating their mistakes which were indicated by their teacher. What they found less interesting was the "essay feedback code." Five students clearly did not like it whereas only one clearly liked it. Almost half of the students (5) somehow liked the process of collaborative revision while there was a balance between the ones that did not like it at all and the ones who definitely did (3 students).

Despite the aforementioned unclear picture drawn from a balanced distribution of answers, items 4–7 yielded more definitive answers. Seven students agreed that they found their flaws and mistakes and only one claimed that s/he did not. They also believed that help was mutual; they both offered help to their partners (6 students) or somehow helped them (2) and also received help by them (7). Overall, supported by the more general question 7, five students were sure they learned from the whole process and four students somehow agreed that they learnt something. Moving on to the open-ended questions (items 8–9), there were only five answers expressing what helped and another five reflecting on what complicated the whole process. Interestingly, cooperation appeared twice in the students' answers both as the aspect that helped them most and as the feature that students found difficulty in. Another answer determining what helped students most was the process of locating the mistakes and correcting them by themselves (2 answers) while limited time and boredom were blamed as the culprits of negative attitude towards collaborative revision. Generally, despite the different instruments used and the scarcity of specific comments, my data confirm the students' positive attitudes towards collaborative revision as found in Memari Hanjani's research.

In reference to the third research question (items 10–11), which sought to compare students' preferred modes of feedback, it was made clear that teacher-correction was by far the most favored mode of feedback by 8 students who agreed and 2 students who somehow agreed. However, six students somehow preferred revising their essays by themselves and two were sure about their preference to self-correction. From the responses it can be assumed that the modes of teacher-correction and self-correction are seen as preferable to peer-correction or collaborative revision.

Findings from Teacher Observation

Let us now see how my brief notes from observing both sessions of collaborative revision supported the moderately positive attitudes of students towards the innovation and how they portrayed their perceptions. Almost all students were thoroughly engaged in the process, cooperating closely, providing various explanations and suggestions to each other and discussing them mostly in Greek. Only one seemed disoriented and bored. The rest seemed to be immensely enjoying it, exchanging their opinions in a relaxed atmosphere with low affective filters (Krashen, 2009). The pairs unconsciously made excellent use of time (30 minutes) choosing to work first on the one partner's essay and then to proceed to the other partner's. They all managed to finish their corrections in time except one group with three students. During collaborative practice there were a few instances of learners seeking my advice and a few others where partners sought the advice and collaboration of neighboring pairs, the latter of which I found extremely satisfactory, as collaboration extended beyond the pair. Time passed very smoothly and, as the students commented, "without even noticing." On the whole, my observations verified benefits which were articulated by the students in the original article, such as the benefit of multiple suggestions. I have to admit that I was profoundly impressed by their engagement in the process but also by the outcome of their work and I daresay that the two sessions of collaborative revision were some of the most rewarding lessons I taught this year.

Discussion and Recommendations for Fellow Teachers

I would definitely recommend this tripartite approach to essay feedback and revision to EFL teachers. Many reasons attest to it. For one thing, the much sought-after collaboration occurred effortlessly although students did not have a lot of experience in working together for a common goal. The pairs were selected on condition that they satisfied two premises: (a) a good relationship between the partners and (b) either a similar—but not very low—level of language or the most advanced students with the weakest ones. From my experience, the two premises are necessary for smooth collaboration and fulfillment of the assigned task with benefits for all participants. Through collaborative work, learners benefited from their partners' way of thinking and the strategies they used to deal with errors (Slavin, 1990), as it was found in Memari Hanjani's study, too. They even benefited from their emotional reactions to failure and success. In this way, learners could enrich not only their linguistic, but also their cognitive, strategic and psychological repertoire and become able to avoid some behaviors while imitating others. However, oral interaction and negotiation of meaning in the target language, as suggested by Long (1996) and Yong (2008), was not observed. I consider it a minor drawback as this was anticipated, and it was not the purpose of the experiment. The main benefits of cooperation, as was mentioned, were obtained.

Additionally, the game-like property of finding something when only a hint is provided (Palmer & Rodgers, 1983), as is the case with the attempt to locate a mistake when only an indication of its type is given by the teacher, made the lesson fun, motivating and effective at the same time. The students did revise their essays, making a second draft, a rare phenomenon in a real classroom! Therefore, I would recommend such game-like features to be incorporated not only to collaborative essay revision but also to various tasks and activities, as they actively engage learners into the learning process.

Finally, the amount of partial autonomy offered to the students shifted the responsibility from the teacher to the learner and it was as much as it was necessary to result in a new improved product—the revised essay. The "two-step revision," as I call it, divides the responsibility of revision among the three participants—the teacher, the writer and the peer—and leaves room for self-directed learning and self-correction. The roles of the students are dynamic, interchanging among the writer, the reviewer and the reader, and learning processes become dynamic, too, alternating between peer-correction and self-correction. In this light, we can visualize collaborative revision in the following equation:

collaborative revision = teacher feedback + peer correction + $\rightleftarrows$ self-correction

Nevertheless, some difficulties were identified both by the students' responses and my observations. One was the feedback code, which was regarded as long and "annoying" although it was specifically designed to be user-friendly and it included only eleven conventions. However, most of its items signified more than one mistake (e.g. wrong/unnecessary/missing article), which probably created some confusion. If a different symbol was used for each type of mistake, perhaps the feedback code would have been unmanageable for teachers and students alike. Another complication was the cases when some mistakes could not be identified and/or corrected—a difficulty also mentioned by the students in the original article. So, the learners had to resort to the teacher or leave mistakes uncorrected.

This observation led to the realization that not all mistakes can be revised by the students alone. Some need guidance from the teacher, especially when they pertain to flaws at sentence and paragraph level, in organization and coherence, and in content and ideas. These aspects of essay writing are also extremely difficult to encode into an easy-to-use feedback code and, additionally, the ones which are not often attended by EFL teachers when they correct essays (Gabinete, 2013; Mahaletchumy, 1994). Writing flaws on the macro-level require more detailed comments by the teacher, which cannot be codified into symbols. These can be added at the end of the essay, a common practice of teachers who do attend this type of mistakes. Yet, an unusual idea, which could possibly make the comments more notable, would be to write comments *before* the essay, provided that students are informed and used to leaving some empty space between the topic and their introduction.

Another issue that needs mentioning is that when a teacher is conducting an experiment in his/her class, the addition of observation can be the key to yielding more reliable results. As we have seen, the data from the questionnaires did not faithfully depict the students' attitudes and perceptions as they were manifested in their behaviors. Both engagement and effectiveness were observed while their opinions from the questionnaire were moderately positive. This discrepancy is common since learners—and especially school-aged learners—quite frequently provide inaccurate answers as they cannot understand their true dispositions (Paschalidou, 2016). For example, although some students claimed they did not like the process of revising collaboratively, all but one seemed to be working perfectly and with unexpected concentration and enthusiasm. It is clear that semi-structured/guided interviews would "force" richer and more reliable responses to be extrapolated from the students, as was the case with the original study, but, unfortunately, it is extremely difficult to find students to volunteer and arrange interviews within a busy school environment. Nevertheless, an attempt to persuade even a few students to participate in such interviews would be worthwhile.

Provided that collaboration, engagement and autonomy are qualities that EFL students need to develop, as contemporary EFL methodology maintains (see, for example, Gas & Mackey, 2012; Larsen-Freeman, 2000; Richards & Rogers, 2014) and taking into account that collaborative essay revision builds upon them, as we have seen from the discussion so far, I would not hesitate to incorporate this innovation as a tool of essay revision into the general EFL curriculum. It could definitely be used several times during a course but not necessarily each time an essay is submitted to the teacher for correction. Limited class time may deter the teacher from implementing it because no one can deny that collaborative revision takes up more time than the usual teacher feedback, which, however, very few students consult. Conversely, revising essays collaboratively ensures that students get involved in the revision of both their own and their partner's essay, even if this means more time allocated to essays. It goes without saying that in cases of specialized essay courses, collaborative revision can be used even more frequently since more time is dedicated to writing.

Additionally, I find collaborative revision to be relevant to various EFL contexts, from young learners to adult courses and from elementary to advanced proficiency levels. The whole collaborative revision process is readily adaptable so that different types of writing can benefit from it. It is not imperative that formal essays are used; other genres of writing, for example narratives, descriptions, informal e-mails, could also be collaboratively revised. Another aspect that could differentiate the process is the different focus of the teacher's initial comments, depending on the level of the learners. The younger or less advanced the learners, the narrower will the scope of the correction feedback be. As learners progress, the goal should shift to include feedback on the macro-level, such as organization, coherence and content deficiencies.

We cannot, of course, argue that the enthusiasm I observed would sustain if collaborative revision was established as the norm. In fact, I doubt it. But, as I see it, it is a realistic alternative to self-correction and teacher feedback with potential success. It is also a way to slightly reduce the workload of teachers and, most importantly, a smart and fun way to persuade students to revise their essays without even realizing it. Finally, by working with such alternative methods of revision we may lay the foundations for student-centered pedagogy because, as we have seen, students still rely heavily on the teacher-expert, as their preferred source of feedback. This student perception is confirmed by numerous studies (see, for example, Ferris, 1995; Goldstein, 2004; Maarof et al., 2011) and needs to be re-thought. Admittedly, who else can be an agent of change but the teacher?

Appendix A: Essay Feedback Code

t/v   error in **tense**/**verb** form, subject and verb don't agree
        e.g. I couldn't <u>came</u>./We <u>comes</u> early.

ar   wrong/unnecessary/missing **article**
        e.g. She is <u>a</u> calm./He is calm person.

prep   wrong/unnecessary/missing **preposition**
        e.g. We went <u>at</u> school.

pron   wrong/unnecessary/missing **pronoun**
        e.g. I told <u>his</u> that he should be ready.
voc   wrong **word**, wrong word-form
        e.g. He is <u>strength</u>./I <u>borrowed</u> my bag to him.
ss   wrong/unclear **sentence structure**, wrong **word order, half-sentence**
        e.g. He has come already. /The kids we called.
link   wrong/unnecessary/missing **linking word**
        e.g. We waited outside <u>but</u> it rained.
punct wrong/missing **punctuation**
        e.g. How old are you.
spel   wrong **spelling**
        e.g. neibourhood
∧   something is missing
!   I don't understand what you're writing!

Appendix B: Student Questionnaire

Collaborative Revision

Circle what you feel the most appropriate for you. For 8–9, write your own answers.
disagree: 1, somehow disagree: 2, somehow agree: 3, agree: 4

1.	I liked the idea of locating my mistakes without their full correction by my teacher.	1 2 3 4
2.	I liked the idea of the "essay correction code."	1 2 3 4
3.	I liked the process of the collaborative correction.	1 2 3 4
4.	I believe we found the mistakes/flaws of my essay.	1 2 3 4
5.	I believe I helped my partner.	1 2 3 4
6.	I believe that my partner has helped me.	1 2 3 4
7.	I believe I have learned something from the process.	1 2 3 4
8.	What helped me most was ...	
9.	What I found difficult was ...	
10.	I would prefer to correct/revise my essay by myself.	1 2 3 4
11.	I would prefer my teacher to correct my essay.	1 2 3 4

Notes

1 Collaborative writing is the process of producing a shared document by a group of
   people. The members of the group engage in interaction and decision-making, and
   are equally responsible for the final piece of writing (Allen et al., 1987).
2 Teacher feedback is the information provided by teachers about student performance in order to minimise the difference between his/her current and the desired
   performance (Hattie & Timperley, 2007).
3 Peer feedback/review is the process whereby peers comment and critique each
   other orally or in written form by assuming the role of teachers as sources of information (Liu & Hansen, 2002).
4 See Eisley, Madden, and Dunn (2000) for a typology of replication studies.

References

Allen, N., Atkinson, D., Morgan, M., Moore, T., & Snow, C. (1987). What experienced
    collaborators say about collaborative writing. *Journal of Business and Technical
    Communication, 1*(2), 70–90.
Bereiter, C., & Scardamalia, M. (1987). *The psychology of written composition*. Mahwah,
    NJ: Lawrence Erlbaum Associates.
Braun, A., Ball, S. J., Maguire, M., & Hoskins, K. (2011). Taking context seriously: Towards
    explaining policy enactments in the secondary school. *Discourse: Studies in the
    Cultural Politics of Education, 32*(4), 585–596.
Cohen, L. M., Manion, L., & Morrison, K. (2007). *Research methods in education*. Oxford:
    Routledge.
Council of Europe. (2001). *Common European framework of reference for languages:
    Learning, teaching, assessment*. Cambridge: Cambridge University Press.
Dörnyei, Z. (2003). *Questionnaires in second language research: Construction,
    administration, and processing*. Mahwah, NJ: Lawrence Erlbaum Associates.
Dörnyei, Z. (2007). *Research methods in applied linguistics*. Oxford: Oxford University Press.
Dörnyei, Z., & Ushioda, E. (2011). *Teaching and researching: Motivation* (2nd ed.).
    Harlow: Pearson.
Easley, R. W., Madden, C. S., & Dunn, M. G. (2000). Conducting marketing science: The
    role of replication in the research process. *Journal of Business Research, 48*(1), 83–92.
Ferris, D. R. (1995). Student reactions to teacher response in multiple-draft composition
    classrooms. *TESOL Quarterly, 29*(1), 33–53.
Gabinete, M. K. L. (2013). Assessment focus on essay of university students: The case
    between language- and non-language based courses in two private universities.
    Language Testing in Asia, 3, 5–23.

Gas, S. M., & Mackey, A. (2012). *The Routledge handbook of second language acquisition.* Oxford: Routledge.

Goldstein, L. M. (2004). Questions and answers about teacher written commentary and student revision: Teachers and students working together. *Journal of Second Language Writing, 13,* 63–80.

Hattie, J. A. C., & Timperley, H. (2007). The power of feedback. *Review of Educational Research, 77*(1), 81–112.

Kern, R. (2000). *Literacy and language teaching.* Oxford: Oxford University Press.

Krashen, S. (2009). The comprehension hypothesis extended. In T. Piske & M. Young-Scholten (Eds.), *Input matters in SLA* (pp. 81–94). Bristol: Multilingual Matters.

Lantolf, J. P., & Thorne, S. L. (2007). Sociocultural theory and second language learning. In B. Van Patten & J. Williams (Eds.), *Theories in second language acquisition* (pp. 201–224). Mahwah, NJ: Lawrence Erlbaum Associates.

Larsen-Freeman, D. (2000). *Techniques and principles in language teaching.* Oxford: Oxford University Press.

Liu, J., & Hansen, J. G. (2002). *Peer response in second language writing classrooms.* Ann Arbor, MI: University of Michigan Press.

Long, M. H. (1996). The role of the linguistic environment in second language acquisition. In W. C. Ritchie & T. K. Bahtia (Eds.), *Handbook of second language acquisition* (pp. 413–468). New York, NY: Academic Press.

Lundstorm, K., & Baker, W. (2009). To give is better than to receive: The benefits of peer review to the reviewer's own writing. *Journal of Second Language Writing, 18,* 30–43.

Maarof, N., Yamat, H., & Li, K. L. (2011). Role of teacher, peer and teacher-peer feedback in enhancing ESL students' writing. *World Applied Sciences Journal, 15,* 29–35.

Mahaletchumy, N. (1994). *What do ESL teachers do when they say they are teaching writing?* (Unpublished MEd thesis). University of Malaya, Kuala Lumpur.

McCurdy, P. (1992). *What students do with composition feedback.* Paper presented at the 27th Annual TESOL Convention, Vancouver, Canada.

Memari Hanjani, A. (2013). *Peer review, collaborative revision, and genre in L2 writing* (PhD thesis). University of Exeter, Exeter.

Memari Hanjani, A. (2016). Collaborative revision in L2 writing: Learners' reflections. *ELT Journal, 70*(3), 295–307.

Palmer, A., & Rodgers, T. (1983). Games in language teaching. *Language Teaching, 16*(1), 2–21.

Paschalidou, G. (2016). *Integrating clil modules of art history into greek secondary education: An investigation of content, language and motivation levels* (Unpublished MA thesis). Hellenic Open University, Patras.

Pedagogical Institute. (2003a). *Cross-curricular framework for the foreign languages curriculum.* Athens: Ministry of Education, Pedagogical Institute. [in Greek]

Pedagogical Institute. (2003b). *Cross-curricular framework for school curriculum: General part.* Athens: Ministry of Education, Pedagogical Institute. [in Greek]

Pedagogical Institute. (2011). *Integrated foreign languages curriculum*. Athens: Ministry of Education, Pedagogical Institute. [in Greek]

Richards, G. C., & Rogers, T. S. (2014). *Approaches and methods in language teaching* (3rd ed.). Cambridge: Cambridge University Press.

Slavin, R. E. (1996). Research on cooperative learning and achievement: What we know, what we need to know. *Contemporary Educational Psychology, 21*(1), 43–69.

Yong, M. F. (2010). Collaborative writing features. *RELC Journal, 41*(1), 18–30.

Zhang, S. (1995). Reexamining the affective advantage of peer feedback in the ESL writing class. *Journal of Second Language Writing, 4*(3), 209–222.

Zhao, H. (2010). Investigating learners' use and understanding of peer and teacher feedback on writing: A comparative study in a Chinese english writing classroom. *Assessing writing, 15*(1), 3–17.

CHAPTER 4

Dynamic Written Corrective Feedback in a Community College ESL Writing Class Setting

Kendon Kurzer
University of California-Davis, USA

Introduction

Dynamic Written Corrective Feedback (DWCF) is a feedback approach that uses a coding system to deliver written corrective feedback (WCF) in which teachers mark student errors on paragraphs written in class (Evans, Hartshorn, McCollum, & Wolfersberger, 2010). In a small quasi-experimental study (treatment n = 28 and control n = 19), students who used DWCF in their classes showed higher gains in accuracy via pre-test/post-test writing samples, indicating that DWCF may positively impact accuracy for multilingual writers (Evans et al., 2010). Many instructors in second language (L2) writing provide WCF on the basis of the belief that multilingual writers need explicit grammatical feedback in order to gain stronger mastery of English linguistic features in their writing (Ferris, 2006, 2011) and have pursued methods of delivering WCF in manners that are well received by students while still being manageable on the part of the teacher (Bitchener & Ferris, 2012; Ferris, 2004; Hyland & Hyland, 2006). DWCF may be one such favorable method of delivering WCF in a student-teacher friendly manner.

The DWCF process includes the following steps, adapted from Evans et al. (2010):

1. Students regularly compose short paragraphs (for approximately ten minutes) on a particular topic in class. These compositions typically are done on a daily basis.
2. The teacher returns the student compositions with the errors coded, per the coding system outlined in Appendix A.
3. Students then individually edit their paragraphs and receive additional teacher feedback via the same coding system.
4. The revision process is repeated until the students ultimately reach an established level of grammatical accuracy on their drafts.
5. Students record their errors from each draft on a log (Appendix B), which then can help them identify and correct personal grammatical error patterns, which may then help them become better self-editors (Ferris, 2006; Lalande, 1982).

I wanted to investigate how feasible it is to implement DWCF in a lower-intermediate ESL writing class I taught at a local community college, marking the intersection of theory/research to pedagogical application (Cain, 2015). DWCF seemed to be an appropriate mode for effective WCF given its foundation in cognitive and second language acquisition (SLA) theories and connection to best practices.

Cognitive and SLA Theories and DWCF

Via DWCF that addresses the personalized needs of their students, writing instructors may better interact with students' Zones of Proximal Development (ZPD)—the difference between what learners can do on their own and what they can do with assistance/scaffolding—and help them internalize (Vygotsky, 1978) and produce linguistically accurate concepts, when their understanding of such concepts may previously have depended on decontextualized grammar instruction. Despite the fact that Vygotsky's work focused on children's cognition, adult learners of a second language may experience similar self-regulated consciousness and mediation via teacher experts (Vygotsky, 1978) that may be done effectively using DWCF.

Along a related theme, teachers' feedback should be targeted at individual students' needs at a comprehensible level only slightly above current mastery, or $i + 1$, per Krashen's (1985) Input Hypothesis. Similarly, teachers can use collaboration to maintain input at $i + 1$ for language learners (Long, 1996). According to Long (1996), feedback—such as that employed by teachers who use DWCF—facilitates language development, "at least for vocabulary, morphology, and language-specific syntax" (p. 414).

While manageable feedback seems beneficial for students, DeKeyser's skill acquisition theory (2001, 2007) further suggests that students need declarative knowledge in order to develop procedural knowledge: what students can actually apply. Students require extensive opportunities to practice, with the ultimate aim of automatic production of the target language features, although successful transfer of these features to new, genuine contexts can be quite challenging for many students (DeKeyser, 2001, 2007). Accordingly, practice should be as authentic as feasible, which may not typically be the case with traditional grammar instruction or common approaches to written corrective feedback. As DWCF uses paragraphs written by the students, students gain genuine experience and practice self-editing with strong scaffolds. This experience may translate to their other authentic writing contexts.

DWCF, grounded in the cognitive and second language acquisition theories outlined above (Krashen, 1985; Long, 1996; Vygotsky, 1978) may be one effective pedagogical intervention that teachers can employ to support meaningful procedural knowledge (DeKeyser, 2001, 2007). This may then result in increased linguistic accuracy.

Established Best Practices of Written Corrective Feedback

"[D]esigned to help L2 learners improve the accuracy of writing by ensuring that instruction, practice, and feedback are manageable, meaningful, timely, and constant" (Hartshorn & Evans, 2012, p. 30) for both teachers and students, DWCF likely matches established WCF best-practices in a number of areas. *Focused* (targeting specific error types) corrective feedback methods are stronger than *unfocused* (all-inclusive) approaches (Bitchener, 2008; Ellis, Sheen, Murakami, & Takashima, 2008; Sheen, 2007). However, teachers may focus too narrowly on a small number of error categories, an established limitation in much of the literature on WCF (e.g. Bitchener & Knoch, 2009a, 2009b, 2010; Ellis, Sheen, Murakami, & Takashima, 2008). Teachers using DWCF can employ an all-inclusive coding system that may better address students' individual needs.

Indirect WCF—only marking the error—may more effectively impact students' long-term linguistic accuracy development than *direct* WCF—marking and correcting the error (Ferris, 2006; Hendrickson, 1980; Lalande, 1982). Teachers who use indirect feedback require students to correct their errors individually, with the scaffold of the identifying code or mark. This individual effort may more strongly lead to increased writing improvement than a provided correction, promoting self-monitoring skills in students (Lalande, 1982). This feedback then may lead to increased automatization of language production that accurately reflects the language features in question (DeKeyser, 2001).

Some errors are considered to be *untreatable*, with rules that are largely idiosyncratic, like "word order, sentence boundaries, phrase construction, word choice, or collocations" (Ferris, 2010, p. 193), while those with more teachable rules are considered to be *treatable* (Bitchener, 2008; Ferris, 2006; Xu, 2009). As students who use DWCF practice editing their own authentic texts, their writing may be more accurate for errors thought to be untreatable (Hartshorn & Evans, 2012). *Explicit* WCF, such as that consisting of a coding approach, may be more beneficial than *unlabeled* corrective feedback, such as simple highlighting or marking of errors (Bitchener, 2008; Bitchener & Knoch,

2010; Ferris, 2006; Foin & Lange, 2007; Sheen, 2007). Coded WCF may remind students of their prior grammar instruction, and thus may help reinforce linguistic accuracy on features for which they have developed prior declarative knowledge (DeKeyser, 2001).

Empirical Evidence on Dynamic Written Corrective Feedback

As discussed earlier, DWCF as a pedagogical approach to develop linguistic/ grammatical accuracy seems grounded in cognitive and SLA theories and matches established WCF best practices based on SLA research. However, the existing research base on DWCF is quite limited, especially in terms of sample sizes. The first study investigating DWCF, outlined earlier, was a small quasi-experimental study with a treatment of $n = 28$ and control of $n = 19$ (Evans et al., 2010). Including this initial study, most experimental investigations of DWCF included only small sample sizes of 12 to 28 students (Evans, Hartshorn, & Strong-Krause, 2011; Hartshorn Evans, 2012, 2015; Evans et al., 2010). In these studies, researchers typically focused on DWCF—as implemented in the original article—in the Intensive English Program (IEP) of a research university; however, Evans, Hartshorn, and Strong-Krause (2011) researched DWCF in non-required grammar classes designed to support matriculated L2 students at this same university.

Taken collectively, this body of literature suggests that using DWCF in language/grammar classes results in statistically significant levels of general increased accuracy (Evans et al., 2010; Evans, Hartshorn, & Strong-Krause, 2011; Hartshorn & Evans, 2015; Hartshorn et al., 2010), specifically in subject/ verb agreement, sentence structure, determiners, lexical/verb/semantic and mechanical/punctuation (Hartshorn & Evans, 2012). However, the control/ experimental group makeups of these studies were typically dissimilar regarding language backgrounds, with students who may acquire the L2 differently (Corder, 1981), making a true comparison difficult.

My previous study investigated DWCF in three different levels of a developmental writing program for matriculated multilingual students at a large research university (Kurzer, 2018). In addition to using larger student samples (treatment $n=214$ and control $n=111$) than the previous studies, the results of this study indicated that students who used DWCF exhibited stronger self-editing skills and more accurate writing on all error categories: global, local, and mechanical (Bates, Lane, & Lange, 1993). The context of this study also adapted the original DWCF approach to the three different proficiency levels of the program, finding that students of all levels showed statistically

TABLE 4.1   Overview of six DWCF studies

Study	Control	Large N (>30)	Context	Longitudinal
Evans et al., 2010	Yes	No	IEP	No
Hartshorn et al., 2010	No	No	IEP	No
Hartshorn and Evans, 2012	Yes	No	IEP	No
Hartshorn and Evans, 2015	Yes	No	IEP	Yes
Evans et al., 2011	Yes	No	University	No
Kurzer, 2018	Yes	Yes	University	No

significant gains in accuracy (thus no ceiling level of proficiency for DWCF has yet been identified).

See Table 4.1 for a brief overview of the six published studies on the DWCF approach.

While the results of these previous studies largely suggest that DWCF is pedagogically effective at helping students gain accuracy, at least short-term, it should be examined more thoroughly, and in new contexts, particularly regarding student and teacher perceptions.

Thus far, DWCF has been integrated into the programs at two different research institutions, with administrators, teachers, and students who, at least anecdotally, have largely responded positively. However, such support for DWCF has yet to be systematically researched and reported. Specifically, we lack studies that have investigated student and teacher perceptions of DWCF as a pedagogical approach in their classrooms. Similarly, we lack evidence on the effectiveness of DWCF in contexts other than IEP and developmental writing programs associated with large research institutions, such as teaching universities or community colleges (CC), contexts that may attract a very different multilingual population than the largely international (e.g., those studying in the United States on an F-1 visa) student population explored in the DWCF literature thus far.

DWCF in a Community College Setting

To begin to address the questions of how DWCF could be implemented in a CC setting, and how multilingual students in a CC respond to it as a method of receiving grammatical support, I adapted the process for use in a lower-intermediate ESL writing class I taught as an adjunct professor at a CC with a sizeable multilingual student population. In this section, I discuss the student population, the context/classroom setting, and how I integrated DWCF in my curriculum.

Student Population

The CC at which I taught is a large, diverse suburban institution that serves the population in one of the urban centers of Northern California. While many such CCs in California may feature a large Spanish-speaking population, my class—and the program at large—was quite diverse, with significant proportions of the students coming from Russian, Middle Eastern, and East/Southeast Asian backgrounds in addition to a robust Spanish speaking population. Table 4.2 contains the home languages of the 25 students from my class who agreed to participate in this study.

Many of the students at this institution, particularly the multilingual students, are non-traditional: students who return to school when they are somewhat older. Of the 25 students in this study, 15 were older, non-traditional students, largely with families at home and occupations or part-time jobs. Several of my students held dual citizenship with the U.S. and elsewhere, such as Iran, Iraq, or Canada. Seventeen had been in the United States for at least four years, with only one having had arrived that year primarily for school. Contrasted with the largely international student population of the previously conducted studies on DWCF, this student population is quite different.

Given the wide range of language proficiencies evident in the class (despite a fairly robust placement system and several different levels of courses into which students could be placed), I did not feel that traditional grammar instruction using only a grammar textbook and inauthentic exercises would adequately serve my students. Quite a few had lived in the United States long enough to develop fairly advanced oral proficiency, in line with many Generation 1.5 students: children from immigrant families who have attended some primary or secondary school in English-dominant countries (Ferris, 2009). However, that proficiency largely did not translate well to written abilities, consistent grammatical/linguistic accuracy in the kinds of texts they were expected to produce, or thorough knowledge of linguistic terms or grammatical concepts.

TABLE 4.2   Home languages of student participants

	Arabic	Russian	Vietnamese	Spanish	Mongolian
Number of students	10	7	1	6	1

Other students more closely matched the typical international student studying temporarily in the United States, with fairly strong awareness of grammatical concepts and terms, evidence of practice using grammar textbooks, and level-appropriate mastery of writing and reading conventions. Such varied student needs made selecting a grammar textbook challenging; relying solely on a grammar textbook to provide all grammar support would likely have been problematic as well, as individual students' linguistic needs may not have been thoroughly addressed. As a result of the tension between traditional grammar instruction via a textbook and providing students with needed, individualized feedback, I ultimately included DWCF as a complement to the textbook.

Classroom Context and Curriculum

This writing class was the second in a series of seven possible writing classes that built on each other to prepare multilingual students for mainstream first year composition courses. The class met twice a week for 15 weeks. The lower-level writing classes all included a grammar component although students also were required to take stand-alone grammar, listening/speaking, and reading classes. The first writing class in the series focused on paragraph writing skills. The lower-intermediate class I taught was the first to introduce the essay, specifically the standard five-paragraph essay format. Prior to this, students had typically written only paragraphs in the lowest writing class of the series. However, of the 25 students who participated in this study, only five had previously taken a writing class. The remaining 20 were placed into my class and were new to the CC that semester.

Following the established program curricula and the suggestions of the program director, I structured my course around two textbooks: an introduction to the essay text and a general grammar book that had been used at this level before. The essay textbook prioritized different genres: description essays, how-to paragraphs, and opinion/argumentative essays. The grammar text prioritized the following grammatical features: verb forms and tenses, noun forms, adjective and adverbial clauses, comparatives/superlatives, and auxiliary verbs.

The bulk of the students' course grades stemmed from timed writing contexts in which students were assigned a particular topic and had to craft a clear argument around that topic. The topics moved beyond simply personal reflection or interest but were not overly academic in nature as they did not require the inclusion of outside sources or other support. Topics for the papers included an argument paper about a meaningful contribution a family member made to a particular society or group of people, a recommendation for a particular place to live, why some students cheat in class, and things that are good/bad for health. As noted earlier, students were expected to write short essays, typically following the five-paragraph essay format, although I encouraged some variability on number of body paragraphs.

DWCF Implementation

Based on my experiences using DWCF in different contexts, I decided to adjust and combine some of the original 20 codes of Evans et al. (2010). Ultimately, I used 16 error codes organized by type: (1) global errors, or those that frequently impede meaning, (2) local errors that typically do not impede meaning but may be irritating to people unaccustomed to working with multilingual writers (Bates, Lane, & Lange, 1993; Lane & Lange, 2012), and (3) mechanical, or punctuation/spelling errors. By grouping the error codes by type, I was able to more strongly stress those features that were more critical for my students to master, or were more appropriate for their level, a strength of my approach to DWCF over the original, which simply addressed all errors as equal. Appendix A contains the DWCF codes I used via a handout I gave to the students and discussed in class. As proposed in the original DWCF approach (Evans et al., 2010), I required students to record their errors on all DWCF drafts written across the semester using a log I provided and regularly checked (Appendix B).

On the first day of the semester, I had students write short, in-class diagnostic paragraphs so I could get a sense for where they were in their writing proficiency as a group. I then used that diagnostic paragraph for the first round of DWCF. The second day of class, in addition to beginning instruction on writing in general, I introduced the DWCF handout (Appendix A). I started off by asking students to work in partners to identify the errors in the example sentences on the handout. We then discussed each sentence as a group to identify the errors, and I informed them of how I would code the errors. In this manner, I was able to make the coding process more salient for the students. I then returned their diagnostic paragraphs and asked them to tally the individual errors of all 16 types they had made in class so we could discuss any questions or concerns they might have had. I then required students to edit their paragraphs at home before the next class meeting.

After students turned in their second drafts, I again coded the remaining errors and returned the drafts to the students for additional recording of the errors in their log and additional editing if required. I required a third draft if a student still had more than two global errors that impacted intended meaning, or more than four errors total. I did not make students edit a fourth time as that may have had a negative impact on student motivation, one concern some other teachers and researchers have shared with me of the DWCF process.

Topics for the DWCF paragraphs ranged from student introductions, to reflection (such as "what was challenging for you on the last practice timed essay?" or "how should you use your time differently on your next essay?"), and to pre-writing activities ("what do you like about your hometown?"). While the original approach to DWCF as proposed in Evans et al. (2010) left the topics quite vague (e.g. "write about the weather"), I thought more specific topics could prepare students for future writing or afford insights into students' struggles and still maintain the necessary grammar/linguistic accuracy focus.

In addition to the topic guidelines, I explicitly directed students to write as much as they could in the ten minutes of class time devoted to the first DWCF draft and encouraged them to keep writing should they finish early. I started by requiring students to write between five and seven sentences, then gradually increased the expectations to between eight and ten sentences by the end of the semester. This pushed students to practice writing a little faster, and thus the DWCF process may have contributed to their written fluency, or speed of writing, as well as their accuracy. As timed essays were responsible for the bulk of the final grade, increased practice on low-stakes assignments likely proved beneficial for these students.

Despite the grammar/linguistic accuracy focus of DWCF, I found that the approach I took to incorporate it into my classroom resulted in benefits to the students beyond just accuracy, such as increased fluency/speed of writing and stronger paragraph organization. Although I did not explicitly provide WCF on writing features other than grammar on the DWCF paragraphs, I requested that students include clear topic sentences, supporting details, commentary on those details connecting to the larger argument of the paragraph, and summarizing concluding sentences. Throughout the semester, as I instructed students on the different features expected within their body paragraphs, the DWCF paragraphs proved to be a good place for them to practice this expected organization, again in a low-stakes context.

Overall, I found that my approach to DWCF in this low-intermediate CC ESL writing class was quite effective. Originally, I had planned on doing 12 rounds of DWCF throughout the semester; that ended up being rather optimistic due to the editing stages for each round and the amount of textbook content we needed to cover. We ended up completing ten total rounds. While having two different types of timed writing assignments (the essays and the DWCF paragraphs) was a little confusing to some of the students initially, after a few weeks they figured things out and were able to productively write in manners that promoted stronger scaffolding using the shorter paragraphs to practice features required in the larger, high-stakes assignments.

I also found that responding to students' DWCF paragraphs was manageable for me as a teacher. The class was capped at 28; over the course of the semester I had two students ultimately withdraw from the class, but it took me approximately an hour to code the errors of all first draft paragraphs, and much faster for second and third drafts. While this did add some work as I was already responding to and grading student essays and grammar homework, it did not prove prohibitive. That said, providing feedback on DWCF paragraphs and the rest of the coursework for larger or multiple classes may be too much of a demand, especially for part-time instructors. In the original study, DWCF was implemented in an IEP's curriculum as a class in and of itself (Evans et al., 2010); such a setting would help ensure that teachers did not become overwhelmed by the copious amounts of feedback expected of them. In my previous study (Kurzer, 2018), DWCF was implemented into developmental writing classes similar to that of this CC, with teachers adapting to the added demands fairly well. In this case, I found that the benefits of DWCF to my students outweighed the costs. Other instructors at this institution also expressed interest in using DWCF in their own classes.

CC Student Perceptions of DWCF

Methods

While I found DWCF to be a meaningful addition to my class from the teacher's perspective, I also investigated my CC students' perceptions of how it impacted their accuracy and writing. In order to determine these reactions, I administered a short survey (Appendix C) at the end of the semester asking about the different facets of grammar instruction in the class. I started the survey by asking five-point Likert scale agree-disagree items about student opinions of the grammar textbook (e.g., I thought the book was a good grammar text; was a good level for me; was effective; helped me improve my grammar). I then asked about student opinions of the DWCF process (e.g., I thought the DWCF process was effective; helped me improve my grammar; helped me improve my writing in general; helped me improve my writing speed; was a good level for me). I then asked students to identify which (the text book or the DWCF approach) they found more effective at assisting with grammar mastery, along with a final open-ended question asking students why they felt the DWCF process or the grammar book was more effective.

Student responses to the Likert scale items were made numeric (Strongly Agree = 2, Slightly Agree = 1, Neither Agree nor Disagree = 0, Slightly Disagree = -1, Strongly Disagree = -2) and tallied, with descriptive statistics calculated. All 25 students took the survey, although only a few answered the open-ended question

Student Perceptions of DWCF: Results and Discussion

Table 4.3 contains the descriptive statistics of the numeric adaptations of students' survey responses.

As seen above, students indicated that the grammar textbook was good, that the book and DWCF were equally helpful at improving their grammar, and that DWCF was more effective overall than the book. These students also generally felt that DWCF helped improve their general writing and writing speed (fluency), which is an important component of this class because much of the curriculum is centered around helping students with timed essays.

Interestingly, with the exception of the first item, student responses to the survey items about DWCF solicited higher overall reactions (with a total average of 1.6) than did the textbook items (total average of 1.46). While these averages were not statistically significantly different (with a calculated t-test p-value of .1), likely due to the limited numbers of data points, the difference still warrants attention. Perhaps most importantly, the fairly low score on the

TABLE 4.3   Student survey response means and standard deviations

Question	Mean	St. Dev.
The book was good	1.72	.46
The book was at a good level	1.36	.76
The book was effective	1.24	.97
The book helped me improve grammar	1.52	.65
DWCF was effective	1.65	.65
DWCF helped me improve grammar	1.52	.77
DWCF helped me improve general writing	1.56	.58
DWCF helped me improve writing speed	1.56	.65
DWCF feedback was at a good level	1.76	.43

Student Preferences

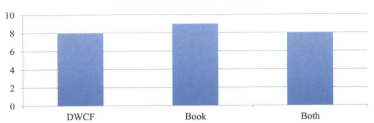

FIGURE 4.1   Student preferences for DWCF, the grammar textbook, or both

item about the book being an appropriate level indicates some dissatisfaction that was not evident in the DWCF item. This may suggest that these students feel that DWCF does indeed match their individual $i+1$ (Krashen, 1985; Long, 1996), at least as implemented in this class, evidence in support of the original DWCF model (Evans et al., 2010).

Students also reported that DWCF positively impacted their speed of writing. As I noted earlier, while the main objective of DWCF is to support students' grammatical/linguistic accuracy, increased fluency may be an added benefit of the intervention. Their response about increased writing speed may support this inference although quantitative evidence would obviously strengthen such a conclusion.

I also asked students which they preferred overall, the DWCF or the grammar textbook as pertaining to their grammar improvement (Figure 4.1).

As seen in Figure 4.1, while more students indicated that they preferred the grammar textbook to DWCF, eight students ultimately indicated that they appreciated both DWCF and the textbook, and eight students preferred DWCF, for a majority of the class (16 out of 25 students). Also, all nine students who preferred the book reported that DWCF had a positive impact on their accuracy overall. Accordingly, including DWCF as a supplement to the grammar textbook for this class was successful.

Conclusion

Dynamic Written Corrective Feedback (DWCF) proved to be a manageable mode of delivering direct, comprehensive, and specific feedback for individual students' needs (Evans et al., 2010). Within my community college setting, DWCF was appropriately used to supplement grammar instruction in a writing class. Students responded well to DWCF while recognizing that they also largely appreciated the grammar textbook and explicit grammar instruction in class. DWCF may be an effective way of connecting grammar instruction to students' own writing production. While I found DWCF to be appropriate in my CC class, my perceptions were not based on empirical evidence as I did not collect data on its actual impact on student accuracy. An experimental study tracking changes in student errors across the semester would lend added weight to my conclusions.

I found that one of the great strengths of adopting DWCF in language/writing classes for multilingual students is its flexibility. In the original study (Evans et al., 2010), DWCF was the sole focus of a language class; however, I used it here as one small component of a writing class with a heavy grammar focus. Teachers in different contexts could easily integrate DWCF principles (using an established, salient coding system, immediate feedback, and regular editing) to provide meaningful, individualized feedback in a manageable manner given contextual appropriateness (small numbers of students/appropriate workload expectations). Using the codes from the original study or the system I adapted (Appendix A) could serve as a foundation. Teachers can further adapt DWCF based on individual contextual needs. Helping students gain linguistic/grammatical accuracy can be challenging, and DWCF may be one fruitful approach to navigating this challenge.

Appendix A: DWCF Writing Correction Marks

	Code	Error type	Example
Global Errors	VF	Verb Form	It was happened yesterday. Psychology expose you to behavior.
	VT	Verb Time	It happen yesterday.
	SS	Sentence Structure (incl. Run-on and incomplete)	They brought the man who them him found. Because they thought it was good. Because friendship takes effort, so it is time-consuming.
	W O	Word Order	Especially, I miss home.
	WC	Word Choice	She says that raising a pet needs responsibility.

(Cont.)

Local Errors	PP	Prepositions	I was responsible of everything.
	D	Determiner (articles)	The trip to United States was enjoyable.
	NF	Noun Form	All family member are supposed to get along.
			She limited the amount of candies I could eat.
	WF	Word Form	Money brings themselves more opportunities.
Other Errors (Mechanical)	SPG	Spelling	I never worried about my teech getting bad.
	P	Punctuation	When I was visiting; one morning scared me.
	C	Capital letter	Students love to party. they also love to eat pizza.
	^	Insert something	A good major helps you earn a lot money.
	ℯ	Omit something	I chose this major is because it is interesting.
	?	Meaning is not clear	He borrowed some smoke.
	AWK	Awkward wording	Candy makes children feel a sweet taste.

(In the "Other Errors (Mechanical)" section, the rows ^, ℯ, ?, AWK are marked "Use with SS".)

Appendix B: Error Log

		1	2	3	4	5	6	7	8	9	10	Total
Paragraph Score:												
Global Errors	VF											
	VT											
	SS											
	WO											
	WC											
Local Errors	PP											
	D											
	NF											
	WF											

(Cont.)

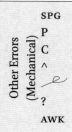

Appendix C: Student Survey Questions

1. I thought the grammar book was a good grammar text.
2. I thought the book was a good level for me (not too hard or too easy).
3. I thought the book was effective.
4. I thought the book helped me improve my grammar.
5. I thought the DWCF process was effective.
6. The DWCF process helped me improve my grammar.
7. The DWCF process helped me improve my writing in general.
8. The DWCF process helped me improve my writing speed.
9. Which did you find more effect at improving your grammar, the book or the DWCF process?
10. Why did you respond as you did?

References

Bates, L., Lane, J., & Lange, E. (1993). *Writing clearly: Responding to ESL compositions.* Boston, MA: Heinle & Heinle.

Bitchener, J. (2008). Evidence in support of written corrective feedback. *Journal of Second Language Writing, 17,* 102–118. Retrieved from http://dx.doi.org/10.1016/j.jslw.2007.11.004

Bitchener, J., & Ferris, D. R. (2012). *Written corrective feedback in second language acquisition and writing.* New York, NY: Routledge.

Bitchener, J., & Knoch, U. (2009a). The relative effectiveness of different types of direct written corrective feedback. *System, 37,* 322–329. Retrieved from https://doi.org/10.1016/j.system.2008.12.006

Bitchener, J., & Knoch, U. (2009b). The value of a focused approach to written corrective feedback. *ELT Journal, 63,* 204–211. Retrieved from https://doi.org/10.1093/elt/ccn043

Bitchener, J., & Knoch, U. (2010). The contribution of written corrective feedback to language development: A ten month investigation. *Applied Linguistics, 31,* 193–214. Retrieved from http://dx.doi.org/10.1093/applin/amp016

Cain, T. (2015). Teachers' engagement with published research: Addressing the knowledge problem. *The Curriculum Journal, 26*(3), 488–509.

Corder, S. P. (1981). *Error analysis and interlanguage*. London: Oxford University Press.

DeKeyser, R. (2001). Automaticity and automatization. In P. Robinson (Ed.), *Cognition and second language instruction* (pp. 97–113). Mahwah, NJ: Lawrence Erlbaum Associates. Retrieved from http://dx.doi.org/10.1017/CBO9781139524780.007

DeKeyser, R. (2007). Skill acquisition theory. In B. VanPatten & J. Williams (Eds.), *Theories in second language acquisition: An introduction* (pp. 94–112). New York, NY: Routledge.

Ellis, R., Sheen, Y., Murakami, M., & Takashima, H. (2008). The effects of focused and unfocused written corrective feedback in an English as a foreign language context. *System, 36*, 353–371. Retrieved from http://dx.doi.org/10.1016/j.system.2008.02.001

Evans, N. W., Hartshorn, K. J., McCollum, R., & Wolfersberger, M. (2010). Contextualizing corrective feedback in second language writing pedagogy. *Language Teaching Research, 14*, 445–463. Retrieved from https://doi.org/10.1177/1362168810375367

Evans, N. W., Hartshorn, K. J., & Strong-Krause, D. (2011). The efficacy of dynamic written corrective feedback for university-matriculated ESL learners. *System, 39*, 229–239. Retrieved from http://dx.doi.org/10.1016/j.system.2011.04.012

Ferris, D. R. (2004). The 'grammar correction' debate in L2 writing: Where are we, and where do we go from here? (and what do we do in the meantime …?). *Journal of Second Language Writing, 13*, 49–62. Retrieved from https://doi.org/10.1016/j.jslw.2004.04.005

Ferris, D. R. (2006). Does error feedback help student writers? New evidence on the short- and long-term effects of written error correction. In K. Hyland & F. Hyland (Eds.), *Feedback in second language writing: Contexts and issues* (pp. 81–104). New York, NY: Cambridge University Press. Retrieved from http://dx.doi.org/10.1017/CBO9781139524742.007

Ferris, D. R. (2009). *Teaching college writing to diverse student populations*. Ann Arbor, MI: University of Michigan Press.

Ferris, D. R. (2010). Second language writing research and written corrective feedback in SLA. *Studies in Second Language Acquisition, 32*, 181–201. Retrieved from http://dx.doi.org/10.1017/S0272263109990490

Ferris, D. R. (2011). *Treatment of error in second language student writing*. Ann Arbor, MI: University of Michigan Press.

Ferris, D. R. (2012). Written corrective feedback in second language acquisition and writing studies. *Language Teaching, 45*, 446–459. Retrieved from http://dx.doi.org/10.1017/S0261444812000250

Ferris, D. R., Liu, H., Sinha, A., & Senna, M. (2013). Written corrective feedback for individual L2 writers. *Journal of Second Language Writing, 22*, 307–329. Retrieved from http://dx.doi.org/10.1016/j.jslw.2012.09.009

Foin, A. T., & Lange, E. J. (2007). Generation 1.5 writers' success in correcting errors marked on an out-of-class paper. *The CATESOL Journal, 19*, 146–163.

Hartshorn, K. J., & Evans, N. W. (2012). The differential effects of comprehensive corrective feedback on L2 writing accuracy. *Journal of Linguistics and Language Teaching, 3*, 16–46.

Hartshorn, K. J., & Evans, N. W. (2015). The effects of dynamic written corrective feedback: A 30 week study. *Journal of Response to Writing, 1*, 6–34. Retrieved from https://doi.org/10.1558/wap.v6i2.251

Hartshorn, K. J., Evans, N. W., Merrill, P. F., Sudweeks, R. R., Strong-Krause, D., & Anderson, N. J. (2010). Effects of dynamic corrective feedback on ESL writing accuracy. *TESOL Quarterly, 44*, 84–108. Retrieved from http://dx.doi.org/10.5054/tq.2010.213781

Hendrickson, J. M. (1980). The treatment of error in written work. *The Modern Language Journal, 64*, 216–221. Retrieved from http://dx.doi.org/10.1111/j.1540-4781.1980.tb05188.x

Hyland, K., & Hyland, F. (2006). Feedback on second language students' writing. *Language Teaching, 39*, 83–101. Retrieved from https://doi.org/10.1017/s0261444806003399

Krashen, S. D. (1985). *The input hypothesis: Issues and implications*. Oxford: Pergamon.

Kurzer, K. (2018). Dynamic written corrective feedback in developmental ESL writing classes. *TESOL Quarterly, 52*(1), 5–33. doi:10.1002/tesq.366

Lalande, J. F. (1982). Reducing composition errors: An experiment. *Modern Language Journal, 66*, 140–149. Retrieved from http://dx.doi.org/10.1111/j.1540-4781.1982.tb06973.x

Lane, J., & Lange, E. (2012). *Writing clearly: Grammar for editing* (3rd ed.). Boston, MA: Heinle Cengage Learning.

Larsen-Freeman, D. (2009). Adjusting expectations: The study of complexity, accuracy, and fluency in second language acquisition. *Applied Linguistics, 30*, 579–589. Retrieved from https://doi.org/10.1093/applin/amp043

Long, M. H. (1996). The role of linguistic environment in second language acquisition. In W. Ritchie & T. Bhatia (Eds.), *Handbook of second language acquisition* (pp. 413–468). San Diego, CA: Academic Press. Retrieved from http://dx.doi.org/10.1016/B978-012589042-7/50015-3

Sheen, Y. (2007). The effect of focused written corrective feedback and language aptitude on ESL learners' acquisition of articles. *TESOL Quarterly, 41*, 255–283. Retrieved from https://doi.org/10.1002/j.1545-7249.2007.tb00059.x

Truscott, J., & Hsu, A. Y. (2008). Error correction, revision, and learning. *Journal of Second Language Writing, 17*, 292–305. Retrieved from https://doi.org/10.1016/j.jslw.2008.05.003

Vygotsky, L. (1978). Interaction between learning and development. *Readings on the Development of Children, 23*, 34–41.

Xu, C. (2009). Overgeneralization from a narrow focus: A response to Ellis et al. (2008) and Bitchener (2008). *Journal of Second Language Writing, 18*, 270–275. Retrieved from https://doi.org/10.1016/j.jslw.2009.05.005

Bringing the *Academic Vocabulary List* into the Classroom: Student Lexical Investigations

Chris Banister
Regent's University London, UK

Introduction

Gardner and Davies's (2014) article introduces their *Academic Vocabulary List* (AVL), a new frequency-based list of academic vocabulary for teachers and learners of English. The authors argue that knowledge of academic vocabulary plays a key role in relation to reading skills, wider success at school and in the negotiation of gatekeeping tests such as IELTS. They point to the increasing body of literature which supports explicit teaching of academic vocabulary, for example via lists, to help learners. They also maintain that a frequency-informed approach to vocabulary teaching can ensure that it is truly reflective of modern academic language (Gardner & Davies, 2014).

The authors trace the recent history of vocabulary lists of academic English and debates in this subfield. Firstly, they acknowledge the important contribution of Coxhead's (2000) *Academic Word List* (AWL). However, they challenge Coxhead's use of word families, a base word and all its derivations, as the unit of measurement, claiming this causes inaccuracies (e.g. counting 'proceeds' as a verb and as a noun together, despite their unrelated meanings). Instead, they suggest the lemma, a base word and its inflectional relationships only, would be a better unit for vocabulary lists to adopt. They contend that lemmas are a more manageable measure (e.g. the verb forms: 'proceed,' 'proceeds,' 'proceeded,' 'proceeding'), especially for lower level learners. Secondly, Gardner and Davies question the AWL's relationship to earlier general English word lists that are now viewed as outdated for analysis of contemporary English. Coxhead omitted some high frequency academic words (e.g. 'company,' 'rate') on the grounds they were included on older general lists, and thus, by association, the AWL is also out-of-date.

The AWL and Gardner and Davies' new AVL both attempt to identify a core of general academic words, that is, a body of lexis deployable across a range of academic fields. The authors address Hyland and Tse's (2007) argument that an academic core is, in fact, a chimera: words may significantly change in meaning as they cross disciplinary borders. For instance, 'analysis' has different meanings in biology and business. Whilst acknowledging the advances in corpus software necessary to solve this meaning-variation issue, Gardner and Davies maintain that vocabulary lists still represent a worthwhile and principled approach to what would otherwise be lexical learning chaos. Reflecting upon these debates, the authors conclude that any new list of academic vocabulary should utilise lemmas and be constructed upon a large representative and up-to-date corpus-base.

Gardner and Davies proceed to outline the new AVL's design. First, a 120-million-word sub-corpus of written academic English was constructed from the Corpus of Contemporary American English (or COCA), a 425-million word digital collection of modern American English. The authors then used several statistical measures including ratio, range and dispersion to extract a list of general purposes academic vocabulary. The resulting list of vocabulary forms the proposed AVL, which the authors contend is "the most current, accurate, and comprehensive list of core academic vocabulary in existence today" (Gardner & Davies, 2014, p. 325). The most frequent 500 lemmas of the AVL are provided at this point as an indicative sample.

When it comes to applying the AVL in the classroom, Gardner and Davies provide only limited suggestions. They recommend the AVL be used with higher level learners of academic English. The authors describe an online interface for the AVL, *Word and Phrase* (henceforth WP). One feature of the WP site, *Word Sketch*, encourages deeper interaction with items of the AVL https://www.wordandphrase.info/academic/frequencyList.asp These Word Sketches comprise definitions, collocates, example sentences with the key word in context and a bar chart showing frequency of use in various academic fields. The second feature, *Analyze Texts*, allows users to input a text and access a breakdown of frequency information about AVL items and technical academic vocabulary that it contains.

Literature Review

Gardner and Davies' article draws upon a number of strands in the literature. Of most direct relevance are: second language vocabulary teaching and learning, the nature of academic language and the notion of an academic core, pedagogic vocabulary lists and classroom use of corpora.

Vocabulary occupies a central role in learning a second language and has been described as "the most crucial component" (Martinez, 2014, p. 121).

Nevertheless, the vast size of the English lexicon can be daunting to learners (Gardner, 2013). Alongside this reality is the lexical shape of English and the fact that not all words are of equal value. Second language learners of English face diminishing lexical returns as they grapple with written texts. This is illustrated by the fact that the 2000 most commonly occurring words of English provide 80% coverage (i.e. understanding) of academic texts while the subsequent 2000 most frequent items add barely more than 5% coverage (Nation & Waring, 1997).

The nature of academic language has been the focus of much discussion. There is a consensus that the language of academic texts is specialised, with academic language defined as the subset of language utilised in academic settings which "facilitates communication and thinking about disciplinary content" (Nagy & Townsend, 2012, p. 92). More specifically, the vocabulary that English utilises in such texts is characterised by its Latin and Greek origins and its morphological complexity (Nagy & Townsend, 2012). In the field of English for Academic Purposes (henceforth EAP), such vocabulary is often classified as general purposes academic vocabulary, as opposed to technical or discipline-specific lexis (Nation, 2001). The notion of an academic core has driven the development of various lists of academic vocabulary which claim to bring order to vocabulary teaching and learning.

Lists like the AVL and AWL represent an explicit teaching and learning approach whereby vocabulary items are a specific focus for instruction. Such an approach stands in contrast to an incidental learning approach, which foregrounds extensive reading as key to natural acquisition of vocabulary (Nation, 2001). Coxhead's AWL has dominated the lexical landscape of EAP in recent years; yet, in addition to Gardner and Davies' criticisms cited above, the AWL has faced accusations by practitioners that it may promote rote-memorisation of academic vocabulary and be misused and misappropriated by teachers and learners alike (Banister, 2016). In particular, there are concerns that use of the AWL may lead teachers to neglect common academic words on general lists (e.g., cause). In addition, learners may be lulled into a false sense of security by the AWL, believing mastery of it is sufficient for all their needs (Banister, 2016). Gardner and Davies' new AVL claims to have addressed such concerns through its dynamic interface, WP, which encourages active learner engagement and interaction with the lexis in the AVL. WP provides examples of AVL words used in context, drawn from the corpus. Thus, WP users may indirectly use the corpus-based data to explore EAP vocabulary (Gardner, 2013). McEnery and Xiao (2011) note that corpus-based data can be used to empower and motivate learners but also note that even pedagogically designed corpus-based tools will need to be teacher mediated for successful classroom use.

At this point, it is perhaps helpful to explain my own interest in vocabulary teaching and learning, lists of academic lexis, and research into these areas in the context of my professional journey and my current teaching role.

An Introduction to Myself and My Students

I have been an English language teacher for 20 years and currently teach EAP and business English to foundation, undergraduate and postgraduate students in a UK institute of higher education. Although I see myself primarily as a teacher, I have recently become research active and am participating in an Exploratory Practice project exploring my students' peer-teaching of vocabulary. Prior to this, my MA research (Banister, 2016) focused on vocabulary and, in particular, teachers' practices, beliefs and attitudes with reference to the AWL. My day-to-day practice has consistently suggested that vocabulary knowledge is central to language learning and is viewed by learners and teachers alike as a tangible indicator of progress and achievement. Given that the EAP teaching contexts in which I currently operate allow only very limited contact hours with students in a week, I was keen to explore ways that my learners could boost their vocabulary knowledge and tools that they could use to extend learning beyond the classroom. Hence, I was interested in the AVL, its online WP interface, and the underpinning research knowledge. I also felt that my familiarity with TESOL vocabulary research would help me to interpret and incorporate it into my pedagogy.

The participants in this research project were undergraduate exchange students from non-English speaking backgrounds on Business English courses. In practice, these courses are a hybrid, focusing on both business and academic language and skills. The small size of these cohorts (6–12 students) facilitates a personalised and student-centred approach. For the students, the modules fulfil a role similar to in-sessional English for Specific Academic Purposes courses, supporting students' performance in their business modules whilst on their exchange. There are three contact hours per week, consisting of a two-hour slot, usually with teacher-led input and a one-hour seminar-style slot. In these one-hour slots students typically generate the materials by selecting a current business news story to present in class. Recent examples include 'Implications of Brexit for the financial sector in the UK' or 'The impact of cybercrime on UK businesses.' Following in-class discussion of the story, students post written comments to an online forum and practice their written academic skills in the process. Weekly feedback slots focus on students' written contributions, covering spelling and punctuation, grammar, vocabulary and academic style. This discussion board component links to a summative assessment, a written report, which is based on one of the business news topics introduced by students themselves.

How I Incorporated the Article into My Curriculum and Pedagogy

For me, the practical implication of the Gardner and Davies paper was that vocabulary learning and teaching should be informed, at least in part, by the notion of frequency. As a teacher, I saw an opportunity to use the AVL research to raise my students' awareness of the useful notion of frequency in vocabulary learning and to focus them on words that would be of the highest value. However, I wanted to do this in a way that ensured that they did not simply go away and memorise a list of words, but instead interacted with and deepened their knowledge of AVL items, avoiding the pitfalls of rote-memorisation inherent in word lists. This explicit vocabulary learning would complement any incidental acquisition whilst students were on their exchange in the UK. The syllabus' pre-existing vocabulary focus had recently been developed with the introduction of a class bank of vocabulary cards as one strand of explicit learning, but I felt there was scope to go further by exploring some ideas underpinning Gardner and Davies' research article and harnessing their newly designed AVL. I aimed to modify my syllabus by boosting the vocabulary strand of the course further and then encouraging my students to reflect on my curriculum innovations.

For teachers, a major consideration is preparation time. So if researchers, in collaboration with materials designers and practitioners, have created ready-made, tailored resources which embody their research findings and when I can locate these resources, I will be happy to test them out with my students. Therefore, encouraging my students to use the online AVL seemed a logical starting point. The *WP* interface has two features, both of which appeared useful. Firstly, there is the frequency list of academic words, the AVL itself, with the *Word Sketch* feature https://www.wordandphrase.info/academic/frequencyList.asp Secondly, the *Analyze Texts* tool provides detailed information on the lexis of entire texts which are entered https://www.wordandphrase.info/academic/analyzeText.asp. When I come across interesting authentic content, I often look for familiar ways to introduce it into my curriculum. In this case, I looked to my teacher's toolbox, my set of trusted templates and techniques, to aid the practical implementation of the research-based ideas into my syllabus.

Independent Student Use of the Word Sketch Feature

As part of their presentations on current business news stories, my students present five useful vocabulary items to their classmates with definitions and sentences exemplifying the chosen words or phrases. I identified this as an opportunity to bring the research into the classroom by encouraging my students to use *WP* to inform their choice of words to peer-teach and also to obtain data through the *Word Sketch* feature. Essentially, I encouraged students to use the site as a kind of super-dictionary, an interactive reference tool. In week one I showed students the WP interface in class to demonstrate its potential, using the word 'market' as an example (Appendix A). I also embedded a link in the online module space with step-by-step instructions.

Lexical Detectives

I wanted my students to try out the AVL and use the WP interface to focus on vocabulary, in particular gain information about its frequency of use in business and also to extend and deepen their knowledge of known words, aspects such as collocation and connotation. I planned for them to use a text sourced by a peer for one of the business news presentations. As their written assessment could potentially relate to this topic, expanded lexical knowledge would also act as an effective revision activity.

Aware of the complexity of the WP site, I wanted to ensure that students had a chance to navigate the site and be on hand to assist as required. This meant that I needed to ensure my own familiarity with the site was sufficient to guide them effectively. For a busy teacher, getting to grips with new technology or web resources can be daunting and entails a time investment. For *WP*, I explored the site's various features and read the Help section. I quickly realised I would need to design a step-by-step worksheet for my students. They could still work individually, but with the teacher as the guide at the side to keep them on task as they completed *the Lexical Detectives* activity.

I designated each student a peer's source text, all articles from business sections of UK newspapers like *The Guardian* or *The Daily Telegraph*. Students briefly read word document versions (I prepared these to alleviate formatting problems and remove online ads) of these and then copied and pasted the whole text into the *WP* text analysis tool. Linking to the COCA Academic sub-corpus, *WP* highlighted the general purposes academic words and discipline-specific/technical words (e.g. for business, history, education etc.) in the inputted text.

An accompanying worksheet (Appendix B) guided students with step-by-step instructions and screenshots, as suggested in the literature on classroom use of corpora-based tools. Students then chose words in their text that they wanted to explore. Whilst the AVL was designed to highlight both technical and academic core items, I did not want to restrict students' natural curiosity about language they encountered, so the worksheet allowed them to choose a mixture of general, academic and technical lexis.

Discussion Wheel

For this activity, I returned to the research article by Gardner and Davies and highlighted what I viewed as the key ideas about vocabulary learning and teaching that the authors either advocated or referred to. For instance, I was interested in the word family construct discussed on page 308 of the article and the learning of multi-word clauses rather than just single items (touched upon in the conclusion on p. 325.). As these ideas are complex and sometimes expressed in a rather complex way in the article, I first rephrased these and similar notions into eight sentences that students could either agree or disagree with, adding italics to help students focus on the potentially contentious aspect and see what I was getting at. For example, sentence 1 related to p. 305 of the article and was presented as:

> Lack of *specific academic* vocabulary is the *major* barrier when trying to understand academic texts.

I wanted to bring research-informed ideas about vocabulary learning and teaching into our classroom discourse to observe students' reactions and responses to these notions. I hoped to encourage them to reflect upon their own vocabulary learning experiences whilst simultaneously developing oral fluency and discussion skills. I believe that most language learners have developed some awareness of their own learning preferences and might enjoy discussing these. It should be noted that by the time this activity took place, students were familiar with terminology like word family or frequency word list through their vocabulary work on the module. For example, I had introduced the word family concept and we had brainstormed examples such as 'produce,' 'productive,' 'productivity,' etc. We discussed the value of this approach to expanding vocabulary knowledge and this consolidated their understanding of the concept.

The eight sentences were presented to students as a *Discussion Wheel*, a template consisting of a circle with four intersecting lines running through its centre, one vertically, one horizontally and two diagonally, creating eight spokes around the rim of the wheel (Peachy, 2002) (Appendix C). I had successfully used the Discussion Wheel framework in the past many times, so I decided to utilise it again. The eight sentences were written at the eight spoke points around the wheel. For the purposes of the activity, I also presented some ideas in the article in a negative form so that there were more likely to be a variety of agree and disagree responses. For example, sentence 2 stated:

> Teachers of academic English shouldn't spend class time *deliberately* teaching academic vocabulary. Reading academic texts and understanding *from context* is enough.

Students read each sentence, considered their view and placed a cross on the line to indicate their stance with an 'x' near to the sentence and edge of the circle indicating proximity and agreement and an 'x' away from the sentence or nearer to the centre of the circle indicating disagreement, with any intermediate position also possible. A Useful Phrases worksheet where students matched discussion expressions (e.g. 'I couldn't agree more' or 'I'm on the fence with this one') with their functions ('Expressing total agreement' and 'Taking a non-committal stance' respectively) accompanied the Discussion Wheel.

Importantly, the three activities described above varied in terms of their delivery and interaction patterns. This promoted learner engagement by catering to a range of learning preferences. Table 5.1 summarises these aspects.

Analysis and Evaluation

I judged the success (or otherwise) of my incorporation of research into pedagogy in the same way as I would any curriculum innovation. Inevitably, practicalities such as whether the WP site and the materials I had designed would prove fit-for-purpose were considered. However, moving beyond this, I considered the following:

1. To what extent did the research-informed syllabus engage my students?
2. What opportunity for language skill development (speaking or writing) or awareness about language learning did the research content promote?

TABLE 5.1   The research informed syllabus: Summary of working mode and interaction patterns

	Word sketch	**Lexical detectives**	**Discussion wheel**
Learning environment/mode	Out of class/ Independent	Language lab with T	Classroom
Interaction	Individual	Individual note taking. Then oral class discussion	Pair/group work, oral discussion, writing follow-up

3.   Did the research-informed syllabus add anything meaningful to my own
      and my students' knowledge about vocabulary learning and related
      strategies?

4.   Did I gain new insights from hearing my students' perspectives on
      research related to vocabulary learning?

I observed my students' reactions and listened to their responses in class.
I also analysed their written responses and worksheets for evidence of
engagement with the key ideas. I am aware that students may not feel comfortable expressing frank views to their teacher about the learning experience, but I believe that the small class size allowed an atmosphere of mutual
trust to develop and mitigate potential issues in this area. In addition to student responses, I kept a reflective journal, which allowed me to construct a
picture of what worked and what did not. Rather than go through each activity one at a time in isolated fashion, the following discussion will draw out
some common themes. This approach reflects the nature of the activities,
which involved recycling and revisiting notions about vocabulary teaching
and learning.

What Worked?

Overall, a small cohort of 6 advanced level students agreed to participate in
this research. This facilitated classroom observation of the new syllabus and
the harnessing of my privileged insider perspective on the classroom.

Working with the Online AVL/WP

The first thing to note is that all six students came to class. They knew in
advance that we would be using the AVL to investigate lexis. This should not be
overlooked as non-attendance is a student's ultimate sanction to demonstrate
a lack of interest. As I monitored and observed them at work, it was evident
that students had completed the preparatory activity for homework, engaging
with WP in the process. They seemed to recognise the value in revisiting the
vocabulary of peers' texts, linked as it was to their end of module assessment.
I noticed my students responding positively as the lexical data revealed itself
with each click.

   From students' completed Lexical Detectives worksheets, I could see
which vocabulary they had investigated. I used the WP site myself to check
whether their selected lexis was categorised as general purposes/academic
core, technical/discipline-specific or general English. The six students selected
three words each, totalling 18 items which were explored (see Table 5.2).

TABLE 5.2   Summary of lexical items investigated during lexical detectives activity

Total words	Academic	Technical	General
N=18	n=6	n=10	n=2

Of the technical words, the majority occurred most frequently in business ('mortgage,' 'earnings,' 'customer') and law ('fraud,' 'sue,' 'crackdown'). In this instance the activity had facilitated exploration of relevant items. Reassuringly, the Word Sketch information provided was accurate. I had been concerned about potential errors as students will swiftly deride inaccurate resources. The fact that students chose words like 'customer' indicated that some of them saw value in deepening knowledge of 'known' words by exploring collocations and synonyms. This deeper interaction with lexis was something I had hoped to promote. The completed worksheets were uploaded to a shared online class space. Upon subsequent reflection, I concluded that the research informed activity had engaged my students, facilitated a review and extension of their vocabulary knowledge and resulted in the production of helpful revision resources.

Vocabulary Research: An Engaging Topic

For classroom discussions, topic engagement is a crucial factor. As a teacher, I gauged interest through the length and depth of discussion provoked, through students extending ideas and drawing upon their experiential knowledge. The amount of language practice and oral fluency development was also important. For the discussion wheel activity, students talked for fifteen minutes, which was in line with my predictions and the time available. As expected, some research-based ideas resonated more with students than others. Student discussion lingered over two sentences in particular, which encouraged personal insights and around which I observed deeper engagement. For instance, sentence 3: 'A scientific, *frequency*-based, list of business English vocabulary could be helpful for learners.' Here, students broadly agreed that a frequency-based business vocabulary list would be useful as a starting point "to make sure the basics are known." Through the discussion wheel activity, it became apparent that my students had started to digest the idea that it could be advantageous to give a little more thought to prioritising some words over others. Similarly, with sentence 4: 'It is usually easy to understand the meaning or meanings of academic vocabulary in different disciplines (e.g. 'analysis' in business vs 'analysis' in biology).' When discussing this sentence, one student identified with the concept of meaning-variation, noting with surprise how scientific vocabulary she had learnt had turned out to have another meaning: "sometimes you misunderstood completely." Of course, students were aware of multiple meanings carried by some words, but here was more evidence that awareness had been raised further.

Upon further reflection, I realised that when engaging and taking a position in relation to these research-based notions about vocabulary teaching and learning, my students had been deploying their critical thinking skills. Alongside this they had been developing their spoken fluency skill in English. Moreover, as they discussed the research-based concepts, I glimpsed the learning experience through the student's lens. Students commented positively on some of the vocabulary learning strategies I had encouraged such as using vocabulary cards and focusing on collocations. Thus, students were simultaneously providing feedback on aspects of their vocabulary learning. I believe that content which encourages critical thinking, self-reflection and provides feedback to the teacher offers multiple benefits: the learners are developing valuable transferable skills whilst the teacher is gaining insights into the teaching and learning preferences of their students and into the way that their teaching is received.

What Did Not Work?

The Complexity of Research-Based Knowledge

Looking at my students' business news presentation materials, I could see that only two students had used WP to source definitions and example sentences whilst others had preferred familiar alternatives. As teachers, we know there are numerous reasons why students may not take up options for independent learning. They may become comfortable with favourite tools and resources, fail to recognise the value in the tasks or lack the time or motivation to complete the work. When I asked, students cited the translation feature their preferred alternatives offered, which WP lacked. Another stated, "realistically, students are more inclined to use easier tools such as Google." I recognise students may have ingrained learning habits, in this case a desire for L1 translations. I make what I believe are useful recommendations for independent learning, but at the same time expect and accept student resistance.

Interpreting the Word Sketch data occasionally proved problematic. It is well-known that corpus-based materials may show but fail to explain, and this means that a relatively high level of student curiosity is required. For example, during Lexical detectives, a student chose the word 'crackdown,' explored the synonym 'suppression,' but struggled to understand in what way(s) it was different. He was at an impasse. I encouraged the student to explore the frequency bars by discipline and the collocates for the two items, which unpacked some clearer differences.

During the discussion wheel activity, students passed over the sentence about the transparency of meaning within word families. I suspect students did not fully grasp the idea or perhaps felt unable to challenge the research, and I could empathise with them in this. Looking back on my reflective journal entries about this, I realised that I had felt the same myself when first confronted with complex linguistic concepts such as lemmas and word families. I can recall feeling intimidated and lacking the confidence to challenge research findings (Banister, 2016). In the face of counter-intuitive research-based evidence produced by academics, I had initially felt very much like an overawed apprentice. Even my extensive experiential knowledge was not sufficient to overcome this until I had engaged in more depth with the literature and had time to consider more carefully the points which might apply and which might be less relevant to praxis.

Negative Student Attitudes towards the Online AVL/WP
Our class discussion following the discussion wheel activity unpacked some insightful student reflections. They broadly agreed that they found the WP site and the Lexical Detectives useful, but one student then revealed "I was against this at first." When probed, it transpired that she suspected that computer-based lessons were an easy option for teachers (perhaps if she had known the amount of time I spent developing the materials for the lesson and familiarising myself with the site she would have rethought). This highlights how something as basic as the learning mode and physical environment can influence students' attitudes as they approach tasks. As it was, she gradually recognised the activity's value as she interacted with her chosen vocabulary.

However, other doubts about the WP interface were apparent in learners' written comments: "It does help ... but ... [t]he layout of the page could be easier on the eyes." From a teachers' perspective, the busy online interface appeared to hinder fully autonomous student use. Researchers deserve praise for attempting to develop tools like WP. There is a clear recognition that learners must interact with the vocabulary, not see it as a disembodied list of lexis. However, researchers must ensure the design of these tools meets the design expectations of digital natives.

Challenges for Teachers
When working with relatively complex research-based online tools like WP, there is a danger that busy teachers with limited time may overlook important

features. There is no teacher's book guide in the design of the research informed syllabus. For example, after the Lexical Detectives activity, I stumbled upon a way that it could be used to obtain a frequency list of business words. Interestingly, this feature was not apparent in any online tutorials or help sections of WP. This left me ruing a missed opportunity (although I hope to use the list in the future). It also prompted me to question whether researchers are always well-placed to highlight aspects of their research most likely to prove valuable to practitioners.

Recommendations for Fellow Teachers Interested in Research Utilization

My own experience of this process prompts me to recommend that teachers choose an area of interest to them as this will clearly help to sustain the effort to incorporate the research ideas into the syllabus and the inevitable additional workload this will entail. However, it is also important to consider how easy or difficult it will be for your learners to engage. My students, like me, found vocabulary a tangible area of language learning prime for discussion. So, my advice would be to choose wisely.

It is also important to consider how you intend to evaluate your research informed curriculum. I attempted to incorporate Gardner and Davies' vocabulary research in a way that provided me with a perspective from my learners and would also suggest this approach to others; build a learner feedback route alongside any syllabus innovation based around research knowledge. It is also important to build the research informed syllabus in a way that features multiple encounters with the concepts and allows reflection and time for the ideas, often complex, to be internalised into classroom discourse. Based on my experience of this project, research-based knowledge suitably presented and packaged has potential to engage learners and illuminate classroom life. Teachers should, of course, exercise their own critical judgement when embedding it in their pedagogy, yet English language practitioners should feel confident handling research findings about language learning, especially if they are able to draw upon familiar teaching frameworks and techniques which then leave them free to focus more on the complexity of the concepts involved. Furthermore, as my experience with regard to my students' critical thinking revealed, bringing TESOL research into the classroom may present additional unexpected benefits which teachers should be alert to and ready to harness.

Appendix A: Word Sketch for 'Market'

Appendix B: Worksheet for Lexical Detectives Activity

Web activity: Lexical Detectives

I see no more than you, but I have trained myself to notice what I see. (Sherlock Holmes, *The Adventure of the Blanched Soldier*, in Searle, 2015)

Aims: This short activity we are going to do today is called Lexical Detectives. It seems an appropriate title given our proximity to 221B Baker Street, the home of the fictional detective Sherlock Holmes, and the way that you will be investigating and making deductions (like a detective) to deepen your knowledge of vocabulary (lexis). Another key aim is to review your knowledge of a business-related topic which may be the topic of your written assignment in week 12.

A: Reading the Source Text (*10 mins approx.*)

1. Go to our module space and open the 'Discussion Board' tab.
2. Find your classmate(s)' PowerPoint presentation and briefly read the slides and some of the posts in the thread to remind yourself of some of the main points, details and the issues.
3. Open the Word document at the end of the thread. This is a simplified version of one of the original presenter's source texts.

4. Briefly read the text and familiarise yourself with its main points (no dictionaries at this stage).

B: Word and Phrase Text Analysis (25 mins approx.)

1. Highlight the whole source text in the Word doc (excluding the yellow highlighted sections).

2. Open a new window and go to http://www.wordandphrase.info/academic/analyzeText.asp

3. Copy and paste the source text (excluding the yellow highlighted parts) into the Text Analysis feature of the Word and Phrase tool (the box in the top left corner of the screen).

4. Ensure 'Word' is selected (as above) and click 'Search.' The text will appear in the top right of your screen and look something like this screenshot below.

5. Click 'Help' (top right of the results box as in screenshot below).

6.   A drop down box will appear. Read through the points 1–6 carefully. (NOTE: COCA = the Corpus of Contemporary American English, a 120 million word database of academic English.)

7.   Follow step 5 in the help box and select 'business' as the discipline.

8.   Choose 3 words to investigate and deepen your knowledge of.
      NOTE: These do not necessarily need to be words that you do not know the meaning of-the aim here is to deepen knowledge. Choose a mix of business, academic and more general English words.

9.   Click on the word and you will see information about meaning, collocations, synonyms and use in different academic areas of study (the bar chart). You can click on most words and the graphics to deepen knowledge. As you click on the collocations, notice how they are used with word you are investigating. Record your findings in the table on the next page (NOTE: the table should expand as you type into it.)

Table for recording information about the words you select

Word	Definition (suitable for the context in the source text)	3 synonyms- remember synonyms are *similar* but never *exactly the same*	3 collocations (word partnerships)	Frequent in ... (top 3 academic disciplines)
e.g. entrepreneur	s/o who organises a business venture and assumes the risk for it	Financier Tycoon Magnate	local (adj) opportunities for (n) seek (v)	Business Law History

C: Upload

Finally, please *save a copy* of this completed worksheet for your own records and also *upload it* to our Blackboard space at the end of the relevant Discussion Board thread.

Appendix C: Discussion Wheel Activity

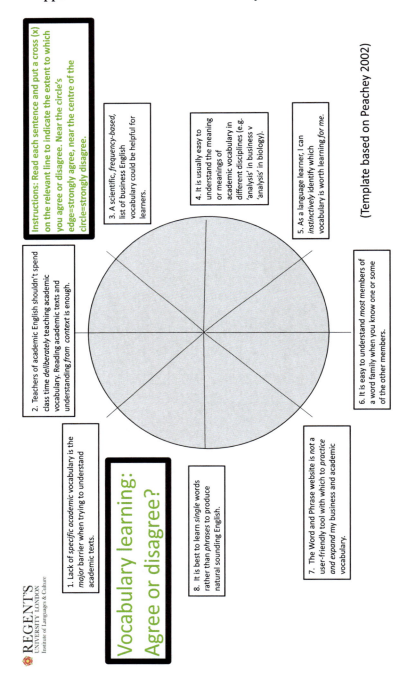

Instructions: Read each sentence and put a cross (x) on the relevant line to indicate the extent to which you agree or disagree. Near the circle's edge=strongly agree, near the centre of the circle=strongly disagree.

3. A scientific, *frequency-based*, list of business English vocabulary could be helpful for learners.

4. It is usually easy to understand the meaning or meanings of academic vocabulary in different disciplines (e.g. 'analysis' in business v 'analysis' in biology).

5. As a language learner, I can *instinctively* identify which vocabulary is worth learning *for me*.

2. Teachers of academic English shouldn't spend class time *deliberately* teaching academic vocabulary. Reading academic texts and understanding *from context* is enough.

6. It is easy to understand *most* members of a word family when you know one or some of the other members.

1. Lack of *specific academic* vocabulary is the *major* barrier when trying to understand academic texts.

8. It is best to learn *single* words rather than *phrases* to produce natural sounding English.

7. The Word and Phrase website is *not a* user-friendly tool with which to *practice and expand* my business and academic vocabulary.

Vocabulary learning: Agree or disagree?

(Template based on Peachey 2002)

REGENT'S
UNIVERSITY LONDON
Institute of Languages & Culture

References

Banister, C. (2016). The academic word list: Exploring teacher practices, attitudes and beliefs through a web-based survey and interviews. *Journal of Teaching English for Specific and Academic Purposes, 4*(2), 309–325. doi:11.111243+004.738.4:159.953

Coxhead, A. (2000). A new academic word list. *TESOL Quarterly, 34*(2), 213–238.

Gardner, D. (2013). *Exploring vocabulary.* Abingdon: Routledge.

Gardner, D., & Davies, M. (2014). A new academic vocabulary list. *Applied Linguistics, 35*(3), 305–327.

Gilbert, J. (2013). English for academic purposes. In G. Motteram (Ed.), *Innovations in learning technologies for English language teaching* (pp. 117–144). London: British Council.

Hyland, K., & Tse, P. (2007). Is there an "academic vocabulary"? *TESOL Quarterly, 41*(2), 235–253.

Martinez, R. (2014). Vocabulary and formulaic language. In P. Driscoll, E. Macaro, & A. Swarbrick (Eds.), *Debates in modern languages education* (pp. 121–134). Abingdon: Routledge.

McEnery, T., & Xiao, R. (2011). What corpora can offer in language teaching and learning. In E. Hinkel (Ed.), *Handbook of research in second language teaching and learning* (Vol. 2, pp. 364–380). Abingdon: Routledge.

Nagy, W., & Townsend, D. (2012). Words as tools: Learning academic vocabulary as language acquisition. *Reading Research Quarterly, 47*(1), 91–108.

Nation, I. S. P. (2001). *Learning vocabulary in another language.* Cambridge: Cambridge University Press.

Nation, I. S. P., & Waring, R. (1997). Vocabulary size, text coverage and word lists. In N. Schmitt & M. McCarthy (Eds.), *Vocabulary: Description, acquisition and pedagogy* (pp. 6–19). Cambridge: Cambridge University Press.

Peachy, N. (2002). Discussion wheels. *British Council Teaching English.* Retrieved May 28, 2017, from https://www.teachingenglish.org.uk/article/discussion-wheels

Searle, K. K. (2015). *Sherlock Holmes quotes* [online]. Retrieved March 17, 2017, from http://sherlockholmesquotes.com/sherlock-holmes-on-problem-solving/

Wikimedia. (n.d.). *Sherlock Holmes* [online image]. Retrieved February 9, 2017, from https://upload.wikimedia.org/wikipedia/commons/1/14/The_Sherlock_Holmes_Museum%2C_Baker_Street%2C_London_-_DSCF0462.JPG

Operationalizing "Defining" from a Cognitive Discourse Perspective for Learners' Use

Nashwa Nashaat Sobhy
Universidad San Jorge, Spain

Dalton-Puffer's (2016) construct of cognitive discourse function (CDF) invites TESOL and CLIL (Content and Language Integrated Learning) educators to make "the process of thought available for learning" and to enable students to verbalize these thoughts. The construct includes seven interdisciplinary academic functions with different macro-realizers and internal structures, which are classifying, defining, describing, evaluating, explaining, exploring and reporting. The point of departure for this chapter was the operationalization of "defining" as a CDF for learner use (Dalton-Puffer, 2016, pp. 29–54). This operationalization took the form of a template that was extended to a group of tertiary students in an English Medium Instruction program that adopts CLIL principles. The definition template, illustrating the possible macro-moves when defining, was incorporated in different activities in a core non-language subject in the degree of education between February and May 2016. Students' perceptions about the template and the activities were surveyed anonymously, which together with the students' actual use of the template and their written definitions were used to determine the usefulness of the initiative.

Summary of the Selected Research

The pedagogical activities reported here are based on Dalton-Puffer's (2016) construct of cognitive discourse functions (CDFs), also referred to as *academic language functions*. The aim from the activities is to contribute to the operationalization of "defining"—one of seven CDFs—for students' use and to explore its role in connecting *content* and *language* learning in a bilingual educational setting. This initiative was motivated by the calls in the European Union (EU) by the Council of Europe (2014) and in North America (cf. Bailey, 2007) to outline students' academic language proficiency in better measures than the existing ones. A quick search for what *academic language proficiency* entails typically leads to literature explaining the difference between Cummin's

(1979, 2004, 2008) concept of Basic Interpersonal Communicative Skills (BICS) and Cognitive Academic Language Proficiency (CALP), and to references concerning knowledge of discipline-specific terminology and rhetorical conventions. Teachers drawing on these resources when planning for teaching and assessing curricular goals wade through over fifty cognitive actions (Anderson & Krathwohl et al., 2001; Bloom, 1956) which students are required to perform verbally across subjects to demonstrate their knowledge of content. This can be particularly difficult for teachers and students who share the status of users of an additional or a foreign language (henceforth, L2), where teachers of non-language subjects may not be in a position to deal effectively with language-related matters.

However, if the linguistic realizations of interdisciplinary cognitive actions—i.e., CDFs—are operationalized and accessible, the gap between content and language teaching and learning could be narrowed (Dalton-Puffer, 2016, p. 30). Because of the potential CDFs have to provide its users with verbalizations of seven cognitive processes as opposed to fifty-four cognitive actions and because the construct approaches academic language proficiency from an integrated content and language perspective, it is the research-based knowledge on which the pedagogical activities in this chapter are based. The following section expands further on the construct of CDFs and its importance in the context of teaching and learning content through an L2. Dalton-Puffer (2016) being the foundation for the work at hand will be referred to in the remainder of this chapter as 'Dalton-Puffer' without further specifications except where stated differently.

The CDF Construct and its Grounding in Content and Language Education

As previously mentioned, CDFs are verbal routines reflecting cognitive processes that teachers and learners need to use in order to convey abstract knowledge. These were grouped under seven main communicative prototypes or categories, namely: *classify*; *define*; *describe, evaluate*; *explain*; *explore* and *report*. Table 6.1 shows the seven categories and the cognitive discourse function verbs subsumed under each.

The left column represents the seven prototypical categories that group the range of verbs underlying a particular category as per Dalton-Puffer. The range of member verbs belonging to each category is spelled out in the right column. It needs to be noted the CDF labels are normal English lexemes whose meanings are activated differently in different contexts (Dalton-Puffer, 2013).

TABLE 6.1   CDF types and their member verbs

Labels of CDF types	Member verbs of the CDF types
CLASSIFY	Classify, compare, contrast, match, structure, categorize, subsume
DEFINE	Define, identify, characterize
DESCRIBE	Describe, label, identify, name, specify
EVALUATE	Evaluate, judge, argue, justify, take a stance, critique, recommend, comment, reflect, appreciate
EXPLAIN	Explain, reason, express cause/effect, draw conclusions, deduce
EXPLORE	Explore, hypothesize, speculate, predict, guess, estimate, simulate, take other perspectives
REPORT	Report, inform, recount, narrate, present, summarize, relate

For example, "define" is *a label* for one of the types of the cognitive discourse functions—*not* a terminology—and is also *one of the actions* (a verb) through which its corresponding CDF is carried out.

Despite the apparent familiarity of CDFs to us as regular features in academic curricula, the linguistic enactments of these processes are not intuitive, and are more challenging in the case of learners and teachers operating in L2 contexts, where content teachers have often voiced that they have limitations concerning language matters. Dalton-Puffer's explorations into CDFs draw on CLIL lesson transcripts from the corpus of the ConCLIL project (Conceptual Framework for Content and Language Integrated Learning), which includes a total of 41 lesson transcripts covering teacher and student exchanges in the subjects of history, geography, science, accounting, business studies, and tourism from Spain, Austria and Finland (cf. Nikula et al., 2016). Her main objective was to identify examples from naturalistic oral classroom discourse that demonstrate the manner and the frequency in which these CDFs are enacted.

Though Dalton-Puffer refers in her work to the context of content and language integrated learning (CLIL) developed in the European Union, it is important to digress and clarify two points. First, CLIL is similar—if not synonymous—to Content-Based Instruction (CBI) in the USA and Canadian French Immersion. Second, both CLIL and CBI have multiple models that can range from being more oriented towards foreign or additional language learning or to content-subject learning through an L2 (Cenoz, 2015; Tedick & Cammarata, 2012).

That is to say, the content of Dalton-Puffer's proposal is equally valid for any educational context where the students learn through a language other than their mother tongue. The proposal put forward by Dalton-Puffer is that cognitive processes across subjects are communicated through language discourse functions, needed by content and language teachers alike. By making the linguistic realizations of these processes visible, the breach between expressing content and language can be bridged and teachers can use them as schemata or scaffolds to help students identify and produce discourse functions necessary for academic progress. CDFs are also seen as a meeting point for language and content teachers to plan teaching and assessment in the bilingual contexts of CLIL, CBI, Immersion or other similar programs.

Dalton-Puffer's (2013, 2016) explorations into CDFs showed that teachers tend to refer to CDFs implicitly; teachers and students use a limited range of linguistic resources to express CDFs; and students have limited opportunities to use them during lessons. As mentioned in the introduction, this chapter focuses on the CDF of "defining" only, which is a vast topic on its own. The following section is a brief review on the importance of definitions and defining for academic literacy, its types, and the constituents or the realizers of each type.

"Defining" as a CDF

A definition is a speech act that expresses the relationship between a term and its exponents (Swales, 1981). "Defining" is a core academic function across disciplines (Beacco, 2010; Vollmer, 2010) and is central to academic writing (Trimble, 1985). Not only is it a function that aids and maintains comprehension in any given situation (Flowerdew, 1992), but it is also beneficial as a language learning skill as it engages students in learning and producing syntactically constrained grammatical features that are representative of academic language. Students analyze their own knowledge and exert control over form(s) when producing information about a target term whether to show knowledge or share information with others; therefore, "defining" can be used to develop students' vocabulary and grammar (Snow et al., 1991). It is important not to generalize the latter statement since definitions come in different shapes and sizes; they can occupy whole pages in specialized text (Trimble, 1985, p. 75), but can also be easily simplified in a word or a short phrase (Dalton-Puffer, 2013).

Syntactically, definitions are classified into three types: formal, semi-formal and non-formal, where formality refers to the structural preciseness of the definition, i.e., a precise definition is considered formal even if the employed register is informal. As shown in Table 6.2, the internal structure of the formal

TABLE 6.2   The linguistic realization of "defining" as found in the ConCLILCorpus, reported in Dalton-Puffer (2016)

Type	Definiendum Term (T)	Definiens Class (C)	Differentia Differences (D)
Formal (Teacher's)	A high involvement decision	is a decision	where a lot of money or a lot of time is necessary to just say yes or no.
Semi-formal (Student's)	A high involvement decision	_____	is for example if you buy a car you will look for a lot of different offers and you won't buy the very first one.

definition is more precise: it depends on (1) identifying the term being defined (the *definiendum*), (2) identifying the class to which the term belongs (the *definiens*), and (3) characterizing the term through descriptions or specifying features that make it distinguishable (*differentia*). These characterizing differences (differentia) can be descriptive, comparative, functional, historical, or any combination of these.

Though the class or definien in the teacher's example is a mere repetition of a category already mentioned in the term or definiendum that does not add to the semantic preciseness of the definition, its explicit use completes the three constituents needed to render the definition as formal.

Dalton-Puffer points to students' enactments of defining as novice when compared to their teachers' enactments, which are more expert-like. Also, she mentions that 'interactive' definitions are more frequent in oral classroom exchanges, where teacher and students or students and students co-construct a definition in turns. Her classification of definition types is originally based on Trimble (1985, pp. 75–84); however, she limits the discussion to types seen in ConCLIL oral exchanges. Trimble's (1985) classification, on the other hand, is based on the analysis of written definitions in science and technology in English with the purpose of demonstrating the linguistic patterns that can be used for teaching definitions to users of English as an L2. As shown in Table 6.3, there are further features attached to the differences characterizing the defined terms, which Dalton-Puffer mentions briefly but does not exemplify. These differences can contain physical descriptions, information on use or purpose, one-word synonyms or antonyms or a combination of both (p. 80).

TABLE 6.3   The linguistic realization of "defining" according to Trimble (1985)

Type	Definiendum Term (T)	Definiens Class (C)	Differentia Differences (D)	Examples of types of differentia
Formal	A spider	is an eight-legged predatory arachnid	with an un-segmented body that injects poison into its prey.	Physical
Semi-formal	An anemometer	_____	is used to measure the speed of the wind	Functional (purpose)
Non-formal	Foreign	_____	is the opposite of 'indigenous'	Synonym or Antonym

Trimble (1985) illustrates two further points, summarised in Table 6.4. First, initial definitions are often expanded in EST by adding further characterizations *after* the differentia. He specifies three types of expansion, by: description, classification and exemplification (pp. 83–84), which we shall refer to here as type A expansions. Second, there are another three types of expansions that make definitions 'special' as per Trimble (1985, p. 81), namely: stipulation, operation and explication, which we shall refer to here as type B expansions. Trimble does not explain the reason why he differentiates between both types. It is my personal understanding that type B leads to writing more complex definitions and is thus found in those developed across several idea units and paragraphs.

Defining may be a "fairly compact affair, which makes them easier to capture than other more loosely structured CDFs" (Dalton-Puffer, 2016, p. 36), but Trimble's (1985) more exhaustive differentiations of this particular academic function shows the intricacies and language difficulties it involves (Table 6.4). It would not be surprising if inexpert learners studying disciplinary content through an additional language were overwhelmed by definitions and defining given the combination of new language and new content (Cummins, 1984). Repeated modeling by the teacher of corresponding rhetoric structures and intensive reading may lead some students to pick up the internal structures of "defining," yet there is no guarantee that this would be the case. In fact, implicit modeling and incidental learning in the case of CLIL learners does not seem to be a promising method for a number of factors. Teachers, often non-natives of 'the language through which content is taught,' do not inject classroom discourse with different registers given that they often use informal

TABLE 6.4   Types of definition expansions according to Trimble (1985)

Type A expansions	Purpose	Example
by Description by Classification by Exemplification	To add further information to the core of the initial defined term.	The average physical product is a [initial functional definition]. *For example, if two variable inputs are required ...,* the average physical product is two units of ...' (Expansion by exemplification).
Type B expansions		
Stipulation	To delimit the meaning being defined to a specific discipline or context.	A spider in *Information Technology* is a program that visits Web sites and reads ... (adapted from Dalton-Puffer, 2016, p. 36)
Operation	To tell the reader what to do to experience what is being defined.	The sound /f/ is a voiceless, labiodental fricative, *formed by placing the lower lip lightly against the upper teeth, closing ...*
Explication	To give information about other terms in the definition, presumably new to the reader.	Agronomy is a science which seeks improved methods of spoil management and crop production. *By crop production we mean new techniques that will increase the yield of field crops ...*

phrasal constructions. Also, they do not announce the cognitive action they are enacting as mentioned earlier, which decreases noticing on part of the student (Schmidt, 1990). Language acquisition requires that noticing be followed by output (Ellis, 1997) as well, which may be scanty, depending on the used materials and the learning opportunities teachers create. This leads to seeing more benefit in making the constituents of defining visible for the students so they may identify definitions practice their different structures with the aim of enabling them to express their understanding of subject-specific terms.

Background

Context: Course, Students and Teacher–Researcher

As previously mentioned, Dalton-Puffer's (2013) CDFs aim to bridge the gap between content and language pedagogy by linking subject specific cognitive goals to their linguistic representation. The course benefitting from this experiment was a CLIL-oriented course in the subject of Theory and History of Education. This subject is taught through English in the first year of the degree program of Early Childhood and Primary Education at a Spanish university. In other words, it is a CLIL course in tertiary education where the students' first language is Spanish (L1) and English is a foreign language (L2). The course is a short three ECTS obligatory subject (European Credit Transfer System) of 75 hours in the Winter Semester (February through June), divided between thirty-four hours of class activities and forty-one hours of autonomous work and study. The assigned readings in this course contain subject-specific terms and definitions that students need in order to discuss education and learning as concepts and processes, and to relate teaching practices to studied theories. Students come across technical terms like *context-(in)dependent learning* and *ecological systems* when discussing forms of education and educational institutions or *reinforcement, (dis)equilibrium,* and *modeling* when reading about learning and teaching practices. It was generally observed that though students could associate key terms to concrete examples and select responses related to the terms correctly when given multiple choice questions, they struggled when asked to define them (a transversal learning outcome). This reinforced the decision to incorporate "defining" in the tasks of this subject.

The participants were twenty-seven first year education students with a heterogeneous level of English, ranging from B1—constituting the majority—through C1 on the CEFR proficiency scale (Common European Framework of Reference). Students attending this course had further exposure to English through another CLIL subject in the first semester (150 hours) and another annual course in "English for teaching" (225 hours) in which students center on English medium instruction skills for early and primary education as stipulated by the National Agency of Quality Evaluation and Accreditation in Spain (e.g., classroom management language and planning activities through English for young learners).

Equipped with a background in linguistics applied to teaching English as a Foreign Language (a Master of Arts in TEFL and a Master in Applied Linguistics) and in integrating content and language in non-language subjects (a Doctoral degree in Philosophy and Linguistics with focus on CLIL programs), my aim was to transform "defining" from its research-oriented form in Dalton-Puffer to teaching materials and learning opportunities for classroom practice. Subjects

I have taught that are relevant to the focus of this chapter include teaching English for academic and specific purposes (ESAP) at tertiary level in different settings, and integrating content and language across disciplines in postgraduate studies and in-service teacher training courses. It was, therefore, natural to be drawn to exploring one of the means Dalton-Puffer suggested had the potential to strengthen CLIL teaching and learning.

Incorporating Dalton-Puffer's Construct of Defining in the Course

Highlighting "Defining" in the Course Outline

To encourage teaching initiatives in the context reported here, an additional in-class one-hour session was introduced into the syllabus so that lecturers could work with the students on any necessary additional skills. Previous experience with this type of sessions showed that students did not feel the obligation to attend when the sessions did not appear in the course outlines. Accordingly, "defining" was planned as an academic skills session in the course outline (Figure 6.1).

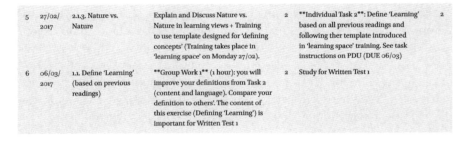

| 5 | 27/02/ 2017 | 2.1.3. Nature vs. Nature | Explain and Discuss Nature vs. Nature in learning views + Training to use template designed for 'defining concepts' (Training takes place in 'learning space' on Monday 27/02). | 2 | **Individual Task 2**: Define 'Learning' based on all previous readings and following ther template introduced in 'learning space' training. See task instructions on PDU (DUE 06/03) | 2 |
| 6 | 06/03/ 2017 | 1.1. Define 'Learning' (based on previous readings) | **Group Work 1** (1 hour): you will improve your definitions from Task 2 (content and language). Compare your definition to others'. The content of this exercise (Defining 'Learning') is important for Written Test 1 | 2 | Study for Written Test 1 | |

FIGURE 6.1   Snapshot of the course outline showing the learning space session in week 5 to teach students how to "define" and extending on it through an evaluated task in week 5

Planning for the Explicit Teaching of "Defining"

Naturally, different reading texts were needed to train students to first help students identify definition constituents with the aim of raising their awareness of the internal structure of definitions. A definition schema-template was used for this purpose. Second, to prompt students to write definitions informed by the previously mentioned definition schema. From a CLIL teaching perspective, it was thought best if students moved progressively through phases that in which content, cognition and language demands were balanced according to Cummins' (1984) quadrant model.

Figure 6.2 shows how reading–defining tasks were planned to proceed from quadrant 2 to quadrant 3; moving from writing formal definitions based on

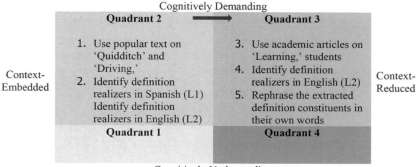

FIGURE 6.2   Activities progression mapped according to Cummins' (1984) quadrants for adjusting language, content and cognition demands

context-embedded texts in which the students are able to draw on their background knowledge to abstract context-reduced texts.

The criteria used for selecting reading texts were: (1) their applicability for the task of defining with its different levels of precision, similar to those found in the genre of humanities (including: class words; physical, functional and historical differentia, or any combination of these; and expansions by exemplification); (2) the degree of topic familiarity to the students; and (3) having short to moderate lengths (100 to 200 words). Throughout the activities, students had access to a template that explained the different parts of definition, which that the lecturer had explained before starting the activities (Figure 6.3).

The first two activities were matching exercises in which students associated parts of text adapted from Wikipedia to their definition constituents. Activity 1 (Figure 6.4) was based on a Spanish text on the fictitious game of Quidditch. Students' first language (L1) was used in this activity to allow students to direct all their attention to dealing with identifying the definition realizers in the text. In Activity 2 (Figure 6.5), students practiced the same process followed in Activity 1, only this time they used an English text, the topic for which was "Driving."

Activity 3 (Figure 6.6), on the other hand, was based on extracts from two subject-specific texts included in students' list of obligatory readings (Schunk, 2012; Young, 2015). In this phase, students moved from identifying definition realizers in popular context-embedded text to define Quidditch and Driving to extrapolating the skills they practiced in the former two texts to a more abstract context-reduced text to define "Learning." Finally, for Activity 4 (Figure 6.7), the students were asked to rephrase the parts of the definitions extracted and tabulated in Activity 3 and were given language support files in the form of sentence starters to help them vary their language.

With regards to this last activity, Activity 4, students were encouraged to test their ability to define subject-relevant terms and concepts (e.g., *learning,*

Column A has the **parts that make up a definition** and **Column B** has explanations of these parts in the form of **questions you can ask to identify the parts make up a definition** in the text the lecturer will give you.

Use the template below to identify the different parts that make up the definitions in activities 1 to 3. This list is extensive: you need not find all these parts in one definition.

A. Parts that make up a definition	B. Explanation of the different parts and ways to identify them
☐ <u>Class</u> of the defined term	• Which 'Class=Category' does the term belong to? (*a process, an object, a method, a person, other*)
☐ <u>Description</u> that distinguishes one term from the other	
▪ Physical	• What visible features distinguish the term? (*components, features by which it is identified, where it is found, when does it occur*)
▪ Functional	• What function does the term have? (*importance of 'x' to us, 'x' is responsible for, other*)
▪ Operational/procedural	• What do you need to do to experience what is being defined? (*Sequence or steps*).
▪ Historical Information	• What historical information distinguishes the defined term? (*origin, other*)
☐ <u>Expansions</u> or additions to the initial definitions	
▪ By Examples	• Are there any examples or different types or names for the term being defined?
▪ By Explanations	• Are there terms within the initial definition that are defined (*a definition within a definition*)? • Are there reasons, effect/cause-effect, and conclusions strongly related to what is being defined?

FIGURE 6.3   A template devised by the lecturer that explains the different parts a definition may have for CLIL students' use

scaffolding, behaviorism, constructivism, ...) in class and in formative out-of-class practice, and it was clarified that their ability to formulate definitions would be essential when tackling an essay question in the final exam. To help students use their own words when defining, they were provided with a language support file. The file provided them with effective practical steps for paraphrasing and avoiding plagiarism as well as a list of alternative parallel structures to: (1) start definitions (e.g., may be defined as; is seen as; *is considered a*); (2) to ascribe a physical description to the term/concept (e.g., *is characterized by*; *occurs when, can be divided into, ...*) or a functional description (e.g., *it is important because*; *without it*); (3) to introduce

Activity 1: Column A. has a text in Spanish adapted from Wikipedia on the fictitious game of Quidditch. Use the template on page 1 to identify the different parts that make up the definition of Quidditch. Sentence 1 and 4 are done for you.

A. Definition of Quidditch	B. Definition Parts
1. ☐ El Quidditch es _un deporte_	Class of the defined term
2. ☐ Donde dos equipos de siete jugadores montados en escobas juegan en un campo del tamaño de una pista de hockey con 3 aros de diferentes alturas a cada lado del campo. ☐ Se juega en todo el mundo	Physical description
3. ☐ El objetivo final es tener más puntos que el equipo rival cuando la snitch es capturada.	Functional description
4. ☐ El snitch es una bola de tenis metida en una media colgada de la cintura de un jugador imparcial oficial (snitch runner)	Expansion by explanation (a definition within a definition)
5. ☐ Cada partido empieza con los siete jugadores titulares de cada equipo alineados dentro de su zona de guardián, con las escobas en el suelo y los ojos cerrados (para no ver a dónde va la snitch) y los balones alineados en el centro del campo. El árbitro principal, tras ver desaparecer la snitch, grita la señal "Brooms up!" a la que los jugadores reaccionan para ir a buscar los balones. Una vez iniciado ...etc.	Operational or procedural description
6. ☐ Creado en 2005 ☐ Es bastante joven ☐ Basado en los libros de Harry Potter	Historical information
7. ☐ Al estar basado en los libros de Harry Potter, Quidditch tiene un crecimiento muy activo.	Explanation (reason, cause-effect)

FIGURE 6.4   Activity 1 is a task devised by the lecturer in which students use popular text on "quidditch" to identify definition realizers in Spanish (L1)

historical information when needed (*is based on*; *comes from*; *is derived from*; *first appears in*); (4) and to give examples (e.g., *for instance*; *to exemplify*; *as in the case of*).

The Joys and Pains of Emergent Definitions

There are two sides to every story, so I will first focus on what students relayed in a survey they were asked to take at the end of the course. Then I will discuss what I observed as a language and content teacher.

Activity 2: Column A. has a text in English adapted from Wikipedia on 'Driving'. Use the template on page 1 again to identify the different parts that make up the definition of 'Driving'. This here defines 'DRIVING'. See if you can identify the different parts

	C. Definition of Quidditch	D. Definition Parts
1.	☐ Driving is a process...	
2.	☐ ....by which the driver manipulates, operates and controls a motor vehicle	
3.	☐ It facilitates transportation and, therefore, speed and ease in reaching one's destination.	
4.	☐ Driving, however, turned into a sport. In other words, people not only drive to get from one place to the other but also for pleasure.	
5.	☐ Women were not seen driving in sports events until the motorized tricycle race in 1897.	
6.	☐ Pioneers in those early days include Madame Labrousse, Italy's Countess Elsa d'Albrizzi.	
7.	☐ As more and more women started driving, General Motors hired female car designers.	

FIGURE 6.5   Activity 2 is a task devised by the lecturer in which students use popular text on "driving" in English (L2) to identify definition realizers

With regards to the survey, students were asked if "defining" was *very easy, easy, difficult* or *very difficult* and the majority (75%) said it was difficult, whereas the remaining students (25%) said it was easy. The majority (75%) also said it was important, whereas the others (25%) rendered it as only slightly important. None, however, thought it was unimportant. With regards to how classifying the phrases helped them decide the extent of information to include in the definitions, half of the students (50%) found that step to be helpful, fewer (37%) found it to be slightly helpful and very few (12.5%) found it to be extremely helpful.

Students were also asked whether they thought practicing with identifying and classifying the constituents of "definitions" (Activity 3) has helped them study and retain information in general during this course. In reply to this

Activity 3: Read the article extract from Xxxx (YYYY) to extract all the sentences that define 'learning'. Determine the function of the extracts and arrange them in the table below then decide which sentences should form part of your personal definition of 'learning'. You do not need to fill the entire table and you can expand the table as needed.

A. Parts that make up a definition	B. Extracts from the article that define 'Learning'
☐ <u>Class</u> of the defined term	☐
☐ <u>Description</u> that distinguishes one term from the other	
▪ Physical	▪
▪ Functional	▪
▪ Operational/procedural	▪
▪ Historical Information	▪
☐ <u>Expansions</u> or additions to the initial definitions	
▪ By Examples	▪
▪ By Explanations	▪

FIGURE 6.6   Activity 3 is a task devised by the lecturer for students to extrapolate identifying definition realizers in popular text to academic text (from Young, 2015)

Activity 4: Use your extractions from Activity 3 (articles A and B) to define 'learning' in your own words. Use the language support file to vary your expressions in accordance with the definition constituent you are rephrasing. Use as many lines as needed.

FIGURE 6.7   Activity 4 in which students rephrase their extractions to define "learning" in their own words with the help of language support materials

question, half of the students (50%) again stated that defining and definitions were helpful in this sense, fewer (37%) found it to be slightly helpful and very few (12.5%) found it to be extremely helpful. Students' answers to this point were important since the task of gathering information from the reading fit to be incorporated into a definition and justifying its inclusion through a process of classification can be quite time consuming when compared to mere reading or reading and highlighting. For this, it was important that the students would perceive the activity as beneficial to their overall learning and retention of content.

Finally, students were asked if they would be using what they learned about "defining" to study for other future courses. Few students (25%) affirmed they would, but the majority (75%) was not sure and chose 'maybe.' Other than those five questions, the survey included another question about the language support file. The majority of the students (87.5%) stated that they used it 'sometimes' as they found it helpful—slightly helpful as opposed to very few (12.5%) who said they rarely used it and did not find it helpful. Students' comments were short and mostly centered on perceiving "defining" as less difficult as they practiced it more. It is worth mentioning that a few students expressed the thought that if defining key terms was expected of them in English, it was only logical that they would receive explicit support to fulfill such expectations. Though this last comment was rather anecdotal, it served as reassurance of my decision to tackle defining.

Dalton-Puffer's research was thus useful in the creation of a blueprint to teaching "defining." It helped communicate content and language expectations that the keener students used in order to study and prepare for different types of assessment. For this, not only was research-based teaching favorable but also essential.

The qualitative analysis of students' answers to the same activity (Activity 3) is very interesting from an applied linguistics perspective. The boundaries between one definition realizer and the other (e.g. different types of descriptions) can be fuzzy, which poses a difficulty when deciding whether a specific constituent is one type of realizer or the other. For example, one of the text extracts that students were given from Young (2015) reads:

> ... but it is the latter [referring to context-independent learning] that *historically* has become increasingly specialized in institutions and has been the source of most human progress and the problems as well as the benefits that this has led to.

Many of the students marked this extract as an idea unit to include in their definition of "learning." The rheme (the predicate) in the above extract is modified by the adverb "historically," which points to the presence of "historical information" (see Figure 6.3) in this unit; however, the extract is answering *where context-independent learning takes place* (physical description) and *what importance it has* (functional description). This fuzziness, and also the fact that these CLIL students are/were learners of English as a Foreign Language (EFL), led students to classify their selections inaccurately—as historical information—in this extract and in similar others.

The task of selecting and classifying idea units from text (Activity 3) was a means to engaging students in analyzing the linguistic functions of the phrases they read: to take note of the category of the term being defined (the class word), its specifying characteristics (different types of descriptions) and of any elaborations (expansions) that may or may not be essential to include, unlike the first two constituents. Eventually, the process leads students to engage more with the text and making meaning of it before they write what they consider a good definition. The following excerpts (Figures 6.8 to 6.11) are taken from students' answers to an essay question based on their course readings in which they were asked to define "learning" in relation to the role schools and teachers play in formal education. The erroneous classifications students did with the different idea units in the tasks completed during the course did not lead to erroneous definitions or hinder the quality of definitional content (Figure 6.8 & 6.9); however, students' lack of understanding of the topic in question or the task at hand did (Figure 6.10) and so did their language proficiency reflected in their short answers and inability to string grammatical sentences (Figure 6.11).

"Learning is a process of knowledge-building that involves social interaction and takes place through two types of experiences: context dependent learning [   ] and context independent learning [   ]."

FIGURE 6.8   A successful approach by a student (FE1-P17/44) to defining "learning" in response to an exam question. In the brackets the student wrote nested definitions of context-dependent learning and independent learning and referred to the role of teachers in the latter

"Young argues that all human learning is an epistemic or knowledge-building activity and inescapably social. There is no learning (that) does not in some sense involve social relations. [   ]."

FIGURE 6.9   Another successful approach by a student (FE3-P10/23) to defining "learning" in response to an exam question. Where the brackets are seen the student briefly referred to Vygotsky and learning from a social constructivist view

"I'm going to define Behaviorism. Behaviorist theory. This theory depends on behavior of the children and is based on reaction-stimuli. [   ]."

FIGURE 6.10   An unsuccessful approach by a student (FE3-P02/23) to defining "learning." In the brackets, the student expanded on stimulus-response and positive and negative reinforcement

"Learning is a process for that acquire knowledge, experience, acttitude, values through the study and experience. For learning we have been (in) contact of other people."

FIGURE 6.11   An unsuccessful approach by a student (FE1-P26/44) to defining "learning." Though there is some truth to what the student says, the student is clearly struggling with grammar and mechanics (including spelling). It is difficult to tell if the student does not know more or cannot convey her knowledge in English

In the examples in Figures 6.10 and 6.11, there is also evidence that students do not use nominalization, which is a central feature of vocabulary abstraction and phrase embedding in academic discourse. Students' inability to use abstract language leads them to discuss agents and actions (e.g., *I'm going to define*; *we have to be in contact with ...*; *all of* us learn in a different way, so it depends on the experiences we've lived—the latter from student FE1-P24/44:) instead of entities and relations (see Snow, 2010). The lacking abstraction in the writing of tertiary students, soon to be natives of their field of study, is awkward and somewhat alarming.

Recommendations for Fellow Teachers

As the variety of pathways and goals for language learning and teaching continue to branch out—as in the case of CLIL that is presented in this chapter—,educators are required to give priority to language functions that learners need to operate successfully in settings where more than one language is at work (TESOL International Association, 2014, p. 7). Teachers' understanding of the role(s) of English in different contexts is an important determinant in this process being the point of departure for deciding what to teach and how. The experience of operationalizing defining from a CDF perspective (Dalton-Puffer, 2016) showed that CDFs can be one of the pathways for learning language in settings where there need to be a concurrent dual focus on subject matter and language. It is, therefore, recommended that these CDFs would be explored in more depth and breadth by both content and language teachers alike, and in different disciplinary genres, as a means to conciliate teaching content and language.

Defining was perceived by the students in this study as a difficult task, despite being tertiary students who have been exposed to many definitional structures throughout their years of schooling. Those who succeeded at defining in the exam needed to employ cognitive and metacognitive steps which they had a chance to pay attention to and practice during the course. For example, they needed to have identified definition realizers for the different important terms earlier while studying then string them together coherently in their own words during the exam, which implies having internalized the syntactic structure of defining. It would, therefore, be fair to say that the other CDFs (describing, classifying, explaining, evaluating, predicting and reporting) are likely to be considered difficult as well if they are equally complex and not spontaneously acquired through mere exposure either. The second recommendation then is for teachers to operationalize the language functions they require of students.

This step has important implications for task and materials design as it most possibly will require more and different planning. It is also strongly recommended that communities of teaching practice create a pool of resources for the different CDFs that teaching members from different disciplines can draw on as well as add to.

The third and final recommendation comes from the observations noted about students' tendency to avoid nominalizations. Some teachers might argue that English as a Lingua Franca—in reference to interlocutors' right to not adhere to native norms and more importantly focus on the message (see Jenkins & Lueng, 2013)—is a more suitable view to appreciating how students express their knowledge of content through English in multilingual settings. Others, however, would argue that lacking in writing conventions can greatly hinder the credibility of an idea or an argument when communicating academic content, which takes us back to idealizing native-norms. Clearly, research that presents practices and methods that would enable teachers to shift paradigms to ELF without jeopardizing students' chances of coming across as academically or intellectually sound is still needed.

References

Airasian, P. W., Cruikshank, K. A., Mayer, R. E., Pintrich, P. R., Raths, J., & Wittrock, M. C. (2001). *A taxonomy for learning teaching, and assessing: A revision of Bloom's taxonomy of educational objectives*. New York, NY: Longman.

Bailey, A. L. (2007). Introduction: Teaching and assessing students learning English in school. In Alison L. Bailey (Ed.), *Language demands of school: Putting academic English to the test*. New Haven, CT: Yale University Press.

Beacco, J. C. (2010). *Items for a description of linguistic competence in the language of schooling necessary for learning/teaching history. An approach with reference points*. Brussels: Language Policy Division, Council of Europe. Retrieved from http://www.coe.int/t/dg4/linguistic/Source/Source2010ForumGeneva/1LIS-History2010en.Pdf

Bloom, B. S. (1956). *Taxonomy of educational objectives: The classification of educational goals* (Handbook I: The Cognitive Domain). New York, NY: McKay.

Council of Europe. (2014). *Education and languages, language policy*. Retrieved from http://www.coe.int/t/dg4/linguistic/

Cummins, J. (1979). Cognitive/academic language proficiency, linguistic interdependence, the optimum age question and some other matters. *Working Papers on Bilingualism, 19*, 121–129. Retrieved May 4, 2007, from http://www.iteachilearn.com/cummins/bicscalp.html

Cummins, J. (2008). BICS and CALP: Empirical and theoretical status of the distinction. In B. Street & N. H. Hornberger (Eds.), *Encyclopedia of language and education: Literacy* (2nd ed., pp. 71–83). New York: NY, Springer.

Dalton-Puffer, C. (2013). A construct of cognitive discourse functions in CLIL and multilingual education. *European Journal of Applied Linguistics, 1*(2), 216–253.

Dalton-Puffer, C. (2016). Cognitive discourse functions: Specifying an integrative interdisciplinary construct. In T. Nikula, E. Dafouz, P. Moore, & U. Smit (Eds.), *Conceptualising integration in CLIL and multilingual education* (pp. 29–54). Clevedon: Multilingual Matters.

Ellis, R. (1997). *SLA research and language teaching*. Oxford: Oxford University Press.

Jenkins, J., & Leung, C. (2013). English as a Lingua Franca. *The Companion to Language Assessment, 13*(95), 1605–1616.

Nikula, T., Dafouz, E., Moore, P., & Smit, U. (Eds.). (2016). *Conceptualising integration in CLIL and multilingual education*. Bristol: Multilingual Matters.

Schmidt, R. (1990). The role of consciousness in second language learning. *Applied Linguistics, 11*, 129–158.

Schunk, D. H. (2012). *Learning theories: An educational perspective*. Boston, MA: Pearson.

Snow, C. E. (2010). Academic language and the challenge of reading for learning about science. *Science New Series, 328*(5977), 450–452. Retrieved from http://www.jstor.org/stable/40655773

Snow, C. E., Cancino, H., De Temple, J., & Schley, S. (1991). Giving formal definitions: A linguistic or metalinguistic skill. In E. Bialystok (Ed.), *Language processing in bilingual children* (pp. 90–112). Cambridge: Cambridge University Press.

Swales, J. M. (1990). *English in academic and research settings*. Cambridge: Cambridge University Press.

Tedick, D. J., & Cammarata, L. (2012). Content and language integration in K-12 contexts: Student outcomes, teacher practices, and stakeholder perspectives. *Foreign Language Annals, 45*(S1), S28–S53.

Trimble, L. (1985). *English for science and technology: A discourse approach*. Cambridge: Cambridge University Press.

Vollmer, J. H. (2010). *Items for a description of linguistic competence in the language of schooling necessary for learning/teaching sciences (at the end of compulsory education): An approach with reference points* (Language and School Subjects: Linguistic Dimensions of Knowledge Building in School Curricula). Strasbourg: Council of Europe. Retrieved April 15, 2013, from http://www.coe.int/t/dg4/linguistic/LangEduc/BoxD2-OtherSub_en.asp

Young, M. (2015). What is learning and why does it matter? *European Journal of Education, 50*(1), 17–20.

CHAPTER 7

From Researchers to L2 Classrooms: Teaching Pragmatics through Collaborative Tasks

Ayşenur Sağdıç
Georgetown University, USA

Robinson's (2001, 2011) cognition hypothesis predicted that cognitively complex collaborative tasks would elicit more interactional features in second language (L2) production, thus facilitating language development. In their politeness theory, Brown and Levinson (1987) also proposed that power, social distance, and the degree of imposition (PDR) influence speakers' politeness strategies in the production of face-threatening acts such as request-making. Kim and Taguchi (2016) set out to test the claims of these theories by investigating the effects of cognitive task complexity and pragmatic task demands on English as a Foreign Language (EFL) learners' pragmatic competence in producing speech acts of request. Their research questions were the following:

1. What is the effect of task-based pragmatic instruction on L2 pragmatic development? Are there any differences in the learning of the request speech act between the collaborative and individual task group?
2. Are there any differences in the frequency of PRES and quality of task performance during instruction between the collaborative and individual task group? (Taguchi & Kim, 2016, p. 419)

The participants in their study were 49 Korean female junior high-school EFL learners whose ages ranged from 13 to 14 (M=13.78). Based on their Test of English for International Communication (TOEIC) scores, the participants were high-beginner to high-intermediate learners (M=131.88, SD=15.35). To examine the effects of task complexity on the L2 learners' pragmatic related learning episodes (PRES), namely the learning opportunities for request-making, the researchers divided the students into three groups: collaborative, individual, and control. In both collaborative and individual task conditions, the participants were asked to write TV drama scripts by using a set of scenarios and pictures provided by the researchers.

In the study, cognitive task complexity was determined based on the amount of cognitive reasoning demands the pragmatic tasks require. Accordingly, cognitively simple tasks provided the participants with detailed descriptions

© KONINKLIJKE BRILL NV, LEIDEN, 2019 | DOI:10.1163/9789004392472_008

of scenarios, matching pictures, and information about main characters and specific events in the storyline. As a result, the participants did not have to deduce the roles of the characters and other sociopragmatic factors to write requests for each scenario. The complex task groups received the same set of pictures, but details about the characters and the scenarios were not provided. Therefore, the learners in these groups had to use their cognitive reasoning skills to analyze the contextual elements to decide what could be requested in each situation. Each group completed PDR-low tasks such as asking a classmate for a pen and PDR-high tasks such as asking a professor for a recommendation letter to ensure that the learners practiced different levels of pragmatic task demands.

The researchers collected data on the L2 learners' oral interactions or self-reflections during their regular English lessons on two consecutive days. Before the participants were directed to complete the collaborative or the individual pragmatic tasks, the researchers gave them a handout that had explicit metapragmatic information about requests and sample dialogues that exemplified PDR-low and PDR-high requests. This pre-task planning stage was completed in five minutes. After this pre-task instruction stage, the participants wrote their scripts for their assigned scenarios in pairs or individually, which took forty-five minutes. Their oral interactions or think-aloud activities during the script-writing tasks were audio-recorded in order to examine the effects of task complexity and pragmatic task demands on the frequency and length of PRES in learners' oral production.

The results of Kim and Taguchi's (2016) study showed that the complex collaborative task facilitated more L2 interaction in both pragmatic task demand conditions. As for the PRES in the students' interactions, complex tasks promoted more discussion about contextual factors, that is the sociopragmatics, in both PDR-low and PDR-high situations. However, task complexity did not affect the amount of pragmalinguistic discussion among the learners. Based on these findings, the researchers suggested that L2 instructors can implement interaction-driven pragmatic tasks that lead to meaningful discussions between learners and opportunities for L2 pragmatic development. The article also suggests that task complexity can vary based on cognitive (simple or complex) or pragmatic (PDR-low or PDR-high) task demands and adds that cognitively complex tasks facilitate more language production and discussions around sociopragmatic variables when it comes to the speech act of request-making. Overall, the study findings highlight the complexity of learning requests and L2 pragmatics in general and illustrate how using tasks with varying complexity can provide L2 learners with practice in different aspects of pragmatic knowledge (e.g., pragmalinguistics, sociopragmatics).

My Teaching Context and Student Profile

This project was completed in an 8-week EAP course that focused on intermediate level listening and speaking skills at an intensive English program (IEP)
based in a public university in the United States. With multiple sets of courses
tailored to different proficiency levels, the IEP aims to develop ESL learners'
English language skills in preparation for pursuing academic studies in North
America. This particular EAP course aimed to help learners identify main ideas
and important details in intermediate level (approximately equivalent to CEFR
B1) lectures and conversations, participate in conversations on familiar topics,
and give short presentations on academic subjects.

In my classroom, there were 12 students (5 female, 7 male), whose ages
ranged from 18 to 42, most being in their mid 20s. All the students held bach-
elor's degrees in various majors. The represented first languages (L1s) were
Turkish, French, Arabic, Spanish, Korean, and Albanian. Although all students
were placed in this course using an in-house language placement test, some
students had slightly higher language proficiency than others. This was a
classroom with mixed-ability learners from diverse backgrounds. Despite their
differences, all were motivated to improve their English for academic and
professional reasons.

Incorporating Research Findings into Curriculum

I chose Kim and Taguchi's (2016) study to inform my curriculum and pedagogical activities because I wanted to teach pragmatics and test whether using
interaction-driven, collaborative tasks at different complexity levels would
lead to pragmatic development. Hymes (1972) listed sociolinguistic/pragmatic
competence under communicative competence, and several influential language competence models have included pragmatic competence as a part of
communicative competence (Bachman, 1990; Bachman & Palmer, 1996, 2010;
Canale & Swain, 1980; Canale, 1983). Since then, it has become clear that pragmatic competence is crucial for L2 learners of English to be successful users of
their target language. However, I observed that many of my students, regardless of their proficiency level, had difficulty in developing their pragmatic skills
because pragmatics had been neglected in their curriculum. Therefore, incorporating interactive pragmatic tasks into my lessons was relevant for my ESL
students because they needed to improve their L2 pragmatic competence to
succeed in their daily interactions, responsibilities, and future goals.

With this goal, I applied the study findings to my curriculum and classroom practices in four steps: (a) needs analysis, (b) pre-task pragmatic instruction, (c) task procedure, and (d) feedback. In the first stage, I analyzed the curriculum and identified that Week 5 was devoted to *polite requests*. In Week 4, I conducted a needs analysis by asking my students to write down situations that required them to make requests. This stage was not present in Kim and Taguchi (2016); however, I wanted to personalize the classroom content for my students' specific needs. According to Doughty and Long (2003), optimal L2 instruction should individualize instruction based on learner needs through a needs analysis. Table 7.1 shows the list of the most commonly listed situations that created the need for my students to make a request in English. By using the pragmatic tasks in the research article as guidelines, I categorized the situations that came from my students into four categories: simple/PDR-low, simple/PDR-high, complex/PDR-low, and complex/PDR-high conditions. Categorization of the six situations in terms of task complexity was made based on Taguchi and Kim's (2016) formula. Accordingly, simple tasks provided the learners with details about the speakers and their relationships while the complex task did not. To determine the pragmatic task demands of a scenario (i.e., PDR-low and PDR-high), I gave a short questionnaire to some of my fellow IEP instructors who were familiar with the targeted pragmatic norms and the socio-cultural environment. In the questionnaire, the instructors were asked to categorize each situation as either PDR-low or PDR-high after being provided with a definition of Brown and Levinson's (1987) politeness theory and PDR constructs.

As shown in Figure 7.1, I turned the situations into task scenarios similar to the scenarios used in Kim and Taguchi's (2016) research. The researchers mentioned that they used scenes from a famous Korean TV show for the task; however, this was not relevant for my students' profile. Therefore, I used copyright-free images available on the internet for the scenarios.

In the second stage, I mirrored the pre-task instruction stage in the research by providing my students with a handout from the research article (see Kim & Taguchi, 2016, p. 48). The handout included metapragmatic information regarding request head acts for PDR-low and PDR-high situations and examples for each type. It also included the pragmalinguistic formulas for PDR-low (e.g., Can you/Could you/Would you give me your eraser? Can I/Could I/May I borrow your eraser?) and PDR-high situations (e.g., I'm wondering if + clause/ I was wondering if + clause). After the students read the handout individually, I elicited the differences between PDR-low and PDR-high situations and had my students underline the request head acts in the given examples. My students also came up with additional

TABLE 7.1   Request situations and their task categories

Scenarios	Task category
1. Asking a small favor of a classmate	Complex Task/PDR-Low
2. Talking to a stranger on the street to make a request	Complex Task/PDR-Low
3. Talking to the IEP director/coordinator to make a request	Complex Task/PDR-High
4. Asking a friend for help with a class project	Simple Task/PDR-Low
5. Asking a professor for an extension on a paper	Simple Task/PDR-High
6. Asking a teacher for a makeup exam	Simple Task/PDR-High

Simple Task/PDR-Low

Instructions: Read the following scenario, look at the picture, and write a script for this situation. In your script, make sure that both speakers say something. It's a conversation!

[The pair receives a picture of a student talking to an instructor at a school.]

Scenario: Salma is an ESL student at an intensive English program in the USA. She got a D on her last grammar exam. She is upset because she really wants to pass the course. After class, she politely makes a request to her grammar teacher, Mr. Jones, on whether she can re-take the grammar exam to make it up.

FIGURE 7.1   A sample task scenario (adapted from Kim & Taguchi, 2016)

requests for various situations. Then, the class had a short discussion about how sociopragmatic factors (i.e., power, distance, rank of imposition) play a role in determining the right request head acts in English. The instruction stage took five minutes in the study; however, learning how to make accurate and appropriate requests is a complex process, as noticing the input requires learners to make connections between forms, pragmatic functions, and social contexts (Schmidt, 1993). Therefore, I allocated two lessons for this stage.

The task procedure stage took place in two consecutive lessons in Week 5. At this stage, I divided the students into three groups to assign them to the collaborative, the individual, or the control group. The collaborative group members worked in pairs to complete the script writing task while the individual group members completed it alone. The control group did not receive any task-based instruction. However, because my goal was to see in my students the positive effects of collaborative, interactive tasks on pragmatic ability in making requests found in Taguchi and Kim (2016), I divided my students into six pairs to complete the collaborative writing tasks. In other words, for reasons of ecological validity, all of my students worked in pairs and there were no individual or control groups. Before writing TV drama scripts for given scenarios, the students in the original study watched a short video modeling the collaborative pragmatic task. Instead of showing a video, I modeled the activity with another student in class to make sure my students understood the expected outcome. Each pair completed four collaborative tasks (simple/ PDR-low, complex/PDR-low, simple/PDR-high, complex/PDR-high) in total. The students completed PDR-low scenarios on the first day and PDR-high the next. The researchers in the study allowed the EFL learners to use their shared L1, Korean, during the tasks. My ESL students, by contrast, used only English, as it was the *lingua franca* between each pair.

Although Kim and Taguchi's (2016) study did not include a feedback session as part of their research design and goal, I wanted to ensure my students received feedback on their task performance for pedagogical reasons. During this stage, I asked each pair to act out one of their scenarios in front of the class. Then, I asked the other students to give feedback on their classmates' requests in terms of their pragmalinguistic and sociopragmatic elements. I also provided explicit corrective feedback when necessary. There were six pairs in total and this stage took one lesson. After this feedback session, I gave my students a test on requests to gauge their understanding of the content. To develop this assessment tool in order to elicit requests, I adapted the four scenarios provided in the appendix of Kim and Taguchi's (2016) study by turning them into written Discourse Completion Tasks (DCTs) (see Appendix A). Finally, I checked my students' responses in the test, provided explicit corrective feedback when necessary, and answered their questions regarding the DCTs in the test.

What Worked?

Kim and Taguchi (2016) claimed that interaction-driven tasks and explicit pragmatic instruction are useful for learning to make requests in English. Based on my research utilization project, I can attest to this claim. However, I also made several adaptations that contributed to the success of my research-informed curriculum. Reflecting on the changes I made to my curriculum, I realized that it was useful for students to have explicit pragmatic instruction about request-making. This is understandable because language learners may have difficulty in decoding the unwritten L2 pragmatic rules that may not be present in their L1, and explicit instruction helps learners develop their L2 pragmatic skills (Jeon & Kaya, 2006; Plonsky & Zhuang, in press; Taguchi, 2015). The pre-task instruction stage in the curriculum prepared the students for the collaborative pragmatic tasks. Additionally, the inclusion of metalinguistic explanations of pragmalinguistic and sociopragmatic aspects of requests, as well as discussions of the importance of pragmatic competence in English, grabbed their attention and motivated them to learn more about making requests. My students told me that they found it helpful to see effective request examples during my modeling and to find the underlying patterns in the sample requests during the instruction stage. I also realized that the pre-task instruction stage made it easier for them to perform the form-function-meaning mapping required for successful request-making.

Another successful aspect of my research-informed curriculum was the use of collaborative tasks that led to meaningful discussions for my students. Although the research simply provided the request scenarios without considering the participants' needs, I implemented a needs analysis, and my students appreciated being able to work on scenarios of their own choice rather than on hypothetical situations that were not relevant for them. Giving them a 'say' in the content of the lessons also increased their motivation to learn to make requests. The feedback stage through role plays was useful in giving my students a chance to use their oral skills to produce requests and to receive corrective feedback on their request-making skills. At the end of Week 6, my students reported that they felt more confident because they knew what to say when they wanted to make a request in various social contexts. Receiving such positive feedback and seeing my students' pragmatic development after a short instructional period confirmed the effectiveness of the collaborative task-based approach and explicit pragmatic instruction with feedback.

I made several adjustments to Kim and Taguchi's (2016) methods and materials to make my instruction not only more effective, but also more manageable to implement. Kim and Taguchi (2016) compared the simple collaborative tasks to complex ones by dividing their participants into two groups. However, I found it beneficial not to divide my students into two groups and to utilize both cognitively simple and complex as well as PDR-low and PDR-high situations in the script writing tasks because my students needed to be exposed to various situations to be successful communicators in their academic and professional lives. Therefore, instead of comparing the effectiveness of pragmatic task types with varying cognitive demands, my curriculum's focus was on using collaborative task-based scenarios and explicit pragmatic instruction to cater to my learners' needs. Another revision of the study was related to the use of L1 between the pairs during collaboration. Because I had an ESL classroom with a variety of L1 backgrounds, it was not possible to have the students use their L1 during the tasks. Even though using English might have made the tasks more challenging, it maximized my learners' opportunities for output in the target language, which is a necessary principle for L2 instruction (Ellis, 2014).

The sequence of the curriculum was also successful. The presence of both pre-task introduction and explicit pragmatic instruction stages, as well as the sequence of PDR-low tasks on the first day and PDR-high on the second day, provided a reasonable challenge for my students. Finally, the inclusion of a formative assessment tool helped me better gauge my students' knowledge at the end of the curriculum unit.

What Did Not Work?

After teaching the curriculum, I recognized several aspects that could have worked better if implemented differently. These were the lack of grammar instruction and the use of written tasks (i.e., script writing, DCTs) for oral communication skills. Although most of my students seemed to do well in writing requests, they struggled more when acting out their scenarios during role-play. One of the main reasons for some of the students' pragmatic troubles was not that they did not understand the sociopragmatic factors in their given scenarios, but that they did not have enough grammatical skills to form accurate sentences or question forms. Not having any grammar instruction as part of the pre-task instruction stage did not work effectively for my classroom context. Despite the fact that my students had already covered modals and question formation before, I observed that some students either could not form grammatical questions or misplaced modal verbs in a sentence, making their requests difficult to understand. The students also had difficulty in the indirect request form "I was wondering if" for the PDR-high situations. This might be due to their lack of knowledge on "if" conditionals. Although I included an example of both direct and indirect requests during the instruction stage, this was understandably insufficient to enable them to produce indirect requests. Therefore, I would incorporate a variety of form-function-meaning mapping exercises before moving to the collaborative tasks to ensure that my students have enough pragmalinguistic competence to produce both direct and indirect requests.

Another challenge was the mismatch between the target language use (TLU) domain and the expected response format in the pragmatic tasks. Although the students improved their request-making skills after instruction and the collaborative tasks, they still had observable difficulty in orally producing the requests in their role-play during the feedback session. This may have happened because practicing writing requests did not lead to development in producing them and the DCT test may not have given an accurate description of their oral pragmatic skills. It is an empirical question whether my students can produce requests orally as successfully as they did in writing during the tasks.

According to Bachman and Palmer (2010), it is necessary for assessment tools to be able to generalize learners' abilities to the TLU domain. Although requests are frequently used as speech acts in real life, the collaborative tasks in Kim and Taguchi's (2016) study required the students to write the expected requests in a given scenario. Bardovi-Harlig (2015) criticizes this mismatch by calling such tasks "written-for-oral" and recommends using "oral-for-oral tasks" (p. 25) because polite requests made in daily conversations are spoken, not written. Therefore, instead of asking my students to write scripts for the scenarios and write requests in DCTs, it could have been more beneficial to ask them to role-play the scenarios during the task procedure, as in the feedback session and give them an assessment task that elicits oral production.

Recommendations for Fellow Teachers

Based on the learning outcomes, my observations, and the students' feedback, several recommendations can be made to utilize Kim and Taguchi's (2016) study findings in TESOL classrooms.

 – *Incorporate teaching pragmatics into the curriculum*
   A quick glance at my curriculum was enough for me to realize that L2 pragmatic skills were neglected in the suggested syllabus for my semester-long listening and speaking skills IEP course. The critical importance of pragmatics lies in the fact that "the consequences of pragmatic differences, unlike the case of grammatical errors, are often interpreted on a social or personal level rather than a result of the language learning process" (Bardovi-Harlig & Mahan-Taylor, 2003, p. 38). As a result, pragmatic failure may have negative consequences such as being perceived as rude and may even reinforce national stereotypes (Thomas, 1983). Encouragingly, however, research has consistently shown that explicit pragmatic instruction does indeed work. In their meta-analysis of the 50 instructional effects studies on L2 pragmatics, Plonsky and Zhuang (in press) have recently found that pragmatic instruction worked with a large effect size and resulted in considerable retention of information over time. Therefore, I recommend providing learners with pragmatic instruction even though the curriculum may not specifically include teaching pragmatics. Corpora (e.g., MICASE, COCA) can be used to analyze texts at the pragmatic or discoursal level, and

collaborative tasks can be implemented to teach pragmatic rules so that language learners know to say (or not to say) the right words at the right time. As for teaching the speech act of requests, I recommend allocating ample time to introduce request head acts and the importance of PDRs of a situation, provide hands-on activities such as role plays, and not expect students to learn to make effective requests solely through exposure to the target language.

– *Use explicit pragmatic instruction with corrective feedback and integrate grammar instruction*
Providing explicit pragmatic instruction is crucial in helping learners understand how to make successful requests. Despite being exposed to requests through other competent English speakers in daily life, L2 learners often have difficulty in producing accurate and appropriate requests in various situations—be it in PDR-low or PDR-high situations. Therefore, explicit instruction that includes metapragmatic information can enable learners to read between the lines and make not-so-salient pragmatic rules more noticeable. It is also necessary to focus on both the sociopragmatic and pragmalinguistic aspects of request-making. During the instruction stage, I had my students find the social factors in the sample scenarios and had them choose the right request formulas based on the pragmatic instruction in the handout. Such form-function-context mapping activities reinforces newly learned knowledge. However, my students still had considerable difficulty in producing requests for PDR-high situations (e.g., I was wondering if ...) due to their more advanced bi-clausal sentence structure. Therefore, I strongly advise including grammar instruction in pragmatics lessons. Finally, explicit instruction should be supplemented with corrective feedback. Meta-analyses on instructed pragmatics studies (Jeon & Kaya, 2006; Taguchi, 2015; Plonsky & Zhuang, in press) consistently found that explicit instruction was more effective when combined with explicit feedback. Although the feedback stage was not present in Kim and Taguchi's (2016) study, its addition ensured that my students knew both the acceptable and the unacceptable requests in each scenario they acted out during the feedback session. Moreover, it led to a lively classroom discussion that engaged the learners with the content. Therefore, metapragmatic information with corrective feedback can be used to increase the effectiveness of pragmatic instruction.

– *Develop tasks that would lead to meaningful interaction and collaboration among learners*

According to the interactionist approach, using tasks that lead to meaningful interaction among learners is beneficial for language development (Gass & Mackey, 2006; Long, 1996), and the collaborative tasks used in this project were proven effective in teaching requests for my ESL learners. Using collaborative pragmatic writing tasks not only led to meaningful interaction among my students but also motivated them to learn even more about L2 pragmatics. Using interaction-driven activities such as role-plays also made the instructional target more memorable for them, as they reported in their reflections at the end of the semester that they still remembered the scenarios they acted out in front of the class weeks after the project. I also recommend using a task-based approach (Long, 2015) when developing materials for teaching requests and L2 pragmatics in general. Existing materials and activities can also be adapted to create a need for learners to negotiate meaning and exchange information. Such activities provide opportunities for L2 use and pragmatic discussions, thus helping learners develop their L2 pragmatic skills.

– *Be aware of the complexity of tasks when planning and sequencing lessons*
The type of tasks and their cognitive demand should be taken into account when teaching pragmatics. In this curriculum, I sequenced lessons from easy to more challenging so that my students would not be overwhelmed with the tasks and the complex nature of request-making. As Doughty and Long (2003) recommended, sequencing PDR-low scenarios before PDR-high ones was necessary for my intermediate level ESL students because gradual increase in task complexity makes the input comprehensible. Besides sequencing tasks, this project also made me realize the importance of using tasks with varying cognitive complexity to enable my students to practice different aspects of language. Depending on language learners' proficiency, using the implications of Robinson's (2001, 2011) cognition hypothesis, the notion that cognitively demanding tasks would lead to more complex and accurate language production, for L2 pragmatic learning can help TESOL instructors create and adapt lesson plans, tasks, and pragmatic assessment tools.

– *Use your sense of plausibility when it comes to utilizing L2 research*
My final recommendation is related to using sense of plausibility in implementing research findings. Prabhu (1990, p. 172) argued decades ago that "teachers need to operate with some personal conceptualization of how their teaching leads to desired learning," and this notion was proven true in my curriculum. Research has shown that incorporating research

findings into classroom practices was a complex process in which instructors adapted the findings using their personal experience and pedagogical knowledge (Anwaruddin, 2016). For example, Cain (2015) found that teachers used narrowly-focused research knowledge and applied it to broader teaching contexts. In their study, Kim and Taguchi (2016) set out to determine the role of task complexity and pragmatic situational demands on Korean EFL learners' number of learning opportunities for request-making skills. Their findings are significant in terms of uncovering the intricate relationship between cognitive and pragmatic task complexity and the development of the speech act of requests. However, as an ESL instructor, my goal was not to isolate independent variables to examine their role on PRES in learners' interaction. Rather, my main aim was to help my students develop their listening and communication skills so that they could succeed in North American academic institutions upon exiting the EAP program. As a result, I focused on using collaborative tasks and explicit pragmatic instruction and made omissions and additions to the original research materials. For instance, I made changes to increase the effectiveness of my instruction by lengthening the instruction, to check my students' knowledge level by adding a pragmatic test, and simply to make the curriculum changes more relevant for my teaching context by using English. Also, the project required approximately 10 hours of additional preparation and grading time on my part, so I made minor adjustments to the research (e.g., using pictures instead of TV show scenes) for purposes of practicality. Teaching is always influenced by contextual factors (i.e., situated, professional, material, external), so any implementation needs to recognize these factors to successfully enact the proposed changes (Braun, Ball, Maguire, & Hoskins, 2011).

Finally, as McMillan and Wergin (2010) underscore the importance of taking ownership of research by critically reading and evaluating the research findings as teachers, I recommend reading each piece of research on L2 learning and teaching with a critical eye. Forming a locally-based interpretive community in which teachers discuss research findings with one another can be a useful approach in transforming L2 research findings into L2 instruction (Anwaruddin, 2015). As every learning context is unique, the positive aspects of this curriculum may not work for other contexts, so interpreting the results and recommendations on the basis of language learners' specific needs and learning context is crucial for language instructors. Overall, Kim and Taguchi's (2016) findings offered a set of activities that provided opportunities for my ESL learners to improve their English pragmatic skills, particularly request-making. Through their emphasis on interaction, collaboration, and a task-based approach, the study also informed my teaching practices and showcased how these can be strategically used to optimize L2 learning and teaching.

Appendix A: Sample Discourse Completion Task (DCT) (adapted from Taguchi & Kim, 2016)

Instructions: Read the following situation and imagine what you would say to the other person in that situation. Then, write your answer next to "you say." Make sure to write your exact words in as much detail as possible. You can include fillers such as "um, well, pauses (…), uh, etc."

Question 1. "Umbrella"

Situation: After school, you are walking outside with your classmate from English class. Suddenly, it starts raining heavily. Your friend has an umbrella, but you forgot to bring yours, and you don't want to get wet. On the way home, you make a request to your friend, whether you can share your friend's umbrella.

You say: [Write your answer here.]

_____

_____

References

Anwaruddin, S. M. (2015). Teachers' engagement with educational research: Toward a conceptual framework for locally-based interpretive communities. *Education Policy Analysis Archives, 23*(40), 1–25.

Anwaruddin, S. M. (2016). Language teachers' responses to educational research: Addressing the crisis of representation. *International Journal of Research & Method in Education, 39*(3), 314–328.

Bachman, L. F. (1990). *Fundamental considerations in language testing.* Oxford: Oxford University Press.

Bachman, L. F., & Palmer, A. S. (1996). *Language testing in practice: Designing and developing useful language tests.* Oxford: Oxford University Press.

Bachman, L. F., & Palmer, A. S. (2010). *Language assessment in practice: Developing language assessments and justifying their use in the real world.* Oxford: Oxford University Press.

Bardovi-Harlig, K. (2015). Operationalizing conversation in studies of instructional effects in L2 pragmatics. *System, 48*, 21–34.

Bardovi-Harlig, K., & Mahan-Taylor, R. (2003). *Teaching pragmatics.* Washington, DC: United States Department of State.

Braun, A., Ball, S. J., Maguire, M., & Hoskins, K. (2011). Taking context seriously: Towards explaining policy enactments in the secondary school. *Discourse: Studies in the Cultural Politics of Education, 32*(4), 585–596.

Cain, T. (2015). Teachers' engagement with published research: Addressing the knowledge problem. *The Curriculum Journal, 26*(3), 488–509.

Canale, M. (1983). From communicative competence to communicative language pedagogy. In J. C. Richards & R. W. Schmidt (Eds.), *Language and communication* (pp. 2–27). London: Longman.

Canale, M., & Swain, M. (1980). Theoretical bases of communicative approaches to second language teaching and testing. *Applied Linguistics, 1*, 1–47.

Doughty, C. J., & Long, M. H. (2003). Optimal psycholinguistic environments for distance foreign language learning. *Language Learning & Technology, 7*, 50–80.

Ellis, R. (2014). Principles of instructed second language learning. In M. Celce-Murcia, D. M. Brinton, & M. A. Snow (Eds.), *Teaching English as a second or foreign language* (4th ed., pp. 15–30). Boston, MA: Cengage Learning.

Gass, S., & Mackey, A. (2006). Input, interaction and output: An overview. In K. Bardovi-Harlig & Z. Dörnyei (Eds.), *AILA review* (pp. 3–17). Amsterdam: John Benjamins.

Jeon, E. H., & Kaya, T. (2006). Effects of L2 instruction on interlanguage pragmatic development: A meta-analysis. In J. M. Norris & L. Ortega (Eds.), *Synthesizing research on language learning and teaching* (pp. 165–211). Amsterdam: John Benjamins.

Kim, Y., & Taguchi, N. (2016). Learner-learner interaction during collaborative pragmatic tasks: The role of cognitive and pragmatic task demands. *Foreign Language Annals, 49*, 42–57.

Long, M. H. (1996). The role of the linguistic environment in second language acquisition. In W. Ritchie & T. Bhatia (Eds.), *Handbook of language acquisition: Second language acquisition* (pp. 413–468). New York, NY: Academic Press.

Long, M. H. (2015). *Second language acquisition and task-based language teaching.* Oxford: Wiley-Blackwell.

McMillan, J. H., & Wergin, J. F. (2010). *Understanding and evaluating educational research* (4th ed.). Upper Saddle River, NJ: Pearson Education.

Plonsky, L., & Zhuang, J. (in press). A meta-analysis of second language pragmatics instruction: Jeon & Kaya (2006) updated and extended. In N. Taguchi (Ed.), *The Routledge handbook of SLA and pragmatics.* New York, NY: Routledge.

Prabhu, N. S. (1990). There is no best method—why? *TESOL Quarterly, 24*(2), 161–176.

Robinson, P. (2001). Task complexity, task difficulty, and task production: Exploring interactions in a componential framework. *Applied Linguistics, 22*, 27–57.

Robinson, P. (2011). Second language task complexity, the cognition hypothesis, language learning, and performance. In P. Robinson (Ed.), *Second language task complexity: Researching the cognition hypothesis of language learning and performance* (pp. 3–38). Amsterdam: John Benjamins.

Schmidt, R. (1993). Consciousness, learning and interlanguage pragmatics. In G. Kasper & S. Blum-Kulka (Eds.), *Interlanguage pragmatics* (pp. 21–42). New York, NY: Oxford University Press.

Taguchi, N. (2015). Instructed pragmatics at a glance: Where instructional studies were, are, and should be going. State-of-the-art article. *Language Teaching, 48*, 1–50.

Thomas J. (1983). Cross-cultural pragmatic failure. *Applied Linguistics, 4*, 91–112.

CHAPTER 8

From False Myths to Achievable Goals: Developing Language Learning Awareness in the L2 Classroom

Lorena Valmori
Università di Modena e Reggio Emilia, Italy

Introduction

Learners enter the language classroom with pre-conceived ideas of how easy or difficult the language they study is, how well they will manage to learn it, and how they will go about learning the language. In other words, learners hold "personal myths" (Bernat & Gvozdenko, 2005, p. 1) about language learning, which affect their "expectations of, commitment to, success in, and satisfaction with their language classes" (Horwitz, 1988, p. 283). Given "the profound influence of learner beliefs on their learning behavior" (Cotterall, 1995, p. 195), it is crucial for language teachers to know what beliefs their students hold in order to understand their receptiveness to learning tasks and instructional approaches. As stated by Cotterall (1995), a primary goal for teachers and learners is to achieve learning autonomy by constructing "a shared understanding of the language learning process and of the part they play in it" (p. 203). Knowing learners' beliefs, raising learners' awareness about them, and adjusting uninformed or counterproductive beliefs are thus fundamental for learners to take responsibility of their learning process and to become autonomous learners.

In this chapter, I focus on Elaine Horwitz's (1988) article, published in *The Modern Language Journal* in 1988. Horwitz developed a questionnaire to assess the extent of certain beliefs among students and "to discuss the potential impact of these beliefs on learner expectations and strategies" (p. 285). I came across Horwitz's study while looking for ways to raise my students' awareness about what learning a language entails, so that they could take responsibility of their language learning process. Although Horwitz's questionnaire was not a complete inventory of learners' beliefs, it sparked my interest because the findings and their pedagogical implications resonated with my experience as a foreign language teacher and learner. The questionnaire dates back to 1988, but it has been widely used ever since in several studies in different cultural settings (e.g., Bacon & Finneman, 1990; Kern, 1995; Mori, 1999; Park, 1995; Tumposky,

1991; Su, 1995; Yang, 1992). For these reasons and because of its manageable size (34 items), Horwitz's questionnaire seemed to be a suitable springboard to start a conversation with my students about their language learning beliefs.

Defining Language Learning Beliefs

Given the same learning environment and stimuli, some learners seem better at learning than others. A great deal of variability in learners' acquisition and ultimate attainment can be attributed to learners' individual characteristics (Dörnyei, 2005). In second language acquisition (SLA) research, learners' beliefs about language learning are considered internal variables or individual differences on a par with aptitude, working memory, motivation, affective factors (e.g., anxiety), willingness to communicate, personality, learning styles, and strategies (Dörnyei, 2005).

After more than thirty years of research on learner beliefs, the construct has emerged as a complex and multi-faceted one, as evidenced by the plethora of definitions and operationalizations provided by researchers. For example, Horwitz (1985, 1987, 1988), the author of one of the most widely used surveys about learner beliefs, speaks about beliefs as preconceptions, preconceived ideas, preconceived notions, and "student opinions on a variety of issues and controversies related to language learning" (Horwitz, 1988, p. 284). Learner beliefs have also been defined as mini-theories (Hosenfeld, 1978), insights (Omaggio, 1978), assumptions (Riley, 1980), filters of reality (Arnold, 1999), and metacognitive knowledge (Wenden, 1987). Flavel (1987) calls beliefs person knowledge, that is, the knowledge learners have acquired about how their cognitive and affective factors influence their learning process. Finally, Miller and Ginsberg (1995) have used the term folklinguistic theories to refer to ideas about the nature and methods of language learning based on common sense and cultural context that help learners to frame and interpret their learning experience. Gregersen and McIntyre (2014) summarized the belief-making process by saying that "beliefs are shaped by perceptions and often assimilated by choice." (p. 32). Simply put, learners hold ideas about who can successfully learn a foreign language, and also why, how, where and when effective learning takes place. These views are accepted, shaped, validated, or rejected by learners' experiences.

Riley (1994) explains the impact of beliefs on the learning process by saying that "in ordinary life people do not go round thinking or taking decisions on the basis of scientific reality, but on the basis of *their* reality" (p. 12). Although no cause-effect relationship between beliefs and learning outcomes can be claimed, a series of studies have shown an influence of language beliefs on language learning strategies (Riley, 1997; Yang, 1992), L2 proficiency (Park, 1995), and L2 achievements (Mori, 1999). Moreover, beliefs are socially constructed, interactive, and variable (Kalaja, 1995), as shown in learners' modification of beliefs as a result of a change in the learning environment such as study abroad experiences (Amuzie & Winke, 2009; Tanaka & Ellis, 2003).

Language Learning Beliefs of University Foreign Language Students

In a series of studies, Horwitz (1985, 1987, 1988) investigated learner beliefs from a normative standpoint by using a Likert-scale questionnaire. In Horwitz's words, her article was based on "a descriptive study of the beliefs of beginning foreign language university students," and her aim was "to sensitize teachers and researchers to the variety of beliefs students hold and to the possible consequences of specific beliefs for second language learning and instruction" (Horwitz, 1988, p. 284).

Horwitz developed a 34-item questionnaire, known as the BALLI (Belief about Language Learning Inventory). This instrument was developed mainly from free-recall protocols of language teachers, students' focus groups, and "additional beliefs supplied by teacher educators from a variety of culture groups" (Horwitz, 1988, p. 284). Horwitz's concern was not the correctness or incorrectness of the beliefs learners held, rather "the extent of such a belief among students and its consequences for language learning and teaching" (p. 284). In other words, the author did not seek to pinpoint how much students knew about the L2 acquisition process, but to draw teachers' attention to possible uninformed, naïve, or ill-advised beliefs that could lead to ineffective learning behaviors, frustration, and ultimately giving up language learning altogether. The BALLI has been criticized for two main reasons (e.g., Kuntz, 1996; Nikitina & Furuoka, 2006). First, the list of beliefs included in the questionnaire were generated mainly by teachers rather than by learners themselves. Second, there has been a lack of statistical backing for the themes under which the beliefs are organized.

Although, incomplete and descriptive in nature, Horwitz's inventory has laid the foundation of research in language learning beliefs. The BALLI included language learning beliefs in five major areas: (1) Difficulty of language learning, (2) Foreign language aptitude, (3) The nature of language learning, (4) Learning and communication strategies, and (5) Motivations and expectations. A total of 241 students enrolled in the first semester of German, French or Spanish at the University of Texas were asked to respond to the items, choosing from 1 (strongly agree) to 5 (strongly disagree). The questionnaire did not yield results in a single composite score or learner profiles, but the percentage of students' agreement with the different items was computed. Horwitz stated that her intention was "simply to catalogue and report the beliefs about language learning of a typical group of beginning university students" (p. 291).

Difficulty of Language Learning

In general, Horwitz noted that "the overall pattern of responses remained strikingly consistent across language groups" (p. 291), and that although popular beliefs could be clearly identified, there were also individuals or minority groups that held differing views. The researcher highlighted a possible link between learners' judgment of the difficulty of the target language, the development of students' expectations and their commitment to learning. A large majority of students agreed that "some languages are easier to learn than others" (p. 285). They were generally optimistic about their success supporting the idea that two years were sufficient to learn a foreign language. These findings are particularly interesting because they show that students may tend to underestimate or overestimate the difficulty of the target language and the time commitment necessary to learn it, creating possible premises for frustration, anxiety, and dissatisfaction about their learning process.

Foreign Language Aptitude

Horwitz identified the belief that learning a language takes some special innate skills as another possible source of negative expectations about learners' own capability that can undermine their commitment and self-efficacy. Many students agreed that "Some people are born with a special ability to learn a foreign language" (p. 287), but they also indicated that they did not see themselves as being particularly gifted. They also agreed that "everyone can learn to speak a foreign language" and rated themselves as having an average ability (p. 287).

The Nature of Language Learning

As for the nature of language learning, many students agreed that learning a language differs from learning other subjects. However, in Horwitz's words, they showed "a restricted view of language learning" (p. 288) that can lead them to invest their time and efforts in only one aspect of language learning (e.g., vocabulary or grammar rules), neglecting the holistic nature of the process. At least, one third of the students in each group believed that learning a language is mostly a matter of learning grammar rules and vocabulary.

Learning and Communication Strategies

Respondents agreed almost unanimously that learning involves repeating and practicing a lot, and they also agreed that it is acceptable to try and speak even somewhat inaccurately and to guess the meaning of unknown words. However, almost half of the German and French students believed that it is important to have an excellent accent and that it would be hard to correct mistakes that are not corrected at the beginning. According to Horwitz, the widespread agreement with the sentence "I feel self-conscious speaking the foreign language in front of other people" is not surprising when learners are over-concerned with correctness. The researcher suggests that these results underline the importance for students to understand the rationale of the activities, in order to prevent clashes between teachers' approaches and students' expectations concerning accuracy and fluency.

Motivations and Expectations

Finally, Horwitz (1988) concluded that the students in the study had only "moderate levels of intrinsic instrumental or integrative motivation" (p. 291), which may not be enough to sustain the students' language learning process in the long run. Instrumental motivation, the practical reason why learners learn a second language, was operationalized as the job opportunities that learning a language could generate. Integrative motivation was operationalized as the desire to know the culture of the speakers of a target language. Motivation predicts and sustains learning (Dörnyei, 2005), and low levels of motivation on a par with misconceived learning beliefs could make language learning a frustrating endeavor.

Summary of the Study

In her discussion of the findings, Horwitz underlined not only the importance for teachers to know their students' beliefs, but also for students to become aware of their own preconceived notions and the possible consequences. Learners build their expectations about the success (or a lack thereof) of their language learning process on what they believe language learning is about (e.g., easy/difficult, innate gift, translating, learning grammar rules and vocabulary, accuracy vs. fluency, long vs. short process). These beliefs may be based on limited knowledge and the instructional practices they experience in language or content classes. Horwitz argues for incorporating discussions about the nature of language learning as a part of regular instruction, for learners to develop awareness of the language as a system and a means of communication, be actively involved in the learning process, and cope with its affective demands (as suggested by Naiman, Frohlich, & Todesco, 1978 cited in Horwitz,

1988). Moreover, as teaching practices "could have a strong influence on the students' own beliefs" (p. 291), teachers' practices should show students the holistic nature of language learning.

Using the BALLI with Italian High School Students

I have been teaching English as a foreign language (EFL) in Italian high schools for more than a decade. Diverse groups of students with whom I have worked have manifested similar patterns and difficulties such as anxiety and self-consciousness when committing mistakes, and too high or too low self-esteem and expectations. During my doctoral work in Second Language Studies, I focused my dissertation on investigating the role of anxiety when interacting in the second language. One of my findings was that the anxiety that the learners experienced was often the result of a mismatch between learners' high (and somewhat unrealistic) expectations of themselves and their real performance in the second language. This highlighted the paramount importance of increasing learners' awareness by working on their beliefs to alleviate language anxiety. Beliefs can thus undermine learners' self-efficacy, but they can also be used as an excuse for learners' failures or disengagement in the learning process. I have often witnessed high-school students in my classes blaming previous teachers' practices or their lack of an innate gift of English for their poor outcomes or performances. They also do not seem to trust the school as a viable way to learn to speak English, believing that a relative short time abroad would grant better and effortless outcomes. These beliefs show that my students do not think they are in charge of their learning process and they misplace responsibilities for their failures and shortcomings.

At the beginning of the school year, I was assigned a new fourth year class composed of 25 students (2 females and 23 males). They were 17-year-old students enrolled in a technical Italian high school, specializing in information technology. Following Horwitz' suggestions, I decided to get to know my students' beliefs. The goal was to discuss their answers to the BALLI together in class and to incorporate consequent activities in the curriculum to increase learners' awareness of and engagement in their learning process.

The Context

The Italian school system consists of three types of high schools: college preparation, technical, and vocational. They differ in language learning goals, levels, types of students, and teaching approaches. Technical schools provide in-depth instruction in one specific area (e.g., chemistry, electronics, business,

information technology), and after graduation students may either decide to
work as specialized technicians or to continue their education at University.
Depending on their future goals, learning English may hardly be their primary
concern. The guidelines of the Italian Ministry of Education (Article 8.3 of
the Presidential Decree 88/2010) set the final proficiency level goal for these
students as B2 of the Common European Framework of Reference (CEFR).
Students should thus be able to understand complex texts in their field of
specialization, explain viewpoints, advantage and disadvantages on a topical
issue, and interact without strain for the speaker and the interlocutor (CEFR,
2001). The National Curriculum for technical schools requires that in the fourth
and fifth year[1] students meet the English proficiency requirements by dealing
with technical and scientific topics, and historical and literary topics related to
English speaking countries. Classes in the final years usually have an English
course book related to their field of specialization.

The Beliefs about Language Learning of Italian Fourth-Year High School Students

For my students, the first homework of the term was to fill out an online version
of the BALLI, which I had translated into Italian to prevent students' proficiency
in English from interfering with the metacognitive task of reflecting on language
learning. To create the online questionnaire, I used Google Form, which gener-
ates a sharable URL. This tool also provides graphs of the results for each item.
Below I present the results from eighteen students who completed the task.

Difficulty of Language Learning

My students' results were similar to Horwitz's in many ways. More than half of
the group believed that English was of average difficulty and that they would
ultimately manage to learn it very well. The other half was evenly divided
between thinking that English was either easy or difficult. The great majority
underestimated the learning process and believed that they would become flu-
ent in one or two years with one hour of study a day.

Foreign Language Aptitude

The great majority believed that some people have a gift for language learning; however, only a third thought they had language learning aptitude, while
the rest indicated having average or poor aptitude. The majority agreed that
everybody could learn a foreign language, even though a few students strongly
disagreed with it.

The Nature of Language Learning

In line with Horwitz's participants, most of my students agreed that to learn a language they should repeat and practice a lot, and more than 40% of the group supported the beliefs that language learning is mostly a matter of learning grammar rules, vocabulary, and translating from their first language.

Learning and Communication Strategies

More than half of the students believed that it was important to speak with a perfect accent and to be correct. Nevertheless, they showed some tolerance for ambiguity as a good percentage agreed with the possibility to guess the meaning of unknown words. The majority of students indicated that they felt embarrassed when speaking English in front of other people.

Motivation and Expectations

Finally, almost 60% of the students seemed to be motivated to learn English in order to get a better job, but only a small portion seemed interested in getting to know English native speakers, showing low levels of integrative motivation.

Summary

Taken together, these results showed that within the same group, my students were going to approach the English class with very different beliefs and expectations. Some general trends did emerge, highlighting that language learning was about aptitude, practicing, being accurate (perfect accent and error-free sentences), and that complete fluency could be obtained in a matter of a couple of years with limited efforts. It is clear that these beliefs could be a recipe for disaster as they create expectations that cannot easily be met. For example, Italian students start learning English in primary school, and when they get to the fourth year of high school, they have usually been studying English for 11 years. Thus, they should have already understood that improvement in language learning is slow and not steady, but many did not seem to realize this. My students might therefore have come to class already disengaged or disillusioned with their learning process on the basis of some beliefs that created unachievable goals and outcomes that I have observed in my previous students' behaviors.

My Research-Informed Curriculum

During the first week of the semester, I showed pie charts and histograms of the class's answers to each item of the questionnaire. I challenged students'

beliefs with some SLA research findings and asked for reasons and explanations for their beliefs. In particular, I targeted those beliefs that might serve
as excuses for learners' disengagement in class activities, such as not having
a gift for languages, or the effortless process of learning abroad compared to
the efforts required by in-class learning. I presented to the students the theory
of individual differences and how aptitude is not the ultimate magic wand
for language learning. I also showed snapshots of case studies of people liv-
ing and studying abroad and their struggle to access the community of speakers. I wanted my students to understand that even for those studying abroad,
language learning requires active engagement in seeking and seizing learning
opportunities. Finally, I introduced some basic notions of the role of input,
output, interaction, and corrective feedback, to discuss the role of the teacher
and learners in the classroom. This was the beginning of a year-long conversation about their language learning process by which I wanted to help them
understand where they were in the process and make them aware of what
steps they should take next.

As my main goal for my students was to increase their awareness about the
learning process so that they could take responsibility, I made changes in the
curriculum accordingly. I took up Horwitz's suggestion to (1) "include discussions about the nature of language learning as regular part of [my] instruction"
and to (2) "show students by example and instructional practice the holistic
nature of language learning" (Horwitz, 1988, p. 291).

Discussions about the language learning process took place periodically,
in particular during feedback sessions before returning students' written and
oral tests. I called the session "common mistakes you made" to convey the idea
that mistakes are actually common to all learners at a certain developmental
level and that they are the stepping-stones to the next level. During the sessions, I presented anonymous samples of erroneous sentences extracted from
the tests and asked students in groups to find and correct the mistakes. Error
correction became a challenging competition and lost its shaming aspect.
Mistakes became a way to reflect on the language as a system and a means
of communication as students' mistakes showed them that speaking a different language does not mean translating words or sentences, but conveying
meaning.

To counteract the belief that "learning a language is ultimately a matter of
learning grammar rules," I deliberately left out explicit grammar lessons from
the curriculum for one semester. Although I taught grammar incidentally, the
class activities focused on developing the students' ability to summarize and
report the content of texts or videos, providing a critical opinion and pros and
cons of the topical issue. Students were evaluated accordingly, with written

tests that included open-ended questions on a known issue. Another type of test required students to read a new text on a known issue and report the main ideas with their own words.

A crucial change in the curriculum was the substitution of oral tests with (video) recorded oral presentations. The Italian high school system requires that at the end of the school year students' final grade in English is the result of three written tests and at least two oral tests. Oral tests are question-and-answer sessions between the teacher and one or two students at a time. These tests generally take place during class time. They are usually dreaded by shy and anxious students who do not feel comfortable speaking English in front of the teacher or their classmates. Recorded oral tests may thus contribute to decrease language anxiety and increase learners' awareness and self-efficacy. I instructed the students to prepare a script based on a given outline and to practice the presentation before recording it. I explicitly told them to listen to their recording, decide if they could improve it, and send me their best performance. Students were also given the evaluation rubric so that they could self-evaluate their delivery, accuracy, fluency, vocabulary, and pronunciation before sending the recording. Finally, after the class feedback session described above, each student received an individual feedback sheet with comments for each item in the rubric and tips on how to improve.

Reflections on the Experience

The changes I made in the curriculum were meant to raise students' awareness about what they were learning, how they were learning it, and how they could improve. One of the main school objectives cutting across all the subjects is for learners to develop an efficient method of work, a sense of responsibility, and the ability to reflect on what they can do. Being aware of how the learning process works and of one's own strengths and weaknesses is the only way to become self-directed learners.

Discussions about language learning beliefs and the collective correction of errors were explicit ways to talk about what learning a language means and its inevitable stages and setbacks. The communicative approach with an incidental focus on grammar was an attempt to provide a more holistic approach to language learning, bridging the gap between learning English at school and speaking it in a realistic setting. Finally, the recorded oral tests had the twofold goal of making students practice and repeat, and making them listen, self-evaluate, and improve their performance. This allowed them to develop both fluency and awareness.

However, students were not familiar with recording and listening to themselves in English, and they were reluctant to do so at the beginning. They also raised concerns about reading from the script. My advice was to keep the script as an outline and to highlight key words. I did not want them to learn the script by heart, but, like news presenters, they could refer to the script so that they did not lose the thread. After sending me the first assignment, a student commented that it took him two hours to prepare a 1-minute-and-40-second recording. Even though this was probably not what every student did, the activity achieved the goal of making students rehearse and practice speaking in English. The parents reported being surprised by hearing their children speaking English in their rooms. As the school year went on, students started to like this new kind of oral test because they were more in control of their performance, they could get better grades, and were less afraid of their classmates' judgment. At the end of the school year, when they were given the option to do the oral test in class or to record it, only two students opted for the class presentation.

Students' Beliefs and Language Learning Awareness at the End of the School Year

During the final week of school, I asked my students to fill in a questionnaire, which included the BALLI and some open-ended questions about the curriculum and their language awareness. As only 12 students filled it in, it is not possible to draw conclusions regarding the whole class's beliefs and awareness. Nonetheless, the students' answers are an interesting form of evaluation that can be helpful in understanding the students' perception of the activities and to improve the curriculum further.

As far as the BALLI is concerned, the percentage of agreement with the items at the beginning of the school year did not differ much from the results at the end of the school year. A small change could be observed though, as the 12 students tended to agree that they would ultimately learn English well, and to disagree that they should be overly concerned about accuracy and correctness. An interpretation of this trend could be that students were gaining more confidence in their ability to learn and gain awareness that language learning is a trial-and-error process.

Feedback on the curriculum suggests that 11 students felt their English improved during the school year, while one student indicated that it became worse. When asked how their English improved, four students indicated their understanding of spoken English improved, while five students wrote they improved their ability to speak and express themselves in English. One student reported feeling more confident. When asked what they were able to do now compared to the previous year, the general response was that they were able to express themselves more fluently. In particular, a student stated that he could "think and build sentences in English from scratch," showing that he probably understood how to communicate in English as opposed to translate from Italian. Finally, I asked students to indicate what their strengths and weaknesses were. Five students felt speaking English was their weakness, while the others stated that they were weak in grammar and syntax. Almost all the students indicated that comprehension was their strength. Two students said that they did not know or did not have any strength.

Students' final questionnaire showed that the system of beliefs that learners had formed over the years was hard to modify. The traditional education system they had been brought up with, based on a product-oriented learning approach, contributed to fossilize students' beliefs about how good or bad language learners they were, leaving little room for possible changes in the status quo. Not everybody was able to see their progress and accept their shortcomings as necessary part of the learning process. As Horwitz warned, "information in and of itself is probably not sufficient to counteract implicit messages students receive from the instructional practices they experience" (Horwitz, 1988, p. 292). Although I made changes in the curriculum, a school year did not seem enough to make all students experience they were in charge of their language learning as a process. Arguably, my aim was not for students to change their beliefs but to become more aware of their learning process. Although some students could not articulate their strengths or abilities they developed over the course of the school year, the majority could. Whether their judgment was correct might be debated, but they did reflect on their path, which would gradually lead them to a better understanding of what they needed to improve and how to go about it.

Conclusion

The teaching practices I described in this chapter were informed by Horwitz's research findings, which reflected what I had observed and experienced in my classes. Following SLA research findings on learner anxiety and beliefs, this year I included in my teaching practices a reflection on how each activity contributed to the students' learning process, so that learners could get actively involved in it. I believe learning awareness is at the core of language learning, as learners' strategies, sustained motivation, success and satisfaction with language learning depend on it. Research findings may sometimes seem unrelated or even irrelevant to teaching practices; however, I experienced that reading how researchers investigated some issues may suggest viable ways to interpret my own context.

In the early stages of my teaching career, I had often felt ineffective, as I had tried to tackle my students' problems in learning English by improving my teaching skills and materials. After engaging in SLA research during my PhD studies, I realized I could tackle my students' learning problems in a different way, namely by developing their awareness and autonomy. I conducted research work as therapy for my frustrations as a teacher, as it enabled me to see my context from a different point of view, and to expand my knowledge of SLA by means of direct access to resources and a better understanding of them.

Teachers may intuitively know what their students need, but changes in the curriculum and the modality of the change may be challenging. I believe that the local community of teachers within each school district is of paramount importance in identifying learners' needs and problems in their specific context. However, to elaborate strategies to change curriculum from within, teachers should be able to consult and refer to relevant educational research and resources, which should be made available and drawn to their attention. By creating a dialogue between theory and practice, micro and macro learning and teaching contexts, it is possible to make effective changes informed by theoretical and practical research findings. For teachers to access resources, relevant databases such as LLBA (Linguistics and Language Behavior Abstracts) should be made freely available.

I hope to continue pursuing the goal of developing learners' awareness and autonomy by improving my teaching practices. In particular, I think that peer evaluation could be a viable resource to increase learners' understanding of the foreign language as a means of communication and a system. Students could listen to each other's recordings and give feedback on what their peers should improve. This activity could help students learn how to give feedback and how the evaluation process works. Another useful development will be to investigate students' learning strategies, by means of questionnaires such as the strategies inventory for language learning (SILL) (Oxford, 1990). The results of the questionnaire could also be discussed in class and the strategies could be challenged and improved over the course of the school year.

In this chapter, I have described how I tried to debunk my students' false myths about how easy or difficult learning a language is. My goal was for the students to have achievable learning goals in accordance with their developmental stages and their efforts. My curriculum was informed by the principles I wanted to convey about language learning. Even though results of my new practices may not be immediately visible, making informed changes in the curriculum has been a challenging and exciting experience. It turned my school year into a real-life SLA experiment, as I brought my SLA knowledge into my classroom, trying to bridge the research-practice gap.

Note

1   In Italy, high school education is for five years. The first year in high school would be equivalent to 9th grade in the U.S.

References

Amuzie, G. L., & Winke, P. (2009). Changes in language learning beliefs as a result of study abroad. *System, 39*, 366–379.

Arnold, J. (1999). *Affect in language learning.* Cambridge: Cambridge University Press.

Bacon, S. M., & Finneman, M. D. (1990). A study of attitudes, motives and strategies of university foreign language students and their dispositions to authentic oral and written input. *Modern Language Journal, 74*(4), 459–473.

Bernat, E., & Gvozdenko, I. (2005). Beliefs about language learning: Current knowledge, pedagogical implications, and new research directions. *TESL-EJ, 9*(1), 1–20.

Cotterall, S. (1995). Readiness for autonomy: Investigating learner beliefs. *System, 23*(2), 195–205.

Council of Europe. (2001). *Common European framework of reference for languages: Learning, teaching, assessment.* Cambridge: Press Syndicate of the University of Cambridge.

Dörnyei, Z. (2005). *The psychology of the language learner. Individual differences in second language acquisition.* Mahwah, NJ: Lawrence Erlbaum Associates.

Flavell, J. H. (1987). Speculation about the nature and development of metacognition. In F. E. Weinert & R. H. Kluwe (Eds.), *Metacognition, motivation and understanding* (pp. 1–29). Hillsdale, NJ: Lawrence Erlbaum Associates.

Gazzetta Ufficiale, Presidential Decree 88 Art. (2010, March 15). Retrieved from http://www.indire.it/lucabas/lkmw_file/nuovi_tecnici/INDIC/_LINEE_GUIDA_TECNICI_.pdf

Gregersen, T., & MacIntyre, P. D. (2014). *Capitalizing on language learners' individuality: From premise to practice.* Tonawanda, NY: Multilingual Matters.

Horwitz, E. K. (1985). Using student beliefs about language learning and teaching in the foreign language methods course. *Foreign Language Annals, 18*(4), 333–340.

Horwitz, E. K. (1987). Surveying students' beliefs about language learning. In A. Wenden & J. Rubin (Eds.), *Learner strategies in language learning* (pp. 110–129). London: Prentice Hall.

Horwitz, E. K. (1988). The beliefs about language learning of beginning university foreign language students. *The Modern Language Journal, 72*(3), 283–294.

Hosenfeld, C. (1978). Learning about learning: Discovering our students' strategies. *Foreign Language Annals, 9,* 117–129.

Kalaja, P. (1995). Student beliefs (or metacognitive knowledge) about SLA reconsidered. *International Journal of Applied Linguistics, 5*(2), 191–204.

Kern, R. G. (1995). Students' and teachers' beliefs about language learning. *Foreign Language Annals, 28*(1), 71–92.

Kuntz, P. S. (1996). *Beliefs about language learning: The Horwitz model* (ERIC Document Reproduction Service, No. ED397649).

Miller, L., & Ginsberg, R. B. (1995). Folklinguistic theories of language learning. In B. F. Freed (Ed.), *Second language acquisition in a study abroad context* (pp. 293–315). Amsterdam: John Benjamins.

Mori, Y. (1999). Epistemological beliefs and language learning beliefs: What do language learners believe about their learning? *Language Learning, 49,* 377–415.

Naiman, N., Frohlich, M., Stern, H. H., & Todesco, A. (1978). *The good language learner.* Toronto: Ontario Institute for Studies in Education.

Nikitina, L., & Furuoka, F. (2006). Re-examining Horwitz's Beliefs About Language Learning Inventory (BALLI) in the Malaysian context. *Electronic Journal of Foreign Language Teaching, 3*(2), 209–219.

Omaggio, A. C. (1978, May 2–3). Successful language learners: What do we know about them? *ERIC/CLL News Bulletin.*

Oxford, R. L. (1990). *Language learning strategies: What every teacher should know.* Boston, MA: Heinle.

Park, G. (1995). *Language learning strategies and beliefs about language learning of university students learning English in Korea* (Unpublished doctoral dissertation). University of Texas, Austin, TX.

Riley, P. (1980). *Mud and stars: Personal constructs sensitization and learning* (ERIC Document Reproduction Service, No. ED20198).

Riley, P. (1994). Aspects of learner discourse: Why listening to learners is so important. In E. Esch (Ed.), *Self-access and the adult language learner* (pp. 7–18). London: Centre for Information on Language Teaching.

Riley, P. (1997). The guru and the conjurer: Aspects of counselling for self-access. In P. Benson & P. Voller (Eds.), *Autonomy and independence in language learning* (pp. 114–131). New York, NY: Longman.

Su, D. (1995). *A study of English learning strategies and styles of Chinese university students in relation to their cultural beliefs about learning English* (Unpublished doctoral dissertation). University of Georgia, Athens, GA.

Tanaka, K., & Ellis, R. (2003). Study-abroad, language proficiency, and learner beliefs about language learning. *JALT Journal, 25*(1), 63–83.

Tumposky, N. (1991). Student beliefs about language learning: A cross-cultural study. *Carleton Papers in Applied Language Studies, 8*, 50–65.

Wenden, A. (1987). How to be a successful language learner: Insights and prescriptions from L2 learners. In A. Wenden & J. Rubin (Eds.), *Learner strategies in language learning* (pp. 103–117). London: Prentice Hall.

Yang, N. D. (1992). *Second language learners' beliefs about language learning and their use of learning strategies: A study of college students of English in Taiwan* (Unpublished doctoral dissertation). The University of Texas, Austin, TX.

CHAPTER 9

Reflecting on Academic Service-Learning Research in a University Intensive English Program

Cynthia Macknish, Tiffany Johnson and Michael McLelland
Eastern Michigan University, USA

I hear, and I forget. I see, and I remember. I do, and I understand. I reflect, and I learn.

　　　　　—CHINESE PROVERB (adapted by Friesen, as cited in Tanya, 2011)

∴

Introduction

As teachers, we believe that our practice should be grounded in theory, which is applied meaningfully in our pedagogy. In light of this, and in our desire to align with our university's philosophy of encouraging academic service-learning (AS-L), we researched how others utilize AS-L in a way that would benefit English for Speakers of Other Languages (ESOL) students. This topic is particularly meaningful to us because in the current climate of less-than-favorable discourse about immigrants in the United States, we are interested in exploring how international students can engage with and make contributions to the local community.

In our literature search we found an article by Bippus and Eslami (2013) published in *TESOL Journal*. Their study inspired us to explore how engaging ESOL students in AS-L and reflecting on it might benefit their learning. Bippus and Eslami concluded that participating in service-learning benefited ESOL students and positively impacted their ability to communicate outside the classroom by making them more active learners, helping build their self-confidence, and instilling an appreciation of learning in an authentic and participatory context. Bippus and Eslami valued student perceptions, and since we were also motivated to give students a voice, we were enthusiastic about applying their research to our course to discover how the experience would affect our students.

© KONINKLIJKE BRILL NV, LEIDEN, 2019 | DOI:10.1163/9789004392472_010

Toward that end, this chapter demonstrates how we attempted to bridge the research-practice gap by utilizing a published study to inform an AS-L project in a university-level ESOL speaking and listening course. We consider existing literature, describe how we utilized the Bippus and Eslami study, and reflect on the results, successes, and challenges. We conclude by offering advice to future ESOL practitioners who desire to apply research to their classroom practice.

Definition and Significance of Academic Service-Learning

Our university encourages AS-L, which is a "teaching and learning strategy integrating meaningful community engagement with instruction and reflection to enrich the learning experience, teach civic responsibility, and strengthen communities" (*Learn and Serve America* [now closed] and the National Service Learning Clearinghouse, as cited in Ryan, 2012, p. 4). AS-L, therefore, goes beyond community service by combining academic learning and service-learning with the goal of creating a transformative experience for all participants.

While Bippus and Eslami (2013) do not explicitly define service-learning in their paper, in her dissertation, Bippus (2011) explains it as "the merging of academic work with real-life community service activities that encourages students to reflect and think critically about their experiences" (p. 1). Thus, she describes the importance of reciprocity and the development of greater civic responsibility. As such, Bippus and Eslami's perspective seems to align with our understanding of AS-L.

Of note is that reflection is highlighted in both the cited AS-L definition and Bippus's (2011) definition of service-learning. Recognizing the benefit of reflection with regard to service-learning, teachers emphasize students' metacognitive processing to solidify their learning (Grassi, Hanley, & Liston, 2004; Heuser, 1999). While there are no accepted metrics for measuring reflection, it can be a powerful tool for students to understand their own learning process, and indeed it may not be the actual *project* but the *reflection* activities afterward that lead to learning (Jacoby, as cited in Cho & Gulley, 2016).

Academic Service-Learning and Second Language Learning

According to Minor (2001), service-learning is well-suited to the second-language classroom because it provides a meaningful learning environment for students, and promotes the values of compassion and kindness as well as the development of humane values. In addition, contributing to the well-being of others has the potential to help students develop a sense of civic responsibility, which can be made evident through students' reflections on their experience. While AS-L as an ESOL learning methodology has not been extensively researched, many of the studies available have resulted in a further understanding of personal growth, empathy, awareness-raising, acceptance, community engagement, and volunteerism (Carr, 2006; Grassi, 2004; Kassabgy, 2013). Askildson (2013) notes that learning outcomes offer a "preliminary yet compelling endorsement for the potential language gains that can be facilitated by an intensive curriculum of formal English language coursework combined with a co-curricular service-learning component" (p. 429). Moreover, the service-learning experience for students and community members reaches its potential when there is reciprocity in their relationship, where students participate in community-based activities that provide them with authentic and meaningful experiences while simultaneously contributing to local residents' quality of life (Smagorinsky & Kinloch, as cited in Cho & Gulley, 2016).

The literature becomes more anecdotal when attempting to quantitatively match AS-L to improvements in ESOL students' speaking and listening proficiency. In one study, success was implied from the students' perspective: "They used reading, listening, speaking, and writing skills in an authentic setting and understood how their language had improved" (Cummings, 2009). The main method for documenting these improvements was through the students' own thoughts on their experience. One conclusion emerging from the literature reviewed is that the relationship between language learning and service-learning needs further study. The Bippus and Eslami study provides further evidence of the benefits of AS-L in an ESOL course by focusing on students' perspectives.

Synopsis of the Bippus and Eslami Study

The purpose of the Bippus and Eslami (2013) study was to explore ESOL students' participation in and perspectives on the AS-L project they conducted. Specifically, they focused on students' oral communication skills and attitudes toward community engagement. They wanted to address a common desire among the more advanced ESOL students, namely that "they want to practice speaking English with native speakers in order to become involved in their communities" (p. 587). Because it can be challenging for teachers to create and maintain authentic learning environments in an academic classroom, Bippus and Eslami implemented a service-learning project to meet this need. The project involved a group of six adult intermediate-advanced ESOL students from five countries enrolled in a 16-week service-learning course at their community college.

Students participated in one of two service-learning projects. One involved weekly interviews with a resident of a retirement community, culminating in a written biography of the resident. As the students' teacher, Bippus scaffolded the interactions between the students and the senior partners by providing resources and discussing interview topics and questions in class. The other project was performing the weekly storytime with pre-schoolers at a local library. For both projects, students kept a journal, wrote reflection papers, and participated in semi-structured interviews about the experience.

Although explicit research questions were not presented in the paper, we delved further into the literature and located Bippus' (2011) dissertation upon which the 2013 paper was based. It listed the research questions as:

1.   What are the perceived benefits of participating in a service-learning course for ESOL students?
2.   In particular, how has participating in a service-learning course impacted the ESOL students' ability to communicate outside the classroom?
3.   What are the perceived disadvantages of participating in a service-learning course for ESOL students?
4.   What common characteristics, if any, are evident in the students who willingly participate in a service-learning program?

To answer these questions, data were collected from students' journals, reflection papers and final projects, as well as observational field notes and interviews. Data were analyzed through coding. Common themes were identified, and results were triangulated.

As a teacher-researcher, Bippus was aware of potential ethical issues of being the students' teacher and was careful to follow proper Institutional Review Board (IRB) protocols. She contended that knowledge of the students may have been a benefit because they had developed a level of trust with her. She believes this enabled them to articulate their honest and open feelings more so than with an unknown researcher. In addition, she was able to observe their growth over a period of time.

The results of Bippus and Eslami's study were consistent in one regard—all students reported that they had gained confidence when speaking English in the outside community, which the authors noted was perhaps the most rewarding aspect to observe. The students stated that they became active participants and were more motivated to take ownership of their own learning due to the "dynamic" and "realistic" nature of service-learning. They concluded that, unlike other ESOL courses, the AS-L course would not allow them to be passive or "hide in the back row." This was impactful for the entire class, as they had all previously described themselves as being shy, timid, or nervous when speaking English. One student reported that due to the spontaneous nature of the informal conversations, she found that doing the homework for class and preparing for the partner conversations was imperative, which was not the case in her other courses.

While students' perspectives were overwhelmingly positive, they did experience some struggles. Most of them claimed they felt self-conscious when compelled to speak English, and half said they had difficulty understanding their senior partners. One student resolved these issues by recording her partner's words and replaying the audio afterward to gain better understanding. She also began passing her written questions to her partner to avoid confusion. Another student said the challenges lessened as his listening skills increased. Other students reported difficulties that were unrelated to the course per se, such as travel time to get to the project sites.

Our Context

Our teaching context is a university Intensive English Program (IEP) in the Midwest USA. Students in the program are placed into five levels: beginning, intermediate, advanced, academic, and graduate. The IEP offers a variety of courses, including: writing, listening/speaking, reading, vocabulary, grammar, and study skills. Our university encourages AS-L and has an office on campus dedicated to assisting instructors in incorporating AS-L into their classes. In addition, the IEP program administrator supports the teaching faculty's efforts to conduct research and engage in research-informed pedagogy with the belief that it can improve our practice. Hence, we were encouraged to embark on this project. We had a team of three researchers: an ESOL/TESOL professor and an MA TESOL practicum student who were directly involved in teaching and research, and a graduate assistant (GA) in TESOL who helped with the literature review, transcription work, and data analysis.

At the time of this research, we were teaching a 15-week listening and speaking course for ESOL students. The class met for 75 minutes twice per week. Unlike the dedicated service-learning course in Bippus and Eslami (2013), ours was a dedicated language course. Due to our university's commitment to AS-L, we wanted to incorporate a project focused on achieving the speaking and listening course outcomes within a community engagement context. Seven adult students were enrolled in the course, which is comparable to the six participants in the Bippus and Eslami study. Similarly, our students had an intermediate-advanced language proficiency, and represented five countries. The syllabus included the following speaking and listening outcomes in which students would be able to:

– *use different elicitation devices and registers in conversation with others*
– *participate appropriately in small group discussions on academic topics*

- *deliver speeches of specified rhetorical types*
- *answer questions and argue own position in response to a prepared speech*
- *raise questions in response to the formal presentation of another*
- *cite source material appropriately when delivering a prepared speech*
- grasp the main idea and some details of authentic media broadcasts
- make accurate notes showing main and subordinate points from a university-level lecture on a topic containing some unfamiliar material
- *demonstrate patterned control of suprasegmental articulation in spontaneous speech*
- *produce speech that is accented but intelligible to most native speakers with minimum repetition*
- *produce longer discourse on academic topics*

Traditionally these outcomes are achieved through various assignments including formal presentations, group discussions, classroom tasks, and exams. After deciding to incorporate the Bippus and Eslami research into our curriculum, we looked for ways to achieve these and further outcomes through AS-L.

Implementing the Study in Our Curriculum

In our approach to linking the research and practice, it was important to start by aligning the course outcomes and the research purpose. Nine of our 11 course outcomes (italicized in the previous section) could be applied to the AS-L project. To reinforce AS-L principles, we added the following outcomes in which students would be able to:
- use the speaking and listening skills learned in the course to initiate and engage in conversation with members of the community
- exchange culture and knowledge with senior citizens
- demonstrate a disposition that seeks similarities and differences, and strengths in other people
- reflect critically on the learning that occurs through this experience
- create and present a narrated slideshow of the experience

The similarities between the Bippus and Eslami (2013) research and our context made it possible for us to fairly closely parallel their research design in terms of method and data collection. Due to our focus on speaking and listening, we modified the type of engagement and final project to reflect this. Our project covered seven weeks, rather than 15; consequently we could only duplicate one of the projects in the Bippus and Eslami study, namely visiting a retirement community once a week. In compliance with research ethics, we first sought and gained IRB approval.

In preparation for the project, we devoted some class time to building an understanding of the AS-L purpose and outcomes. We also spent class time scaffolding the students' interactions with the senior residents by working on presentations, brainstorming questions, developing conversation skills, and role-playing. Prior to meeting the seniors, we took the students to the retirement residence to meet with the community partners and build an understanding of each other's roles, orient the students to the environment, and give them an opportunity to ask questions.

In the first of the two weekly classes, students visited the retirement community, where they delivered a ten-minute prepared speech about their culture and then engaged in cultural exchange with senior residents. Since more seniors participated in our project than in the Bippus and Eslami study, we conducted informal group conversations and discussions, rather than interviews. In the second class each week, we discussed the experience together before students wrote their weekly reflections. Bippus and Eslami did not provide details of the journal or reflection prompts in their paper, so we developed prompts relevant to our context. Rather than written biographies, our final project involved the creation of an individual two-minute oral reflection and a three-minute narrated slideshow about the AS-L experience. For the narrated slideshow, students could work individually or in pairs. Some chose to focus on a senior citizen they connected with, while others chose to reflect on their experience as a whole. They all incorporated photos and music with their narration. At the end of the course two of the researchers conducted individual, semi-structured interviews with the students to gain more insight about their experience. We utilized the questions provided in Bippus' (2011) dissertation with some modifications based on our specific context. Each interview lasted half an hour, was audio recorded, and transcribed.

Similar to the Bippus and Eslami study, we collected data from student journals, reflection papers, final projects, researcher observations, and interviews. Then we coded and analyzed the data in order to identify emergent themes. Successes and challenges that emerge from the findings will inform future iterations of the course.

Successes

This experience took us one step forward in bridging the research-practice gap. Working with a published study gave us confidence to embark on research that would benefit our students and align with our university's philosophy of encouraging community engagement. In addition, the Bippus and Eslami

(2013) study provided a research design to follow and, despite some minor differences in context, we successfully duplicated elements of their study. Importantly, our findings confirm those of the original study, which helps build and strengthen the literature in the field, and motivate us to continue working on similar projects in the future.

Responses to the Initial Briefing and Orientation

In a briefing, we explained the study and invited our students to participate. Like Bippus, as teacher-researcher, our familiarity with the students added a level of trust so students were quite forthcoming in sharing their opinions and anxieties about the experience. We made it clear that their participation—or lack thereof—would not affect their grades in any way. All seven of our students appeared to be interested in the research because at the briefing they asked questions, willingly signed the consent forms, and even requested that we share our findings with them. At the orientation visit to the seniors' residence before the project began, the students responded to the community partners enthusiastically and asked many questions about the seniors and their lifestyles.

Participation in the AS-L Project

After admitting some initial apprehension about meeting native English speakers outside the comfort of the classroom, our students actively participated and engaged with a group of senior Americans with whom they would not normally have an opportunity to meet. As the project progressed, they showed continued enthusiasm for engaging with the seniors. In debriefings and journals, students shared that they enjoyed getting to know the seniors and being able to practice their speaking and listening skills with them. The quote below is representative of all students' attitudes:

> I had an opportunity to have interesting, fun and joyful conversations with seniors ... I want to thank them for my speaking and listening skills improvement, because they give me ability to practice and improve those skills every week, and this is not all what I have improved. I also improved how to be patient while having conversations with others and how to make myself understood. I want to mention that from now on I will not be afraid to present or to start conversation with others, because I know after practicing with seniors it is easy to be confident no matter what, and also it is easy to make myself comfortable with unknown people. (GN, journal entry 4)

It was not just the AS-L project students were engaged in, but also the research study itself in terms of producing data to be analyzed. Students actively participated in the de-briefings and used these discussions to inform their written and oral reflections. Many students commented that they appreciated the way we took time in class to brainstorm conversation prompts, explicitly teach relevant linguistic expressions, and role-play specific situations. We observed that this helped lower their affective filter when they met with the seniors. Students' affective filter refers to Krashen's (1985) claim that language input (and subsequently acquisition) can be filtered or blocked by aspects of emotion (affect), such as anxiety, motivation, and self-confidence. They also enjoyed being able to choose the focus for their narrated slideshow and seemed very proud of their finished products. Whether it was engaging with native speakers outside the class or awareness that the data would be used for research, students seemed more invested in the AS-L project than in traditional coursework.

The most telling evidence of a positive response to the AS-L project emerged when a student voluntarily returned after the course had ended to visit one of the seniors he had befriended. This implies that the AS-L experience may have been transformative for this student because he took ownership of the interaction beyond the requirements of the course and developed a deeper friendship with someone he would not have otherwise met. The project thus created the opportunity for the learning to transcend from an academic experience to a more personal, life-affecting experience.

As in the original study, our findings reveal that all of our ESOL students had positive perceptions of the experience. They said they liked the authentic context of the retirement residence and, similar to Bippus and Eslami's (2013) findings, all of our students claimed that the experience helped them build more confidence in speaking outside the classroom. They also reported that they perceived an increase in their oral skills, despite occasional communication challenges. They did not identify any disadvantages of participating in the service-learning project.

Benefits to Using Research in Practice

Our study was able to fulfill the purpose of determining ESOL students' perceptions of the AS-L experience and, in our view, implementing this research enhanced the AS-L experience. In normal classroom practice we would not have conducted formal interviews to collect data; yet, this gave the students an opportunity to express their opinions and share with us what was important to them. The data provided reliable information that compelled us to reflect more deeply on the students' perceptions. For example, had we not conducted the interviews, we may not have learned that one of the students returned to the retirement community on his own time to visit with a senior resident.

The students' interview responses also provided feedback that we will use to improve our course in future semesters.

This project enabled us to transform research knowledge into practical, pedagogical knowledge (Cain, 2015). First, the positive results of the Bippus and Eslami (2013) study aroused our curiosity about how research could impact our teaching. The similarities in our contexts inspired us to explore AS-L in our course, which we may not have done otherwise. Any apprehensions we may have had about implementing the study—such as increased workload, logistical challenges, risk of unsatisfactory outcomes—were overcome by the willingness of our students to participate in the research. Admittedly, seeking approval for compliance with research ethics could be arduous, but it reminded us as teachers, not to take our students' wellbeing and participation for granted. We depended on our students for their insight in the form of reflections, which were simply a source of data initially. However, the increased frequency of reflections required for our study had a positive impact on our classroom. Reflecting on the authentic language experience led to meaningful in-class discussions which were much more relevant than those based on contrived topics in our speaking textbook. Our findings and the success of our project now inform discussions about student learning, specifically the importance of authentic language experiences. They also give us a syllabus framework for implementing and improving future AS-L projects. Though the sample size in both studies was very small, we are encouraged that this research has the potential to influence teacher beliefs about teaching and learning and contribute to the literature in the area of AS-L in ESOL courses. Finally, using this research knowledge motivates us to explore other published research that can inform our pedagogy in similar ways. For example, beyond revealing the students' perspectives of the AS-L experience, we are now interested in exploring further benefits of AS-L in terms of language development.

Challenges

Time Constraints
As with any research, there were challenges. Perhaps our biggest challenge was dealing with time constraints. After finding a relevant study and determining how to apply it in our practice, we had to apply for IRB approval and work around some required teaching to meet the expectations of the teaching practicum. These factors delayed the start of our project and limited the amount of time we could devote to preparing our students for AS-L. This may

be one reason why our students had some difficulty defining and explaining AS-L at the end of the project and why their reflections were occasionally superficial.

Limited time may also have affected the ability of some students to achieve the goal of transformation. While one student took the initiative to revisit one of the senior citizens, none of the students indicated that they had definite plans to participate in further forms of community engagement. Indeed, Bippus and Eslami (2013) criticized research on service-learning experiences of short duration. Nevertheless, we believe that seven weeks—though not ideal—was enough time for useful data to be collected.

Duplicating the Research Design

Some challenges involved aligning the research design to our context, but they were not insurmountable. The Bippus and Eslami (2013) paper did not explicitly present the research questions, interview questions, or coding scheme—perhaps due to a limited word count. Bippus' doctoral dissertation (2011) on which the paper was based gave us some guidance in doing this. We did find a few of the original interview questions somewhat vague and this may have impacted results. For example, one interview question was: "How would you describe your personality when you are talking in your language? When you are talking in English?" With the lack of context, we thought this question had little meaning, so we decided not to use it.

A limitation with our study, and potentially any research done with ESOL students, was that language proficiency may have restricted the depth and precision of students' responses in interviews. In addition, a power differential between the research practitioners and the students may have impacted students' responses. We attempted to mitigate this by not grading the presentations or conversations with the seniors. We did grade the narrated slideshows, but students had time both in class and out of class to work on these, as well as use detailed feedback on their drafts from peers and teachers to guide them in making improvements before the final submission.

Related to this, another limitation is that self-reported data potentially lack credibility. That said, the purpose of the research was to identify students' perceptions, not verifiable facts. Here, being research practitioners worked to our advantage in that we were able to build strong rapport in teaching this class, and we felt we were able to put the students at ease during the interviews. Due to the forthcoming and seemingly honest responses we received in interviews, we believe that the self-reported data we collected was credible. For example, many of our participants willingly admitted that they could not fully explain what AS-L was. This suggests that we were not very effective in teaching the principles of AS-L. One student also admitted that she did not know if her engagement with the seniors helped them in any way: "So maybe I help them, maybe not. I don't know" (HZ, final interview). This latter example indicates that the goal of reciprocity in AS-L may not have been wholly realized.

In summary, we discovered that our students' perceptions of AS-L were positive in ways that matched the original study, particularly in building confidence in engaging with native speakers in the community. Importantly, these findings now motivate us to continue to implement AS-L projects in future ESOL classes and pursue further research.

Recommendations for Teachers

Despite the challenges we faced, we highly endorse applying research to classroom practice and facilitating an AS-L experience.

Duplicating Research

Applying research to classroom practice can be adapted and modified to fit different contexts. Where appropriate, research design aspects can be modified in terms of project duration, skill focus, and methods of data collection and analysis. One of the most important considerations when applying research to classroom practice is aligning the course outcomes. Teachers should carefully select a research project that successfully achieves outcomes without a significant amount of extra work for students.

A second major consideration is ensuring that there is sufficient time to conduct research. Before the study begins, time must be budgeted for securing research ethics approval, administering informed consent briefings, interviews, etc. During the study, teacher-researchers should devote time to ensuring that both the participants and researchers are reflecting at every step of the project. This is crucial for drawing out learning processes that might remain unstated in regular classroom interactions. One lesson we learned from our research experience is the importance of teaching students how to reflect in a meaningful way. It is not enough to simply provide reflection prompts. Teachers should take the time to model, evaluate weak and strong examples, and practice writing reflections with students. Reflection is also essential for AS-L.

Academic Service-Learning

In terms of AS-L, teachers should know that it is something that can be modified to fit different teaching contexts. Based on our experience we have three main recommendations for teachers seeking to implement AS-L in their ESOL courses. The first is to spend significant time defining, explaining, and reinforcing the concept of AS-L with students. It is important for students to understand both the academic and community service aspects of the project in order to see how it can benefit both their English skills and ability to contribute to the community. It is also essential to work with their community partners to make sure that everyone has similar goals and expectations.

The second recommendation for teachers is to ensure that students are prepared for success. We found it important to brief students on what to expect and brainstorm language that they may need. If possible, take students to the venue to meet the community partners and have a pre-project orientation. It is equally important to make time for regular debriefings after the community visits. This way, teachers can monitor progress, discuss issues, and clarify expectations for reflections and subsequent visits.

Finally, in terms of fostering a more transformational experience, we recommend that teachers maximize opportunities to remind students of their positive contributions, as well as emphasize the progress they are making in their learning. When the project is finished, teachers can encourage students to continue to engage with the community by making them aware of further service opportunities.

Conclusion

In this chapter, we have reflected on how our ESOL speaking and listening course was informed by Bippus and Eslami's (2013) study. By duplicating elements of this research in our practice, we could reflect on it in an informed way that, importantly, had relevance and meaning for our context. We can now add our own empirical data to the original published data, which provides meaningful support for future decisions about implementing AS-L projects in ESOL courses. Bridging the theory-practice gap by incorporating published research in our course in this way has helped strengthen our practice and contribute to the knowledge base of the field.

References

Askildson, L., Kelly, A., & Mick, C. (2013). Developing multiple literacies in academic English through service-learning and community engagement. *TESOL Journal*, *4*(3), 402–438.

Bippus, S. L. (2011). *Adult ESL students and service-learning: Voices, experiences, and perspectives*. Retrieved from http://ezproxy.emich.edu/login?url= https://search.proquest.com/docview/909001861?accountid=10650

Bippus, S. L., & Eslami, Z. R. (2013). Adult ESOL students and service-learning: Voices, experiences, and perspectives. *TESOL Journal, 4*(3), 587–597. doi:10.1002/tesj.89

Cain, T. (2015). Teachers engagement with published research: Addressing the knowledge problem. *The Curriculum Journal, 26*(3), 488–509. doi:10.1080/09585176.2015.1020820

Carr, N., Eyring, J., & Gallego, J. (2006). What is the value of service-learning for ESL teacher preparation? *CATESOL Journal, 18*(1), 66–80.

Cho, H., & Gulley, J. (2016). A catalyst for change: Service-learning for TESOL graduate students. *TESOL Journal, 8*(3), 1–23. doi:10.1002/tesj.289

Cummings, S. (2009). Purposeful language development through service learning. *Essential Teacher, 6*(3–4), 45–47.

Grassi, E., Hanley, D., & Liston, D. (2004). Service-learning: An innovative approach for second language learners. *Journal of Experiential Education, 27*(1), 87–110.

Kassabgy, N., & Salah El-Din, Y. (2013). Investigating the impacts of an experiential service-learning course. *TESOL Journal, 4*(3), 571–586.

Krashen, S. D. (1982). *Principles and practices in second language acquisition*. Oxford: Pergamon Press.

Minor, J. M. (2001). Using service-learning as part of an ESL program. *Internet TESL Journal, 7*(4). Retrieved from http://iteslj.org/Techniques/Minor-ServiceLearning.html

Ryan, M. (2012). *Service-learning after learn and serve America: How five states are moving forward*. Denver: Education Commission of the States. Retrieved from http://www.ecs.org/clearinghouse/01/02/87/10287.pdf

Tanya, P. (2011, October 5). *184 days of learning blog—day 24*. Retrieved from http://www.psdblogs.ca/184/2011/10/05/184-%E2%80%93-day-24-tanya-p-educator/

"I Saw Wonderfull Things in There": Reflection on an Art Museum Field Trip for High School English Language Learners

Donna M. Neary
Jefferson County Public Schools, USA

Introduction

"Art makes you smart" was the title of the relatively short article that described a massive study undertaken to establish evidence that art does make kids smarter. The article referenced a provocative study conducted by researchers, Greene, Kisida and Bowen, which had established a "causal relationship" between "arts education and a range of desirable educational outcomes" (Greene, 2013, p. 12). As the authors express, asserting that students exposed to art benefitted in the classroom was not new thinking. Educators and museum professionals had long believed in links between exposure to art and positive carry-over to student learning.

As a former museum professional, I share the belief that visiting museums and cultural sites holds enormous potential for students' language development and critical thinking skills. As a Social Studies and English as a Second Language (ESL) teacher in the largest school district in Kentucky, I understand that students learning English require multiple methods for engaging with the new language through subject content. After reading the study, I realized that it held the potential to justify, or at least support, the inclusion of field trips to art museums for the ESL students enrolled in my Social Studies courses. As a public historian, I was confident that students would make critical connections to culture and the past by being exposed to authentic artifacts and sites.

Overview of the Student Population and Neighborhood

I teach in a high school located in a neighborhood that serves as a settlement area for immigrants moving to Louisville, Kentucky. Known as Iroquois High School, it enrolls approximately 1350 students annually. The majority of

© KONINKLIJKE BRILL NV, LEIDEN, 2019 | DOI:10.1163/9789004392472_011

students and their families confront high poverty rates, and the school leads the state in the percentage of students receiving Free and Reduced Lunch at nearly 100 percent (Holbrook, 2016–2017).

Students attending the school face many challenges on a daily basis. Iroquois High School is home to the largest population of students requiring Exceptional Child Education (ECE) services in the district, the largest number of students with Functional Mental Disability, and a large population of English learners. Almost one-half of enrolled students are English Learners. Students speak approximately 40 distinct languages, have emigrated from at least 35 countries, and bring a range of educational experiences. ESL students and mainstream English-speaking students attending the school are identified as exhibiting gaps in their learning. The population of English learners at Iroquois has increased by more than 500% since 2012, and the ongoing issues for most students of poverty, lack of adult support outside of school, food insecurity, and truancy due to multiple factors are realities in this learning community. Of the English learners eligible to earn a high school diploma, only 58 percent completed the necessary credits to graduate in May 2017. Sixty percent of the eligible mainstream students at the high school graduated during the same period (Holbrook, 2017–2018).

The overall statistics of the neighborhood shows a transient population experiencing high poverty rates. The neighborhood is annually identified as having among the city's highest murder rates, and other crimes. Within the neighborhood is an entrenched category of residents who have lived there for decades, and who are financially secure and intend to remain, creating an aspect of stability in the area around the school. Restaurants, coffee shops, and markets catering to the immigrant populations thrive, and have become popular with patrons from across the city. Neighborhood amenities include a 739-acre public park within walking distance of the school, and The Speed Art Museum. Less than two miles from the high school, the museum's Education staff is focusing on outreach efforts to residents in the neighborhood, including students attending the high school and their families.

My students in the International Academy, a newcomer program providing sheltered instruction, study World History, Exploring Civics and Humanities. Newcomer students range in age from 14 to 21 years old. This disparity from traditional high school students is due to the fact that many students arrive at our school as older teens with few, or no transferrable high school credits. Students bring a range of educational experiences and exposure to formal education. Some students are enrolled in school only days after arriving in this country. All students' English language acquisition in reading, writing, listening and speaking is tested annually by standardized Access Testing based on the WIDA framework. Once used as the acronym for World-class Instructional Design and Assessment, that designation has been dropped and WIDA is now simply WIDA. Its primary goal is to advance "academic language development and academic achievement for children and youth who are culturally and linguistically diverse through high quality standards, assessments, research, and professional learning for educators" (WIDA, 2017, p. 2). Students' language abilities range on the WIDA performance definitions scale from Entering to Developing, and classes are often mixed with students who have varying levels of formal education (WIDA, 2016).

Lessons for my students follow Social Studies curriculum and focus on English language acquisition in the content, using strategies such as vocabulary development, comparing and contrasting, designing timelines, and conducting small group discussions. The number of high school credits earned by students identify each as being in the Ninth to Eleventh grades, and students of all grades and ages take courses together to earn needed credits. The academic year is divided into two semesters, and summer school may be offered based on available funding. I teach approximately 130 students each semester, divided between six class periods. Additionally, students reading, writing, speaking and listening skills range on the WIDA Can Do Descriptor scale from Entering and Emerging to Developing (WIDA, 2016).

Purpose

I set out to design instruction for my students that would integrate a field trip to an art museum as a central component of the semester. I was intrigued by the work of Greene et al. and saw their work as an attempt to provide results that I could use to justify art museum field trips for my students. It was clear that this work was potentially different and meaningful because the study evaluated the value of art within the educational context. By collecting and analyzing data, the authors formed assertions about the learning outcomes their study recorded for students exposed to art and art museums (Greene, 2014). The results of the impact of art education on students reported by Greene et al. was so powerful that I selected the study to guide my work with students.

The journal article provided discussions and details of the project, the methods used and the outcomes experienced by students (Greene, 2014). The article detailed the trend, supported by data, of school districts foregoing field trips to museums during the school year due to financial constraints on schools and students, and another to discount the field trip as superfluous to the student's education. The researchers found no other study that had sought to collect data to measure the value of field trips on students' learning. They questioned the decisions by some schools to forego field trips by asking, "If schools are de-emphasizing culturally enriching field trips, has anything been lost as a result? Surprisingly, we have relatively little rigorous evidence about how field trips affect students" (Greene, 2014, p. 80). This void became the focus of the research.

Greene et al.'s article appeared to support my plans to include a field trip to the Speed Art Museum for students in my Social Studies classes. The newly redesigned and reopened museum is located near our school adjacent to the University of Louisville. New educational programming at the museum offered field trips, and classroom visits by museum curators with "Art Detective" kits. Arrangements were made the first year of the program to bring "Art Detectives" to our classroom and to visit for a tour. The second year, as word spread in the district about the program, the calendar filled quickly for Art Detectives, and we relied on our field trip and online sources for our museum exposure.

Once my project began, travel bans were imposed on residents of seven countries in January 2017. My students expressed confusion, fear, and sadness about this identification of immigrants and refugees as dangerous. Students expressed their dismay that people feared them because of their faith or their country of origin. They asked, "Why my country?" Students expressed uncertainty about their new home, and wondered aloud why their new neighbors did not like them.

To address these questions and to support the students, I worked with the museum staff to explore two ideas for our field trip and accompanying classwork. The exploration of *being lost and found* and identifying *why each of us matters* were selected as themes for the art that would be created by students. As the project developed, American born students enrolled in Art classes were included in the project and worked with these themes, further emphasizing the universality of loss, and necessity for seeking our place in the world.

Discussion of the Related Literature

The Greene et al. (2014) study was undertaken at The Crystal Bridges Museum in Bentonville, Arkansas, opened to the public in 2011. The staff at this newly opened museum took the opportunity to collect data about museum field trips. The privately funded study collected data from approximately 11,000 students, many of whom had not previously visited an art museum. Crystal Bridges Museum—built and funded by Alice Walton, an heir to the Walmart retail fortune—had funds to offer free field trips to school children in the area.

There quickly arose a shortage of openings for teachers seeking access to tours and the demand far-exceeded the capacity of the museum. The museum staff called on the researchers to devise a fair and equitable way to choose which students were selected to visit the museum. The team designed a lottery system to achieve equity. In addition, the museum wanted to know if it was possible to identify tangible links to learning by students who visited on a field trip. The study that these researchers conducted was "the first large-scale randomized-control trial designed to measure what students learn from school tours of an art museum" (Greene, 2014, p. 80). This study provided empirical data, not just speculation or conjecture, about the value of students' exposure to art education and field trips.

The authors relied on a survey sent to students and teachers following their tours of the museum. The collected surveys were evaluated with a rubric and the team grouped the data into four categories of impact: critical thinking, historical empathy, tolerance, and interest in art museums. A significant finding indicated that students from rural areas and those attending high-poverty schools benefitted the most in their academic performance from their access to the museum. The data revealed that students who attended a field trip consistently outperformed peers who had not had the opportunity to visit. The results of the study showed that in critical thinking assignments following the field trip, students who had been to the museum were much more likely to participate in discussions about art and other topics (Greene, 2014).

The results of this study were so conclusive that I may have stopped there to construct my project. However, I examined additional research to compare the studies and the data collected by similar research projects. I was deliberate in my selection of studies, and chose to review the work of researchers cooperating and collaborating with classroom teachers. These authors, like Greene et al., included real-world application for me to follow with my students. I reviewed many articles but discarded more than I selected because of a disconnect I found between the researcher's approaches or perspectives, or their voice in the reports, and the work I am doing with students in the classroom. Importantly, I sought articles that included students who were English learners, where available, or addressed language acquisition in their studies.

Relatedly, Teacher Gayle Smith Padgett, working with English language learners, described her work developing a three-pronged approach to teaching strategies, including taking students on field trips. The field trips—not only to museums but a variety of locations in her community—served as the foundation for student work where they were exposed to content. She then used the material learned by students to support their language acquisition with writing assignments and other creative endeavors. She assessed progress with written work, a student portfolio and student conferences. Ultimately, Padgett's students showed progress in language acquisition by being exposed to real world experiences, and opportunities to use their academic language outside of the classroom (Padgett, 1994).

I also sought articles written by museum professionals, such as the one detailing how the Leigh Yawkey Woodson Art Museum in Wausau, Wisconsin actively worked to develop strong relationships with the large Hmong community in that city. The museum staff developed an exhibition to directly appeal to this immigrant community and actively invite them into the museum. School field trips were a large component of the programming and the museum hosted most children of Hmong descent enrolled in the school district. The tour was based on storytelling and required students to interpret a piece of art in the exhibition (Lang, 1997). The assessment of students' work showed that

> These novice viewers went far beyond the superficial scan, finding qualities in art that they had never been formally taught. As they shared their work, discussion was lively. All the students were exposed to points of view about the work. They became questioners, clarifiers, supporters, arguers, skeptics, and believers—in effect part of a thinking team. (Lang, 1997, p. 26)

Similarly, a field trip program at the Philadelphia Museum of Art was relevant to my study because it was designed for English learners. This program, funded by a foundation, was created to develop a curriculum unit in the arts based on the collections from the museum for area students identified as English learners. Museum professionals identified three goals for their program: to introduce students to museums and the collections, to teach students the art curriculum, and to embed language acquisition into their art experiences. An important component of their overall plan was to provide museum educators with strategies for teaching English learners. Students in this study took multiple trips to the museum and the museum staff required teacher collaboration over the course of the project to ensure the coordination of assignments before and after the field trip, carried out in the classrooms. The author points to evidence of the impact on students as shown in their recall of facts, the art they made, and the writing samples collected (Shoemaker, 1998).

Informative for its emphasis on English learners, the work by Berho and Defferding (2005) focused on art making in ESL classrooms. The authors found, "Using art in the L2 classroom presents opportunities for students to become acquainted with the target culture and appeals to different learning strengths not tapped by traditional grammar activities" (Berho & Defferding,

2005, p. 271). The authors cite their own experience working with English learners and classroom observations as evidence of the impacts of art making on students' language acquisition and academic performance.

Summary Statement

Review of these materials not only supported the assertion that including art education advanced students learning, but also offered a solid foundation for designing strategies for integrating art education into Social Studies courses for high school English learners. Importantly, the Greene et al. study's focus on the impact on students of high poverty was meaningful for the student population served by the high school where I teach.

The evidence offered for showing the value of field trips varied in the studies consulted. The financial resources available to Greene et al. afforded a large-scale study allowing the researchers to examine broad implications for the impacts on students of visits to art museums. Lang, Padgett, and Shoemaker all recorded positive outcomes for students who took part in the arts education programs they studied. These studies' evidence for success was based on teacher observations of students after exposure to the art education and field trips, as well as written reflections. Padgett's is the only study to connect the field trips to advances in students' language acquisition. In all the reports examined, authors attest to the value to the academic and empathic growth in students exposed to art education and field trips to museums, but the evidence offered to support the value of the field trip in students' academic achievement is inconclusive.

Design and Research Method

The goal for using the Greene et al. study was to support integrating art education into the course curriculum focusing on Deeper Learning. The practice of Deeper Learning is defined as:

> an umbrella term for the skills and knowledge that students must possess to succeed in 21st century jobs and civic life. At its heart is a set of competencies students must master in order to develop a keen understanding of academic content and apply their knowledge to problems in the classroom and on the job. (The William and Flora Hewlett Foundation, 2013, p. 1)

Determining the value of the field trip on students learning directly supports implementing a deeper learning framework in the classroom. This educational theory places students at the center of the instruction, and the teacher operates as their learning partner providing content, resource, and ongoing support. In this model, students are actively involved in their own learning. The teacher is no longer the lecturer at the front of the classroom, but performs in the role of a coach, guiding students to mastering the learning. Represented graphically by three interlocking circles, the overlapping circles place the student in the nexus where the three circles overlap. The three circles represent:

- Caring—the power to relate constructively to self and other
  - Perseverance
  - Compassion
  - Respect
- Thinking—the power to think critically, creatively, and productively
  - Innovation
  - Reflection
  - Problem-solving
- Communicating—the power to interpret, express, and influence
  - Negotiation
  - Voice
  - Collaboration (JCPS, 2016).

Deeper learning components directly correlate to the categories of growth identified by Greene et al. (2014) to evaluate student's critical thinking, empathy, tolerance, and future interest in museums. The Greene et al. data served as a guideline of what pieces of evidence may be meaningful to include and how I might prepare lessons in my classroom. A key difference between their study and my work in the classroom was the inclusion of semester-long art education lessons taught to students versus the single field trip offered to the students in their study. Evaluative rubrics were used to assess key assignments completed by the students including:

- A student-created work of art,
- an essay written to address an empathy prompt,
- an art critique of another student's work,
- a group presentation, and
- a thank-you letter written to museum staff following the field trip.

To meet the standards of learning required for the field trip, overall course standards were integrated into all field trip and art lessons. These included the following: the use of geographic tools, students investigating the interdependence of international activities, and describing movement and settlement patterns of people and the causes of those patterns. In the vein of Deeper Learning, the skills students would be evaluated on by the end of the semester were identified and linked to field trip and art lesson designs. For example, skills included students being able to describe in detail, use new vocabulary, write complete sentences, collaborate in groups, including choosing a leader and agreeing on procedures. Students were expected to know how to compare and contrast using graphic organizers such as Venn diagrams and other visual models to map out meanings.

An important aspect of Social Studies for students is the necessity to recognize and identify divergent perspectives. This was a key connector to the art lessons and field trip to the museum. Students were continuously encouraged to think critically and to evaluate and analyze facts as active participants in their learning. During the semester, lessons were designed to push students to choose a position, and then argue to support that position, first in written form and then in presentations to a small group. This skill development culminated in each student selecting and critiquing the art work of a classmate, providing their opinions about the work, its execution and how the piece made them feel. Critical to organizing historical facts and events, students needed to be able to create timelines, and understand graphs, charts and other tools for organizing data. These skills were integrated into the art content, so students were able to see real world applications of the skills they were learning in their respective Social Studies class.

Analysis and Reflection

Students were informed at the beginning of the semester that we would be visiting the art museum, and that many of their lessons would prepare them for the field trip. Most students were excited when they learned they would tour the museum. We began by discussing who in the classes had visited a museum before, in the United States or in other countries? Very few students indicated they had been to a museum; so, it was critical for students to understand the meaning and purpose of museums in general. Time was also devoted to setting parameters for acceptable behavior and museum etiquette, such as not touching works of art, no running in the museum or speaking in loud voices, and no food or drink in the galleries.

In order to activate the student's prior knowledge, small groups of students discussed the question, "Why do cultures need or want to collect their art and artifacts?" Students then shared examples about their own cultures, and the things they valued that may be preserved. After group discussions ended, and museum definitions were established, many students realized they had visited a museum or other cultural sites in their own countries or in the United States. Importantly, many students detailed their experiences of seeing valuable or important artifacts on display.

In order to create a context for students, I asked them to view and evaluate works of art recognizable around the world. Several lessons in the classroom incorporated images of works of art housed in museums primarily in the United States. Students viewed online collections of the Museum of Modern Art (MOMA), the Chicago Art Institute, and the Speed Art Museum—the location of the field trip. Classroom discussions focused on questions about whose culture was being portrayed in the artwork, and who the people in the paintings were. Students commented on how the painting looked, and their colors and techniques. They also discussed how they felt about specific works of art, and if they liked, or disliked them, and why.

Students' observation skills appeared to increase as they became comfortable and gained the vocabulary to participate in discussions. Initially as students viewed slides of famous works of art the words they chose to describe the works focused on color or shapes. The continued practice of examining images of famous art began to illicit responses that moved past description and into feelings and emotions. For Starry Night by Vincent Van Gogh, words selected by students were lonely, village, storm, darkness, and beautiful. Students described the painting as "so beautiful it inspires me" and "I like the picture but it looks a little scary" (Student writing prompt). For Monet's Water Lilies, one student wrote, "This picture is beautiful and makes me to miss my country because in my country have a lot of water lilies" (Student writing prompt). Students speculated on the motives of the painters and their emotions in their responses. When viewing the painting known as Whistler's Mother, one student said, "Maybe the painter missed his mother so he draw a picture of her" (Student writing prompt). Another student commenting on the same painting speculated that, "she is a Muslim woman" (Student writing prompt). A student responding to Cezanne's Still Life with a Basket said, "I think in that village they have many fruits and vegetables. And it looks like a celebration of thanks giving" (Student writing prompt).

Throughout the semester students were supported in developing language skills to become active participants in the student-led discussions. They responded to the question: "what do you need to be an active participant in your culture?" This question prompted dynamic discussions in the small groups around the room. Connecting to the familiar allowed students to think about ways to be active in discussions, and to transition to discussions about art, and Social Studies topics. They agreed that to be active participants they needed to be able to recount things that happened, explain events, argue their positions, and discuss their differences. These realizations by students directly supported their ongoing development of the Deeper Learning framework.

Beginning the discussions of famous works of art by talking about students' cultures created a connection to the academic language necessary for critiquing others' work. Efforts were made to ensure students who spoke different languages were grouped together to ensure that they spoke English. Students who expressed discomfort at offering criticism learned the language to express their position while not offending anyone. Some students expressed the desire not to offend others or were concerned about hurting someone's feelings with their comments. Classroom discussions supported and encouraged empathy, with these discussions allowing students to express their understanding and acceptance of their own work and that of their classmates.

Each student created a drawing or painting as part of the field trip-related assignments. Students' skill at art or their abilities as an artist were not assessed. The rubric evaluated the creation of a piece of art based on the themes "why I matter," or "lost and found." An unintended outcome of creating art and exposure to art education and the field trip was the creation of a safe space for some students to work out events of the past that may have caused trauma. One student whose family fled a war-torn country created a graphic collage of war and death. A student from an agricultural background drew a peaceful field filled with crops ready for harvest. Many students chose to place their countries' flags into their artwork.

Each student was assigned an essay to be written around the themes of "why I matter" or "lost and found." The Museum staff chose these themes to allow these newly arrived immigrants to express their own value to the world, including their families, school and the larger community in which they live. The theme of lost and found focused students' writings and works of art on what students had lost in their lives as refugees and immigrants, and what had been found in their new homes. These themes were designed broadly enough to allow students room for their own interpretation of the themes. An important aspect of the partnership with the museum was allowing students an authentic voice in their writing and art making. Students were assigned themes depending on which class period they attended.

Many of the student essays referenced pain, sorrow and hope. Prior to the field trip students shared their essays with one another. The essays produced by students revealed raw emotion and evoked honesty about how they felt about themselves, the situations they now found themselves in, and in the lives they left behind. Essays revealed students' deepest feelings, including, "I was so crying fir many hours in one day. I was so sad because I left my family and my school and my friends ... I found someone speak same my language in my new school ... now I feel amazing because I have real friends" (Student essay). Another student who wrote about why she matters said, "my goal is to success because I need to see my family forget about those adversity time in the past and have an amazing moment in the future" (Student essay). Providing students with opportunities for authentic expression of their voice is a critical factor of Deeper learning. Essays were compiled into a binder and displayed at the museum. Students were given the option to withhold their piece from public access.

In letters written to the museum staff following the field trip, students expressed gratitude at the welcome they had received. One student wrote, "We really enjoyed it, it was a safe place" (Student letter). Another student who is an artist, thanked all the teachers and the bus driver for making the field trip possible. She wrote, "Thank you so much to the Speed Art Museum that welcomed all of us inside itself" (Student letter). One student indicated just how isolated some students can be in their lives outside of school by writing, "I happy to go there because I at home, I don't go anywhere just stay home to clean and I thank you so much ... and I hope I we will go there again" (Student letter). Another student said, the students "were invited there to watch or look for some pictures from all over the world ... It makes you wonder and wanted to learn more about those things." One student thanked the staff for the opportunity to visit and said, "Thanks to you we enjoyed a beautiful educational visit" (Student letter). Another student expressed an immediate reaction to visiting again, and said she would, "plan to return maybe next week on Sunday because I am curious to know many things than what I saw" (Student letter). This comment, and similar ones in other letters indicated that students understood that they could visit the museum for free on Sundays, a message communicated to students throughout the semester and the day of the field trip. Other students commented directly on the museum collections, as one student wrote, "the museum was having a beatiful picture that changed my feelings" (Student letter). Another commented on the breadth of what he saw, "I wish to go there again because it's amazing they are from famous art they come from African." Another student moved by his visit wrote, "Thanks everyone at the Speed Art Museum for allowing us to come there. I saw wonderfull [sic] things in there. I appreciate it. May we meet again" (Student letter).

Conclusion and Implications

In retrospect, I am not sure that I clearly communicated the connectivity of the work students would complete in art across their Social Studies content.

It became evident that some students regarded the class periods in which we did art education lessons as unrelated to our coursework. Only at the completion of the semester and a review and overview of all the work the students had accomplished did most students understand the overarching theme and how their work was related to this bigger theme. In the future, I will integrate the art education lessons and field trip much more deliberately into the curriculum so that they do not appear as such an outlier set of assignments or experiences.

Like the students in the study by Greene et al., students who went on the field trip displayed awareness in the growth categories identified by their research: critical thinking, empathy, tolerance, and an interest in future museum visits. However, unlike that study, no control group was used, so I did not compare students who had attended the field trip against those who had not. Importantly, a shortcoming of my inquiry was the fact that none of the students' levels of awareness in these areas were measured prior to their exposure to the museum or before going on the field trip.

Incorporating a field trip to the art museum connected English language acquisition to the History and Humanities core content. Like Padgett's students, these students learned about art, history and the museum through inductive learning and project-based learning (Padgett, 1994). The field trip added a cultural context to the lessons and provided opportunities for ESL students to connect their home cultures with the culture of the United States. One object in the Museum in particular—a large, gilt bronze sphere located in the center of a gallery—provided the opportunity for students to illustrate their recently acquired museum vocabulary and critical thinking skills. Called the Armillary Sphere (Cycle of Life) by Paul Manship, the sculpture prompted students to wonder aloud what the object was, and if perhaps it was a globe, a compass, or a magnet. The group of students worked together, describing the object in detail, referencing its size and decoration and using many of the new vocabulary words learned in class, such as shiny, sculpture, artifact, and valuable. Like Lang's observations about the Hmong students, this group of students moved past the superficial in their evaluations and brought real depth of thinking and expression about the objects they saw in the Museum (Lang, 1997).

Importantly, I learned how to integrate Art education and field trips into my content area, bringing an enhanced cultural and language dimension to students learning. An important outcome of this study is the realization that the field trip and art lessons could be incorporated into the existing course curriculum, allowing teachers to expand students' engagement potential. Students responded with enthusiasm to the written reflections, and they responded favorably to the themes created. These reflections required students to think critically about their experiences both on the field trip and in the classroom.

The most valuable indicators of the students' critical thinking and assessment were the thank-you letters written to museum staff. These letters were critical for learning from the students themselves the impacts the museum experience had on them. These letters evoked unguarded responses, perhaps seeming less like a school assignment. The letters were indicators of students' abilities to communicate their thoughts and ideas in writing. Although some of the students required the scaffolding of sentence frames, the letters yielded insights into how they felt about the field trip experience, and what pieces of art they viewed as most valued. Notably, writing the letters gave students a chance to show gratitude for the experience.

Finally, I observed students' empathy and increased critical thinking skills as positively impacted by their exposure to art and the museum field trip. However, because no pre-assessment of these traits was conducted, the evidence produced may be inconclusive. Nevertheless, Iroquois High School English learners are benefitting from a powerful relationship with the Speed Art Museum, providing access to field trips and classroom visits. Entering its third year, the partnership is evolving into a program that supports and develops students' understanding and appreciation of art by providing them access. As an educator, turning to published research was helpful to find insights and strength to connect arts, museum, and language education.

References

Berho, D. L., & Defferding, V. (2005). Communication, culture, and curiosity: Using target-culture and student-generated art in the second language classroom. *Foreign Language Annals, 38*(2), 271–276.

Franklin, M. B. (2014). A review of research on school field trips and their value in education. *International Journal of Environmental and Science Education, 9*(3), 235–244.

Greene, J. P., Kisida, B., & Bowen, D. H. (2013, November 22). Art makes you smart. *The New York Times*, p. 12.

Greene, J. P., Kisida, B., & Bowen, D. H. (2014). The educational value of field trips: Taking students to an art museum improves critical thinking skills, and more. *Education Next, 14*(1), 79–86.

Holbrook, H. C. (2016–2017). *Comprehensive school improvement plan for priority schools*. Frankfort, KY: Department of Education.

Holbrook, H. C. (2017–2018). *Comprehensive school improvement plan for priority schools*. Frankfort, KY: Department of Education.

Jefferson County Public Schools (JCPS). (2016). *JCPS deeper learning framework with initial focus capacities and dispositions*. Retrieved from https://www.jefferson.kyschools.us/department/academic-services-division/professional-learning-support-services/deeper-learning

Lang, G. C. (1997). Bridging a cultural gap: A museum creates access. *Curator: The Museum Journal, 40*(1), 15–29.

Padgett, G. S. (1994). An experiential approach: Field trips, book publication, video production. *TESOL Journal, 3*(3), 8–11.

Shoemaker, M. K. (1998). "Art is a wonderful place to be": ESL students as museum learners. *Art Education, 51*(2), 40–45.

Students, I. H. (2017). *Student evidence folder*. Louisville, KY: University of Louisville.

The William and Flora Hewlett Foundation. (2012). *Deeper learning strategic plan summary education program*. Retrieved from https://www.hewlett.org/wp-content/uploads/2016/09/Education_Deeper_Learning_Strategy.pdf

The William and Flora Hewlett Foundation. (2013). *Deeper learning competencies*. Retrieved from https://www.hewlett.org/wpcontent/uploads/2016/08/Deeper_Learning_Defined__April_2013.pdf

WIDA. (2016). *WIDA can do descriptors key uses edition grades 9–12*. Madison, WI: WIDA.

WIDA. (2017). *Mission statement*. Madison, WI: WIDA. Retrieved from https://www.wida.us/aboutus/mission.aspx

Wright, S. (1997). Learning how to learn the arts as core in an emergent curriculum. *Childhood Education, 73*(6), 361–365.

CHAPTER 11

Blending the Styles: Exploring Students' Views on the Merging of the Creative with the Academic

Leigh Yohei Bennett
Akita International University, Japan

Introduction

Creative thinking is encouraged from an early age and continues to be a valuable asset in later life in many domains. Yet, in education, creativity is often marginalized and ignored since "institutions are dependent on a control paradigm, and thus resistant to anything which threatens that control" (Maley, 2017, p. 85). In foreign language education, there is a progressive shift from situational and structural approaches to communicative language learning, but creativity remains ostracized. For example, within the institutionalization of teaching where maintaining assessments, objectives, prescriptive curricula, and administrative responsibilities are rigid. Despite these restrictions, a teacher's concept of what creativity is and whether or not it can be applied to the classroom are personal impediments in viewing themselves as creative practitioners. Lin (2011) categorizes the implications of creativity into three aspects. Firstly, creative teaching concerns the provision of innovative content, approaches, materials and activities stimulating multiple intelligences amongst students. The second concerns the environment which encourages motivation and enthusiasm. The third aspect focuses on the teacher's ethos or credibility where he or she remains open-minded towards ideas and behaviors as opposed to being rigid and inflexible. In essence, creativity in education consists of teachers teaching creatively. Teaching for creativity involves encouraging students to express their innovation by providing opportunities for such habits to shine in the classroom.

Defining Creativity

Demonstrating proficiency in writing can be a difficult and an anxiety provoking task for L2 students (Matsuda, 2001). Attention is spent on grammar and vocabulary instruction leaving out the humanistic, communicative intent of what the student wants to say. In academic essays, described by Strum (2012) as monolithic and archaic, the limitations imposed by the conventions stifle how students write. In order to address this, Hanauer (2012) suggests meaningful literacy, e.g., personal autobiographies, as a step to build motivation and for students to notice the creative expression and language often lacking in academic prose. Such writing offers more choices in how students can express ideas and is an essential ingredient in good writing (Sword, 2012). In order to narrow down creativity to a more manageable and relatable concept, a definition of creativity is taken from Koestler (1964) who views creativity as something which "uncovers, selects, reshuffles, combines, synthesizes already existing facts, ideas, faculties and skills" (p. 120). This definition is suitable given the context of my study, since all participants have experience in writing in different genres for creative, expository, and/or academic purposes.

Turning to Academic Research

Desmond Allison's (2004) research with students and teachers at a university in Singapore explores their views concerning the application of creativity in English for Academic Purposes (EAP) pedagogy. Historically, creativity is mainly associated with psychology and philosophy with occasional reference to education. In terms of conducting academic research and producing academic compositions, creativity is relevant especially if it "is conceived and pursued as a means of encouraging students' legitimate peripheral participation in research minded activities rather than as mere accommodation towards the expectations of academic teachers in reproductive assignments" (Allison, 2004, p. 193). The two reasons deterring creativity in academic writing are, firstly, its association with creative and expressivist writing pedagogy. Allison cites John's (1995) recognition of how process approaches to the teaching of writing have resulted in limitations to the linguistic and structural forms of academic writing in English. Also there is a tendency to ignore the cultural and discursive backgrounds of non-native speakers of English writing academic composition in L1 institutions. Secondly, creativity is often associated with "creative thinking"—a term connected to the enhancement of individual learning and education, often through the application of information technology.

Allison's keyword search of "creativity" and other cognates are words rarely found in EAP literature. The reasons for its absence are partly due to an accommodationist stance teachers take to ensure that students follow the linguistic, structural and discoursal expectations. For example, EAP students are often taught to write a standard five paragraph essay, instead of choosing their own structures as well as implementing formulaic chunks of language which are commonplace in academic writing. Comments on creativity in general and academic writing stem from a social constructionist perspective, establishing one's own expressive voice and demonstrating membership of the academic community by abiding by the written conventions and teacher expectations. A final concern is a common perspective held in EAP. The L2 learner cannot be expected to be left to their own devices in how to compose academic papers, especially in terms of producing essays of innovate or creative substance, whereas more experienced writers may have more success in tweaking the academic with more expressive language, hence playing with the institutional discourse (Bhatia, 2002). Despite this, the genre of academic papers remains impersonal and objective. L2 students can quickly identify and often produce essays which are rhetorically structured, objective and impersonal in tone containing appropriate linguistic features such as hedges, modal verbs, minimal personal pronouns and the use of active and passive structures. Although creative expression is met with skepticism in the academic domain as Allison reported, it remains a powerful resource worthy of examination and discussion in relation to students' academic writing.

Student and Teacher Comments on Creativity

The method employed in Allison's (2004) study involved analysis of a questionnaire and interview data taken from an earlier study by Allison and Wu (2002). The questionnaire consisted of 5 questions aimed at eliciting views from students and teachers concerning what constituted good writing (question 1), whether students felt their writing had improved during the English Language degree program (question 2), documentation on good writing (question 3), and finally, the helpfulness of writing guidelines and feedback (questions 4 & 5). The total responses received from this study consisted of 44 from first level module, 44 from third level module and 18 teacher responses. These responses were reviewed in order to search for lexical items that related to "creative," other cognate terms as well as other lexical terms (examples given include "fresh" and "captivating"). From the initial 88 participants, 28 (14 students and 14 teachers) agreed to participate in the follow up interviews.

From the interviews with students, the reported use of creativity and other terms related to demonstrating originality instead of mimicking answers shared amongst other students. Although this interpretation of creativity as ingenuity was deemed positively, 4 interviewees expressed caution relating it to the possibility of being penalized especially in tertiary education. Reasons given focused on the notion of creativity as more applicable and acceptable for primary or high school where writing conventions are looser or non-existent. A further concern is the view that attempts to show flair may hinder clarity and before creativity is applied, clarity of meaning is the priority. Other notions of creativity involved comments referring to encouraging students to "pursue academic enquiry more reflectively, creatively and critically for their own intellectual growth" (Allison, 2004, p. 201).

Implications for EAP

Overall, Allison makes an argument explaining why creativity can be a powerful notion within EAP pedagogy, specifically within academic writing pedagogy. He concludes that creative content is more acceptable in the minds of teachers whereas their reservations to creative form is partly due to the risk of sacrificing clarity in an attempt to show lexical or stylistic uniqueness. The other point of view places creativity as an essential component of academic work, essential for content and writer's mental thread. Yet, equally seen as important is to follow the existing convention as a means for the student to illustrate that he or she is aware of the institutional expectations.

The implication for the EAP practitioner is to re-examine a common belief that student writing styles should abide by those socially constructed in the academia. The author advocates the integration of creativity in EAP pedagogy in the context of "thinking, inquiry, interpretation, verification and argumentation" and not just as an extra add-on for the pedagogy. From this, the author draws two implications for its integration: the importance of students to understand the reasons behind academic expectations, which at times appear to counter the notion of creativity in their minds, and diversification of task expectations within the undergraduate curriculum. Furthermore, the author shares his concern with the misconception by the participants in assuming that academic guidelines are unquestionable and unchallengeable. Although the author does not completely condone conventional academic writing and enquiry, calls for experimenting in different ways in writing about academic issues are encouraged. Lastly, the article implies that because conventional EAP pedagogy is often restrictive and accommodationist, creativity should be added to its discourse in order to pay more attention to the holistic aspects of the writer's sense of self, identity, and voice. The implications are, firstly, to encourage students to understand the nuances and reasons behind academic expectations, and secondly, to introduce writing tasks and task expectations which enable students to experiment with content and form.

Background to My Teaching Context

Teaching Context

Research reported in this chapter took place at a liberal arts university in Japan. The university is one of many universities which established an English mediated curriculum whereby courses and programs are taught and assessed in English in an educational environment where English is a second language. English mediated instruction (EMI) was initially introduced as an incentive by the Japanese government in 2009 in order to make significant increases in the number of international students as well as to assist in the promotion of internationalization (MEXT, 2008). Like many academic institutions, preparing non-native English speakers to the demands of academic study is supported by EAP tutors. The role of these tutors is beyond language instruction and involves developing L2 receptive and productive skills.

Academic Writing Courses: Aims and Assessments

The opening academic writing course (EAP-105) for incoming first year EAP students is 15-week long with approximately four hours of classroom time per week. The main aims of the course are for students

- to present facts, feelings and informed opinions in written English,
- to learn and apply the basic rhetorical modes in formal written communication,
- to find, evaluate and incorporate academic sources, and
- to produce definition, cause and effect and argument of increasing length (700–1000 words).

The subsequent course (ENG-100) involves more advanced reading and research as well as demonstration that formal academic writing moves away from experiential and towards source-based support. Amongst other, the course aims include:

- to increase student autonomy in critical thinking, writing and revising,
- to respond to a variety written texts in essays and other kinds of academic genres,
- to improve writing in informal and formal rhetorical modes, and
- to produce rhetorical analysis, argument synthesis and a problem-solution of increasing length (1200–1500 words).

Overall, the transitional aims of the two courses introduce students to the typical macro and micro features of the academic essay, process of writing, employing fellow students as readers and reviewers as well as other institutional support systems. For example, one to one assistance from senior students, writing clinics and feedback from faculty are available to all university students. The more advanced course which targets the nature of argument via producing essays applying source based knowledge involves greater use of the university academic databases instead of the previous general, non-academic sources. Greater student attention is drawn to the functions and types of citation practices as well as strategies of effective argument (the role of ethos, logos, pathos) and the avoidance of logical fallacies. Finally, in each course and for all essays, students have full autonomy in identifying a topic of their personal/academic interest.

Student Demographics

The ENG-100 course consisted of ten students, five of whom offered to participate in the end of course group interview. Out of the ten students, five were in their first semester at the university and were classified as Bridge students. They had attained a higher than average score on the TOEFL (near-native English speakers in the majority of cases), had two or more years in formal education in an English-speaking country, or passed the university's oral and written examination. Out of the remaining 5 students, all were home students having completed the formal Japanese education system and were in their third year. These students, unlike the Bridge, enrolled for the EAP courses and had successfully completed the EAP courses in their first semester. A needs analysis of the cohort revealed the Bridge students had minimal experience in academic writing. They reported writing mostly in preparation for the university entrance exam. Only one of the Bridge students reported writing for academic purposes namely a book review, narratives, and reflective essays. The experiences of the EAP were similar insofar that prior to entering the university, these students had close to zero experience in writing academically in English. Their writing in English was purely for English language test purposes.

Utilization of Allsion's Research in ENG100

Previous Course Objectives

In previous semesters, the course opened with revision for EAP students and an introduction for Bridge students on the recurring stylistic and discoursal features of academic writing. Johns' (1997) text analysis of research articles identified these as use of transitional phrases and conjunctions, denoting objectivity by avoiding personal pronouns and judgmental or emotive adjectives and lastly, the inclusion of cautious and tentative language. Additional lesson time was spent on expanding academic parts of speech, noticing and practicing the salience of nominalized and passive syntactic structures and the textual features of cohesion and coherence. As mentioned in the previous section, the Bridge students were unfamiliar with academic written discourse (evident from the needs analysis and opening diagnostic), whilst for the EAP students, this opening section of the syllabus acted as a reminder of the conventionalized features students are expected to continue to demonstrate.

Several sample essays written by university faculty and students illustrating the typical characteristics of the academic essay had been introduced as models throughout the course.

Rationale of Sample Selection

In order to demonstrate how creative language and linguistic/structural playfulness can be applied to academic compositions, I opted to apply the models given in section 3.3 which represented the rhetorical modes students are assessed on. The rationale for incorporating these essays is that unlike the essays taken from previous texts by faculty and students, the language displayed more rhetorical flourishes. For instance, they applied primary data sometimes in the form of narrative, added further color to the text by using figures of speech, metaphor, analogies, rhetorical questions and humor. Additionally, each essay demonstrated a hybrid of formal and informal language, which were deployed in attempt to persuade or occasionally, entertain the reader. Wyrick (2002) warns of overusing creative expressions such as figurative speech and that adding too much "spice" (p. 16) may inadvertently spoil the broth. Regardless of the reader's taste buds, rhetorical freedom should be encouraged. The essays cited in the following section portray a range of creative devices in action thereby raising student awareness that nothing should be off limits but at the same time maintains an academic nuance by embedding the typical linguistic features evident in academic prose.

Influence and Application of Allison's Research

Allison's (2004) research outlined an aspect of writing which was overlooked in my academic writing curriculum. He wrote, "EAP discourse community is more concerned to show students how to follow conventions than to encourage them to be creative in research terms" (p. 194). He advances the idea that creativity can be a concept which removes the shackles on teachers and students allowing greater freedom in teaching and writing more expressively. The curriculum to date stressed register, style and structure illustrated in model essays written by previous students and university faculty. These samples represented the prevailing university expectations as to what constitutes good academic writing with creative writing being viewed as an optional addition rather than as an essential trait of high quality composition. A significant change to the curriculum therefore involved exploring communicative forms which differed from the conventional essay.

The changes to the syllabus involved replacing previous sample essays from students and faculty with those written by students, novelists and journalists for purposes other than pure academic inquiry. The samples were a rhetorical analysis essay of a Tommy Hilfiger perfume advertisement "Marketing the girl next door: A declaration of independence?" (Rossenwasser & Stephen, 2006), an opinion piece from *The Guardian* titled "How a corporate cult captures and destroys our best graduates" (Monbiot, 2005), and a problem-solution essay by Alan Patrick Herbert (1921) "About bathrooms." Therefore, in each of the above three essays, the samples used reflected the rhetorical modes students needed to produce but deviated from a standard academic essay on a structural and linguistic level. Incorporating sample essays into a writing syllabus as models that students can understand and reproduce has been thoroughly documented in the literature. According to Pincas (1982), during the product approach students go through the stages of familiarization (awareness of certain features of a text), transforming (manipulation of the salient linguistic features), then expanding (paragraph construction), and lastly composition of a final product. The advantages of the product approach, especially for the academic genres, are that the model texts explicitly highlight the differences between academic and general texts and encourages active student reflection as to whether their own essays successfully represent the model.

However, a major criticism of the product approach is that it encourages imitation. It lessens innovation in how the writer may structure the text and express their ideas. In addition, personal aspects of voice and stance are limited in the writing process. The former is defined by Blommaert (2005) as "the capacity to make oneself understood as a situated subject" (p. 222). Stance is defined as "the ways that writers project themselves into their texts to communicate their integrity, credibility, involvement, and a relationship to the subject matter and their readers" (Hyland, 1999, p. 99). The product approach remains a highly frequent and arguably an essential ingredient to successful teaching and learning of L2 composition. However, models which illustrate variation and expose students beyond the prototypical academic micro and macro features can act as a means to cultivate student discovery by expressing their voice and stance instead of mere replication (Ferris & Hedgcock, 2014). In a similar vein, the impersonal nature of academic prose can mean that linguistic options are minimized hence ignoring other paths to express oneself (Carter, 1997).

Allison's research revealed a number of issues which the current syllabus had ignored. The main impact of his research was the decision to include samples which blended creative and academic writing, described by Forché and Gerard (2001, p. 4) as "creative non-fiction," a writing style which is factual and literary. The analysis of these samples aimed to assist students in noticing how academic genre can contain a more creative style of writing as a means to write in their own self, identity, and voice. The following sections report student views on whether such a style was deemed favorable, as well as their perspectives on what constitutes good academic writing in higher education.

Effectiveness of Course Changes

In order to measure the effectiveness of the changes outlined above, student essays were analyzed to find examples of expressive and creative language introduced from the three sample essays. The only example of such devices was the inclusion of narrative as a means to introduce the relevance and importance of the essay topic. The "rhetorical flourishes" and the adding of "spice" were extremely rare and, if present, difficult to identify. The limited use of creative expressions suggested student reservations and difficulty in integrating this type of writing, hence, I conducted group interviews with the students to identify the reasons why and to explore their attitude towards its applicability. An email asking students to attend an informal discussion concerning thoughts toward the course was sent at the end of the semester. Five Bridge students (Mai, Kensuke, Aoi, Sota, Jun) agreed to be interviewed and have their opinions audio recorded. The following section opens with the question asked and provides extracts of student responses as well as my commentary and analysis of opinions pertaining to creativity in academic writing.

What Is Good Writing?
Mai: Good writing is probably something people want to read. And think that's kind of interesting. So to make interesting it has to have some colour not dull or boring and has some unique ideas which make people think.

Aoi: Yeah not narrowing down but thinking about the audience when you write is really important. Making sure that you write it in a way which makes that group of people want to read it. Like target a group of people you are writing for not just for the teacher.

Kensuke: I think when I want to read something but when I find an article interesting is when I see who the author is and the way he or she writes is unique in some kind of way I want to read that.

All three participants describe good writing as representing an aspect of uniqueness which encourages the reader to read the text. Similar to Allison's students who described creativity as demonstrating originality, Mai and

Kensuke describe uniqueness as related to content where ideas stand out and are deemed "interesting" with a feeling of "I want to read that."

Kensuke views good writing as a means to cater for a specific audience instead of writing purely for academic audiences. Although this comment does not directly relate to creativity, it does nevertheless echo a feature of the sample essays, i.e., each essay was written with a particular community in mind (female consumers, soon to be graduates, residence in 1920s Great Britain).

Continuing with this question, Mai began to elaborate on good writing by stressing that a text which contains humor and sarcasm is worthy of reading. It is interesting to note here that responses to good writing considered the perspective of the reader. Students on the whole did not respond introspectively, i.e., by asking themselves "what is good about *my* writing?" In each of the above given responses from Mai, Aoi and Kensuke, good writing is seen as entertaining, exhibited by original ideas, sarcasm, and humor.

Sota: First one it has to be accurate. It's the most important thing.

A feature of good writing according to Sota is writing which is accurate, explained as a text which reports facts and informs rather than amuses the reader. It is also representative of mainstream academic prose as Sota's later responses illustrate. The comment made concerning *kuse* (literal translation is *an unconscious habit* or *tendency*) draws the discussion to stylistics, specifically feelings of inadequacy by Kensuke where she struggles to express her voice. All participants follow with the micro features of the essay, suggesting that good writing is manifested by avoiding informal, conversation language, and incorporating academic vocabulary and a succinct organizational structure as a means to deliver an effective argument.

Were the Sample Essays Helpful?

The responses toward this question were generally positive. The selected essays contained a mixture of formal and informal expressions, and student responses given below identify how academic and creative expressions could be integrated into their own compositions. For example:

Kensuke: The bathroom one was interesting because the content wasn't that academic but the style he writes was made to entertain the audience ... yeah how to write fun.

Mai: The Guardian one was a lot of numbers and stuff so I mean it was kind of interesting because there was one point of view of students, there is a tendency of students to do something and they are influenced by the society and stuff so I could understand that but I thought it was only one way of thinking overall. I don't want to say biased but similar to that.

The comments above illustrate the distinction students made concerning self-expression in writing "to entertain the audience" and "how to write fun" while Mai refers to the article's content lacking alternative insights. Similar to their opening responses for the first question, student responses tend to focus on more on the content rather than the language. The two participants below, however, explained their reluctance to apply more expressive language:

Jun: I did find it interesting because all the samples opened up a different style, structure and tone in delivering effective arguments but I actually thought I had to write in a more strict or more academic format and I felt more comfortable writing in an academic format.

Sota: They were useful especially in knowing the structure. But I didn't want the readers to misunderstand that I wasn't taking it seriously or that I was goofing around. Because I wasn't used to finding the balance between writing creatively and academically. If I tend to write creative I think I will lose the focus of the topic itself as well the go off route for an academic paper which is why I didn't actively engage in those kind of expressions.

The comments above from Jun suggest that the range of "different styles, structures and tone" generated insights into his writing; yet, he felt that doing so would damage the character he wished to portray. For example, by not being taken seriously or be perceived as "goofing around" as well as losing focus and going "off route." Even though Jun hopes to merge the two styles of writing, the response suggests that creative and academic expressions are distinct, and the inclusion of the former is a hindrance both to his identity as an academic writer and in regard to his concerns of giving the wrong impression to the reader.

Do You Think Creativity Helps Students Write Essays?

Despite their compositions seldom illustrating the use of literary devices, some participants were more aware of the type of creative expressions available. This, as can be seen from Mai's comment below, empowered students to see how a variety of rhetorical features can play a role in their academic writing.

Mai: I don't know but some of the essays shows how I want to write. I want to write like that more freely at times.

Other participants, however, reported the opposite. Students were discouraged to apply a stylistic form of writing believing it to fly in the face of the conventions of academic writing, seeing it as unsafe with the possibility of losing marks:

Jun: Yes in that I have to come up with an original argument but in order to write a good academic essay, I also have to follow the rules if I just write the way I want then I will lose marks. Plus, because I chose to write about my own topic on autism I feel that that narrows the context encouraging me to apply an academic style whether it be from source information or my own ideas.

Sota: I don't think it helps me very much. Academic writing needs to be professional. I think if it is understandable and logical enough it might work but writing creatively is hard thing to do so I think it's very risky. Once I have confidence in my writing then maybe I can write more freely.

The risk-reward comment above taps into the expectations held by teachers and the institution at large. The comment also suggests that the participant believes his writing is a deficit and needs mastering before he is permitted to write more expressively. This point resonates with other participants. The general consensus from the participants appears to be a desire to write more loosely with expression and creativity yet, like the comment given by Sota, there remains a reluctant but necessary need to abide by a more formal, objective way of writing.

Conclusion

Using Allison's (2004) research, the aim of this chapter was to elucidate participants' views on using creative expressions in their academic essays. Allison's research enlightened my own practice in terms of giving students more opportunities to experiment in different ways of writing about academic issues. Similarly, the comments made by the participants illustrate concerns with their inability to deliver a familiar voice and identity. Hence, imposing the typical nuances of the academic genre may in practice add more detriment than good. This raised a further question concerning how the assessment rubric needs to be adapted in order to accommodate different styles to reduce debilitating their freedom to express. It is also interesting to note that creative form was viewed positively much more so than the academic. Although this is unsurprising given its flexibility, it undoubtedly raises student motivation to write by minimizing negativity toward writing. The introduction of broadening writing tasks and sample essays are further changes made. A fixation with applying samples which deliver an academic style was substituted with essays which blended the traditional academic argument with rhetoric, humor, and journalese. It is crucial that this kind of genre-bending and rhetorical playfulness be made clear especially since EAP students are often in the process of developing their understanding in academic writing. The definition of academic writing needs to be expanded, not fixed or static, and to recognize writing as multimodal. Overall, the impact of Allison's research drew my attention to the writer with less importance placed on texts demonstrating academic style.

Suggestions for Teachers Utilizing Research

Similar to critical thinking, creativity encompasses a variety of meanings and actions for students and teachers. Upon reading Allison's (2004) research, my interpretation of how creativity can be applied to the academic writing curriculum and as a salient feature in student essays involved introducing sample essays which steered away from the traditional model to ones which outlined a bending of the academic genre. From the perspective of enhancing my curriculum, utilizing Allison's research was not a means to formulate an effective method to teach writing but as a process of questioning what good writing is and how best to incorporate the answer to this question into the classroom. Although Allison's research does not contain a recipe on how to apply creative form in the classroom in different contexts, the research did however awaken my understanding of a problem which remained ignored, i.e., encouraging the use of creative forms and rhetoric in order to accommodate student voice and identity.

For teachers intending to use research in their practice, it is necessary to turn the impersonal, theoretical aspects of research to a personal and humanistic perspective given the interpersonal nature of teaching. Discerning whether the research ideas presented can be applied in one's own context followed by interpreting how the ideas can be merged within the curriculum are necessary steps. A key aspect of constructing a research-based pedagogy involves considering what teachers already do and believe. It involves challenging tacit habits in order to give ground for new actions and concepts thereby cultivating one's craft. The utilization of Allison's research made me question my pedagogy in regard to whether solely focusing on an academic register and the associated conventions was a disservice to students, and whether creative language can be placed within an academic writing course.

A Way Forward?

Creativity is a viable and desirable option for some, but for others the concerns of appropriateness and coming across as casual or informal with the risk being penalized are equally valid. The chapter has demonstrated that students welcome sample essays reflecting argumentation underpinned by rhetoric, injection of narrative and playing with the tone of the genre. Although this study reported the views of a limited number of participants, teachers should recognize that creative and academic writing need not be regarded as opposites but as a hybrid. Rarely is an essay composed of a single style or discourse. Rather than structuring texts according to a model essay which fixes the style and discourse for students, introducing and responding to a range of academic, creative and expository writing can assist writers in developing and understanding the functions of writing in their personal and professional lives. Finally, the discussion given earlier concerning the limitations of the product-based approach calls into question whether a model clarifying the linguistic, stylistic, and structural elements of an academic essay best serves students entering disciplinary courses. For EAP and the majority of the Bridge students, such models provided scaffolding, but a variation of samples for different audiences and purposes can remind students that academic writing need not be as rigid as many believe.

References

Allison, D. (2004). Creativity, students' academic writing, and EAP: Exploring comments on writing in an English language degree programme. *Journal of English for Academic Purposes, 3*(3), 191–209.

Bhatia, V. K. (2002). A generic view of academic discourse. In J. Flowerdew (Ed.), *Academic discourse*. Harlow: Longman.

Blommaert, J. (2005). Bourdieu the ethnographer: The ethnographic grounding of habitus and voice. *The Translator, 11*(2), 219–236.

Carter, R. (1997). *Investigating English discourse*. London: Routledge.

Dudley-Evans, T., & St. John, M. J. (1998). *Developments in English for specific purposes*. Cambridge: Cambridge University Press.

Ferris, D. R., & Hedgcock, J. S. (2014). *Teaching L2 composition: Purposes, process, and practice*. New York, NY: Routledge.

Forsché, C., & Gerard, P. (2001). *Writing creative nonfiction: Instruction and insights from the teachers of the associated writing programs*. Cincinnati, OH: Story Press.

Hanauer, D. I. (2012). Meaningful literacy: Writing poetry in the language classroom. *Language Teaching, 45*(1), 105–115.

Herbert, A. P. (1921). *About bathrooms*. Retrieved from
http://interpretiveliteature.blogspot.jp/2013/11/about-bathrooms.html

Hyland, K. (1999). Disciplinary discourses: Writer stance in research articles. In
C. Candlin & K. Hyland (Eds.), *Writing texts, processes and practices* (pp. 99–121).
London: Longman.

Johns, A. (1997). *Text, role, and context. Developing academic literacies*. Cambridge:
Cambridge University Press.

Koestler, A. (1964). *The act of creation*. London: Penguin.

Lin, Y. S. (2011). Fostering creativity through education: A conceptual framework of
creative pedagogy. *Creative Education, 2*(3), 149–155.

Maley, A. (2017). In search of creativity. In R. Breeze & C. S. Guinda (Eds.), *Essential
competencies for English-medium university teaching*. Madrid: Springer.

Matsuda, P. K. (2001). Voice in Japanese written discourse: Implications for second
language writing. *Journal of Second Language Writing, 10*(1), 35–53.

Ministry of Education, Culture, Sports, Science and Technology. (2008). *Study in English
at Japanese universities*. Retrieved from http://www.uni.international.mext.go.jp/
global30/

Monibot, G. (2015, June 3). How a corporate cult captures and destroys our best
graduates. *The Guardian*. Retrieved from https://www.theguardian.com/commen-
tisfree/2015/jun/03/city-corporates-destroy-best-minds

Pincas, A. (1982). *Writing in English 1*. London: Macmillan.

Rossenwasser, D., & Stephen, J. (2006). *Writing analytically* (4th ed.). Phoenix: Thomson
Wadsworth.

Strum, S. (2012). Terra (in) cognita: Mapping academic writing. *Text Journal, 16*(2),
173–181. Retrieved from http://www.textjournal.com.au/oct12/sturm.htm

Sword, H. (2012). *Stylish academic writing*. Cambridge, MA: Harvard University Press.

Wyrick, J. (2002). *Steps to writing well*. Orlando, FL: Harcourt.

Fostering Teacher Agency and Ideological Awareness

Brian Morgan
Glendon College/York University, Canada

Knowledge Mobilization in TESOL: *Connecting Research and Practice* is a most welcome and timely contribution to the field of English Language Teaching and its varied acronyms of setting and purpose (i.e., ESL, EFL, EIL/ELF). The parameters of connection established by the editor, Sardar Anwaruddin, serve to illustrate the decision making of practitioners in ways that resonate with a number of current developments in the fields of TESOL and Language Teacher Education (LTE). For one, the many chapters in this book attest to the importance of post-method pedagogies (Kumaravadivelu, 2006, 2012a), a shift from prioritizing universal methods in TESOL/LTE towards encouraging local responsiveness and variability in curriculum planning. Kumaravadivelu's (2012b) post-methodology is also openly ideological, linking knowledge production/mobilization in TESOL to (post)colonial power relations that sustain the dominance of center-based theories and practices and that continue to marginalize the work of periphery language professionals in the field (see e.g. center-based epistemic dependencies in TESOL). While not explicitly framed in decolonizing terms, many of the practitioners in this book demonstrate a necessary willingness to question the received wisdom and appropriateness of academic research for their own classrooms. By posing such questions, greater equality between researchers and practitioners is also claimed though not necessarily recognized within academic circles or by powerful stakeholders in the broader society.

Of course, a major related challenge here is for language teacher educators: how might we foster such critical engagement and effective advocacy amongst new practitioners, particularly in a field in which theory/practice dysfunctions stubbornly persist (Clarke, 1994; see also the editor's introduction) and growing job precarity and deprofessionalization serve to reduce interest in the kinds of knowledge mobilization promoted in this book (Morgan, 2016). Elsewhere, Anwaruddin (2017) has explored this challenge for LTE, drawing on both Kumaravadivelu's post-method approach and Rancière's emancipatory politics, a radical egalitarianism in which instructional hierarchies based on the perceived "ignorance" of the student/learner/practitioner are reversed. The specific focus of Anwaruddin's exploration is a teacher development project in Bangladesh known as English in Action (EIA), which aims to develop locally appropriate, learner-centered curricula for language and literacy. The broader focus relates to significant shifts in current thinking around TESOL and LTE, in particular, the recent emergence of *language teacher agency* as a desirable if not essential goal/aspiration of pre-service/in-service LTE programming (Miller & Gkonou, 2018; Morgan, 2010).

Towards the goal of advancing language teacher agency, this book makes a unique contribution, arguably in the form of a bottom-up corrective to the more typical top-down flow of research knowledge emanating from universities and academic journals. Rather than belaboring theoretical debates and underpinnings—i.e., is teacher agency an innately human and universal quality, or is it instead the product of discourses and subject/identity negotiation, contingent and ecological in realization (e.g., Miller & Gkonou, 2018; Priestly, Biesta, & Robinson, 2015; Wernicke, 2018)—a particular strength of this collection is in the ways that it extends our understanding of *agency in action*. Across a rich diversity of international settings and programs, readers are invited to see not only how practitioners mobilize research knowledge but also, of necessity, how they mediate (supplement or resist) the same in light of local conditions and constraints and based on pedagogical and identity-based experiences. In terms of understanding and fostering agency, I am reminded of Ilieva's (2010) impressive study of an intensive summer LTE program for international English language teachers and her interview data, which shed light on the participants' engagement and selective uptake of official curricula—an active transposition from *authoritative discourses* to *internally persuasive discourses*, following Bakhtin.

In Ilieva's article, as in this book, displays of practitioner engagement and agency are to be commended. Still, we should remain cautious regarding any claims of researcher/practitioner equality made in respect to knowledge mobilization in TESOL. What might appear to be a two-way, reciprocal relationship at one level or scale of activity may, on another, serve to reaffirm existing norms and hierarchies. Or in other words, when research knowledge is mobilized to accomplish short-term curricular goals more efficiently, questions regarding the broader social and moral purposes of education can be left unexamined as they may appear incidental to the ways in which both student "success" and teacher professionalism are measured in particular settings. In respect to second/additional language education, and depending on the types of high-stakes assessment to which students are subject, this can result in lingua-centric preoccupations with lexico-grammatical accuracy or academic writing conventions and less on intrinsically motivating or socially relevant content that engages with the life chances and desires of students. Language and texts become fragmented, carved up into discrete units, taught separately and in linear, predictive ways over a defined period of time.

The metaphor of the factory and its controlled processes of throughput and production might be an exaggeration here,[1] but I worry that the "connections" being made between research and practice, on the one hand, are growing disconnections, on another, in part a reflection of increased research specialization/fragmentation, itself driven by neoliberal pressures in our increasingly competitive, academic marketplace (e.g., the "terrors of performativity," Ball, 2003). For example, I read Kurzen's chapter on Dynamic Written Corrective Feedback with great interest, especially in my professional role as an EAP writing instructor concerned about the quality and effectiveness of the written feedback I provide on graded assignments. Perusing Kurzen's references for my own knowledge mobilization needs, I came across a publication in the *Journal of Response to Writing,* whose title struck me as particularly narrow/specialized. This journal is certainly not alone in its tight specification. Others come to mind: The *Journal of Second Language Pronunciation*, or the forthcoming *Journal of Second Language Teacher Education*. With the advent of e-journals and open access publishing, the viability of these relatively narrow-focused journals is evident. Yet, there is a risk that they encourage a TESOL research agenda in which we come to learn more and more about less and less, a fragmentation and disconnection of concern when we consider the complex social realities of second/additional languages classrooms and the multifaceted relationships teachers need to negotiate with their students. If anything, an argument could be made for greater holism, emotional engagement, creativity, and inter/transdisciplinarity in TESOL when mobilizing knowledge for students who have experienced the trauma of forced migration, increased racism, Islamophobia, environmental degradation, and fewer and fewer decent paying jobs.

Many of the chapters in this fine collection do in fact mobilize research knowledge in ways that complement and extend a notion of language as a *social* practice: chapters integrating a service-learning or arts-based component, come to mind. And it is not my intention to fault practitioners whose research priorities fall more in line with cognitive and/or lexico-grammatical concerns. Perhaps, what I'm arguing for is a greater *ideological* awareness of both, of how the same research knowledge can be mobilized for multiple purposes: some linguistic, some ideological, and often for strategic and transformative purposes. Returning to the notion of practitioner agency raised above, such awareness of the potential duality or multivocality of research mobilization is worth greater attention in LTE settings.

My earlier experiences around the duality/multivocality of research mobilization are worth briefly sharing here. In a chapter titled *Writing Across the Theory/Practice Divide: A Longitudinal Confession* (Morgan, 2003), I describe my growing awareness of the power of academic research in arbitrating difficult ESL program decisions. One example took place in an adult ESL program where I was teaching in the 1990's while doing graduate studies at the Ontario Institute for Studies in Education (OISE). At the community center that housed the ESL program, classroom/office space was scarce, and one of the center's head administrators argued that too much L1 use and bilingual instruction in the ESL program (actually trilingual: Cantonese/Mandarin/English) was delaying progress in English, resulting in an excessive and unnecessary demand on center resources. In the chapter, I then describe how I brought in research publications by Auerbach (1993) and Cummins (1996) that spoke to the value of L1 use in L2 instruction. We also had an established professor from OISE on the center's board of directors, who corroborated the research evidence provided. Fortunately, soon after, the English-only rationale was no longer advanced as a reason to limit classroom space for the ESL program. In this case, the mobilization of academic knowledge had important material effects and community consequences not directly related to the content of the research.

Another example in the 2003 chapter deals with one of my earliest publications as a young scholar, an action research account of a unit of lesson plans on Teaching the Gulf War in an adult ESL program, first published in the *TESOL Journal*, a publication specifically oriented towards practitioners' interests (Morgan, 1992/1993). As described in the 2003 chapter, the final edits of my manuscript were highly contentious. Throughout the article, outcomes and goals that I had perceived to be social and critical were re-defined by some of the editorial team. Several summative statements of specific lessons addressing language, power and identity, for example, were subtly reframed to focus instead on affective barriers and skills-based instruction. It was a difficult process at times, the editors indicating that I was being unreasonable and unwilling to cooperate with normal editing procedures; moreover, as a practitioner I was unqualified to be making such editorial demands. On more than one occasion, I was told, "That's not done in ESL; its conjecture—not academic." But from my perspective, I felt that ideas that were foundational to my way of teaching were either being removed or trivialized in the editing process. In terms of knowledge mobilization, I spoke with the editors about emerging research in Critical ESL Pedagogies and Critical Applied Linguistics that underpinned my practice. I referred to key research articles by Pennycook (1989) and Norton Peirce (1989) in the organization's flagship research journal, *TESOL Quarterly*, to explain/justify an alternative approach to adult ESL instruction in community-based programs. Without this critical theoretical precedent to cite, I doubt that my practitioner-based arguments would have been accepted. Eventually, we arrived at a final version with which we could all agree.

A related observation I make regarding the Gulf War article is on the structure of practitioner-focused publications such as *TESOL Journal* (that is in 1992!), in which space constraints (shorter article lengths) and an emphasis on lesson plans, syllabus design and curricular issues tend to re-affirm the ideological and paradigmatic status quo. Under such preconditions there isn't the allocated space or expectation to claim an alternative/transgressive set of epistemologies and aspirations for the language lessons on display, hence rendering them incoherent to those unfamiliar with the critical/alternative theories that underpin them. In short, the power of research presents/ hides itself in complex ways. When mobilized, it can be both a tool and a weapon, both options always worth exploring in support of language teacher agency and the possibility of greater reciprocity between researchers and practitioners.

Though I remain skeptical regarding the forms of reciprocity and equality that might be achieved, I agree with the editor that there are several positive developments that have occurred. A recent narrative turn in the writing up of academic research (e.g., Barkhuizen, 2017; Vandrick, 2009) is a welcome development, which can enhance the reception and mobilization of research findings. For practitioners, action research on their own classrooms and programs can be a revelation, an exciting new window onto a world less considered. In this regard, I appreciated Valmori's (Chapter 8) comment on research work as "therapy for my frustrations as a teacher to see my context from a different point of view." Therapy indeed! As noted above, there are already sufficient frustrations and challenges in the current state of TESOL as a viable career path. Conceptual boredom should not be one of them. My compliments to the editor and contributors for the engaging set of perspectives presented in this important collection.

Note

1 My metaphor of factory production processes refers to earlier work on call centre language practices in India (Morgan & Ramanathan, 2009) and their affinity with the principles of rationalization characteristic of scientific management or Taylorism (Braverman, 1974).

References

Anwaruddin, S. M. (2017). Methodism versus teacher agency in TESOL. In D. J. Rivers & K. Zotzmann (Eds.), *Isms in language education: Oppression, intersectionality and emancipation* (pp. 144–164). Berlin: De Gruyter Mouton.

Auerbach, E. R. (1993). Reexamining english only in the ESL classroom. *TESOL Quarterly, 27*, 9–30.

Ball, S. J. (2003). The teacher's soul and the terrors of performativity. *Journal of Education Policy, 18*, 215–228. doi:10.1080/0268093022000043065

Barkhuizen, G. (Ed.). (2017). *Reflections on language teacher identity research.* New York, NY: Routledge.

Braverman, H. (1974). *Labour and monopoly capital: The degradation of work in the twentieth century.* New York, NY: Monthly Review Press.

Clarke, M. (1994). The dysfunctions of the theory/practice discourse. *TESOL Quarterly, 28*, 9–26.

Cummins, J. (1996). *Negotiating identities: Education for empowerment in a diverse society.* Ontario, CA: California Association for Bilingual Education.

Ilieva, R. (2010). Non-native english speaking teachers' negotiations of program discourses in their construction of professional identities within a TESOL program. *Canadian Modern Language Review, 66*, 343–369.

Kumaravadivelu, B. (2006). *Understanding language teaching: From method to post-method.* Mahwah, NJ: Lawrence Erlbaum Associates.

Kumaravadivelu, B. (2012a). *Language teacher education for a global society.* New York, NY: Routledge.

Kumaravadivelu, B. (2012b). Individual identity, cultural globalization and teaching english as an international language: The case for an epistemic break. In L. Alsagoff, W. Renandya, G. Hu, & S. McKay (Eds.), *Teaching english as an international language* (pp. 9–27). New York, NY: Routledge.

Miller, E. R., & Gkonou, C. (2018). Language teacher agency, emotion labor and emotional rewards in tertiary-level english language programs. *System.* Retrieved from https://doi.org/10.1016/j.system.2018.03.002

Morgan, B. (1992/1993). Teaching the gulf war in an ESL classroom. *TESOL Journal, 2*(2), 13–17.

Morgan, B. (2003). Writing across the theory/practice divide: A longitudinal confession. In C. Casanave & S. Vandrick (Eds.), *Writing for scholarly publication* (pp. 223–235). Mahwah, NJ: Lawrence Erlbaum Associates.

Morgan, B. (2010). Fostering conceptual roles for change: Identity and agency in ESEA teacher preparation. *Kritika Kultura, 15*, 34–55. Retrieved from http://kritikakultura.ateneo.net/images/pdf/kk15/fostering.pdf

Morgan, B. (2016). Language teacher identity and the domestication of dissent: An exploratory account. *TESOL Quarterly, 50*(3), 708–734.

Morgan, B., & Ramanathan, V. (2009). Outsourcing, globalizing economics, and shifting language policies: Issues in managing Indian call centres. *Language Policy, 8*, 69–80.

Norton Peirce, B. (1989). Toward a pedagogy of possibility in the teaching of english internationally. *TESOL Quarterly, 23*, 401–420.

Pennycook, A. (1989). The concept of method, interested knowledge, and the politics of language teaching. *TESOL Quarterly, 23*, 589–617.

Priestly, M., Biesta, G., & Robinson, S. (2015). *Teacher agency: An ecological approach.* London: Bloomsbury.

Vandrick, S. (2009). *Interrogating privilege: Reflections of a second language educator.* Ann Arbor, MI: University of Michigan Press.

Wernicke, M. (2018). Plurilingualism as agentive resource in L2 teacher identity. *System*. Retrieved from https://doi.org/10.1016/j.system.2018.07.005